# Exploring LGBT Spaces and Communities

"This important work, critically approaches a vexed topic that of 'community' in an informed, innovative and rigorous way. Its cross disciplinary approach and clear writing style means that it will be of interest to all who are interested and work with not only lesbian, gay, bisexual and trans communities, but also those who are interested in social cohesion, identities, exclusions and marginalisations. This is also a must read for policy makers and the LGBT community and voluntary sector."
—**Katherine Browne**, *Professor Human Geography at University of Brighton, Uk*

"*Exploring LGBT Spaces and Communities* interrogates the complexities that lurk behind the deceptively simple idea of "community." Page after page, Eleanor Formby shatters the stereotype of singularity and shows us the manifold experiences of communities—in the plural—for LGBT people. This book is sure to poke and provoke as it traverses tensions between sameness and difference, hostility from the outside and safe spaces within, forced labels that misalign with lived experiences, on-line and offline encounters, cynicism and celebration about membership, demanding conformity or celebrating individuality, and in broad strokes, whether sexuality is primary or peripheral in our lives."
—**Amin Ghaziani**, *University of British Columbia*

The phrase 'LGBT community' is often used by policymakers, service providers, and lesbian, gay, bisexual and trans (LGBT) people themselves, but what does it mean? What understandings and experiences does that term suggest, and ignore? Based on a UK-wide study funded by the Arts and Humanities Research Council, this book explores these questions from the perspectives of over 600 research participants.

Examining ideas about community 'ownership', 'difference' and diversity, relational practices within and beyond physical spaces, imagined communities and belongings, the importance of 'ritual' spaces and symbols and consequences for wellbeing, the book foregrounds the lived experience of LGBT people to offer a broad analysis of commonalities and divergences in relation to LGBT identities.

Drawing on an interdisciplinary perspective grounded in international social science research, the book will appeal to students and scholars with interests in sexual and/or gender identities in the fields of community studies, cultural studies, gender studies, geography, leisure studies, politics, psychology, sexuality studies, social policy, social work, socio-legal studies and sociology. The book also offers implications for practice, suitable for policymaker, practitioner and activist audiences, as well as those with a more personal interest.

**Eleanor Formby** is a Senior Research Fellow at Sheffield Hallam University.

**Routledge Advances in Critical Diversities**
Series Editors: Yvette Taylor and Sally Hines

# Exploring LGBT Spaces and Communities

## Contrasting Identities, Belongings and Wellbeing

**Eleanor Formby**

Routledge
Taylor & Francis Group

NEW YORK AND LONDON

First published 2017
by Routledge
711 Third Avenue, New York, NY 10017

and by Routledge
2 Park Square, Milton Park, Abingdon, Oxon OX14 4RN

*Routledge is an imprint of the Taylor & Francis Group, an informa business*

© 2017 Eleanor Formby

*British Library Cataloguing-in-Publication Data*
A catalogue record for this book is available from the British Library

*Library of Congress Cataloging-in-Publication Data*
A catalog record for this book has been requested

ISBN: 978-1-138-81400-4 (hbk)
ISBN: 978-1-315-74779-8 (ebk)

Typeset in Times New Roman
by Apex CoVantage, LLC

Dedicated to my much-loved Mum, and in memory of my much-missed Dad, who both taught me about the world's inequality and diversity from an early age

# Contents

# Acknowledgments

I need to thank many people in connection with this book. First, thank you to all those who supported and/or participated in the research on which this book is based. Thanks also to the Arts and Humanities Research Council (ref AH/J011894/1) for funding the research, and Sally Hines and Yvette Taylor for accepting it within the edited series *Advances in Critical Diversities*.

On a more personal note, thanks to (in no particular order) supportive colleagues at Sheffield Hallam University (particularly Nick Hodge for reading draft chapters, and Guy Merchant for reading the whole thing!), my family who encouraged me, friends who have been neglected during the course of writing the book and Catherine Donovan, who was always so supportive at the end of a phone. Last but by no means least, my eternal love and thanks to Jo Woodiwiss—for reading chapters and so much more—without whom I never would have started working in academia in the first place. To quote Bob Dylan, if not for you, I couldn't find the door . . .

# 1 Introduction

The word 'community' derives from the Latin *com* (with or together) and *unus* (the number one or singularity) (Delanty, 2010). As Delanty (2010) and others have argued, the term is widely used in popular and academic discourse, but is also contested. It has been suggested, for example, that "community . . . means all things to all people" (Dalley cited in Crow and Allan, 1994: xv), and that "it seems to describe everything, and therefore nothing" (Mayo, 1994 cited in Day, 2006: 19). Whilst sociologists and others may have poured scorn on the concept, the term remains much used and 'abused' within politics and policymaking (Day, 2006). This partly explains my interest in the notion of community when it is applied to lesbian, gay, bisexual and trans (LGBT) people. This book is therefore an exploration of the concept of 'LGBT community'. In the UK, government documentation has begun to refer to LGBT communities in the plural (e.g. see Government Equalities Office, 2010), which at least seems to acknowledge the diversity amongst LGBT people, even if this acknowledgment is not then (re) enacted in practice. To denote the necessary caution required in any use of the word 'community', following Crow and Allan (1994), throughout the rest of this book I invite readers to place mental scare quotes around the word.

In the mid 1990s, Weston (1995: 280) suggested that television and film often presented gay characters as "bereft of community". Though widespread images of the 'tragic gay' (Monk, 2011) still exist, I would argue that there is now also—at least in certain policy and practice arenas—a contrasting assumption that LGBT people automatically belong to ready-made communities. There are parallels here with other 'minority' groups, for instance, Mallett and Slater (2014) have pointed to disabled people's dissatisfaction with the homogenising term 'disabled community'. Frost and Meyer, in their study (2012: 40), explicitly told their participants that when using LGBT community they were not referring to particular areas or social groups but "in general, groups of gay men, bisexual men and women, lesbians, and transgender individuals". In other words, they were using community as a proxy for people or population. However, some people may have LGBT friends but not see these as forming a community, whilst others may feel part of one or more communities but these may not include any (other) LGBT people. The assumption of any (singular) LGBT community in existing research is therefore problematic. How people see and experience their own sense of belonging to any particular community can be spatially and temporally specific—as I will go on to explore—and may contrast with how others, including researchers, perceive and describe this (assumed) belonging/community.

Whilst identity is a factor, whether implicitly or explicitly, in much of the literature I discuss in this book, existing work tends to draw on particular understandings of community (see below), with varying degrees of acknowledgment of this. Some of these understandings are of course influenced by authors' subject disciplinary backgrounds and/or epistemological standpoints. However, there are also examples of work where community is used and discussed with little engagement with what community might have meant to study participants, or study authors. I would argue that any research that seeks to examine community must first address how community is conceptualised in order to identify if and how understandings are shared. This is not to suggest that any particular viewpoints are 'right' or 'wrong', but to acknowledge that the concept is open to interpretation. In Rothblum's (2008) study linking community to lesbian and bisexual women's experiences of stress and support, for example, community itself was not clearly defined, but appears to have been understood, or interpreted, as women's friendship groups and immediate geographical social networks. In her later article, Rothblum (2010) asked participants how they understood (their) community, dividing participants up into 'founders', 'finders' and 'flounderers' according to their roles and respective 'success'. Her participants tended to relate community to people or organisations, linking these to support, similarity and/or physical proximity. Despite these somewhat problematic examples, there are many other scholars who question the use of the term community. Rothenberg (1995), for instance, critiqued some geographers' use of community and neighbourhood interchangeably, whilst Hines' (2007) research with transgender people also indicated that community cannot be assumed based on shared identity or collective participation, as both are likely to be more complex and varied than is sometimes presumed.

This book draws on an Arts and Humanities Research Council funded research project on understandings and experiences of LGBT communities (ref AH/ J011894/1). In this introductory chapter I give an overview of the research aims and methods (with further detail on participants and research methods within in an appendix), but first I provide a broader context for how community has been conceptualised in previous research. Existing literature can be loosely divided into several common patterns of usage, largely revolving around communities understood as spatial, cultural, imagined, based on friendships and personal connections and/or as virtual. In this opening chapter I begin by outlining each of these understandings within both a general and LGBT research context. Though the book looks at the concept of LGBT communities as a whole, I do draw on individual work that has examined 'gay communities', 'lesbian communities' and so on.

## Spatial Communities and 'Gay Ghettos'

Typically, community has been understood to be highly spatialised (Delanty, 2010). Having something 'in common' has often been related to shared geography, hence 'territorial' and 'place' communities (Willmott, 1986). This tradition emerged within early sociological studies of particular localities, such as Lynd and Lynd's study of 'Middletown' (Muncie, Indiana) in the United States in 1929 (Day, 2006). To some degree, the tradition continued in the development of community studies, and more recently community re-studies, which seek to update and revisit previous studies/locations (Crow, 2012; Phillipson, 2012). Sometimes these communities are known as 'communities of fate' because people are unable to choose where they are born (and probably where they are raised), though clearly some people have more ability to choose where they (continue to) live as adults. The notion of certain places providing a space where particular people can enjoy relaxing with other people 'like them' was noted 50 years ago (Patterson, 1965 cited in Crow and Allan, 1994), and whilst problematised, continues to this day (Ghaziani, 2014).

Drawing on spatial understandings of communities, early work on homosexuality emerging within geography and urban sociology in the late 1970s and 1980s tended to focus on specific geographical areas, often in America. Frequently these were known as 'gay ghettos' (Bell and Valentine, 1995a; Binnie, 1995; Levine, 1979; Rothenberg, 1995; Valentine, 1993a), 'gay Villages' or more recently and particularly in the US, 'gayborhoods' (Brown, 2014; Ghaziani, 2014; Reiter, 2008). As representations of 'gay communities', these locations were/are densely populated with gay housing and businesses, with some writers linking this to broader patterns within the functioning of capitalism, urbanisation and/or gentrification (Castells, 1983; Knopp, 1995; Rothenberg, 1995; Smith and Holt, 2005). The Castro district within San Francisco is probably the most famous example, where a concentration of gay voters facilitated Harvey Milk becoming the first openly gay elected official in America (played by Sean Penn in the Hollywood film *Milk*, which depicts his life and subsequent death). Ghaziani (2014) recently outlined that gayborhoods are characterised by four key features: a distinct geographical focal point, a unique culture, a concentration of gay and lesbian residences and a cluster of commercial spaces (e.g. comprising gay-owned and gay-friendly businesses, nonprofit organisations and community centres). He suggested that as such they offer gays and lesbians a space of freedom, and "enable social networking for a group of people who face unique challenges in not being physically identifiable to one another" (Ghaziani, 2014: 126). It should be noted, however, that not all studies of 'gay' life have focussed on urban settings, although there is a preponderance, as work has also sought to explore rural gay and lesbian geographies (e.g. see Bell and Valentine, 1995b; Browne, 2008), which will be returned to in further depth in Chapter 5.

Valentine (1994) has pointed to the extent to which 'ghettos' are often dominated by gay men. Explanations that lesbians had/have less economic power to own or run their own businesses in these (or other) areas may have some credence (Casey, 2007; Moran and Skeggs, 2001; Rothenberg, 1995). However, Castells' (1983) suggestion that women have less 'territorial aspirations' than men has been robustly critiqued (Bell and Valentine, 1995a; Valentine, 2000). His argument that women are more concerned with personal relationships and social networks than seeking spatial 'superiority' or 'domination', for example, has been contradicted by a range of research demonstrating that there are areas of lesbian concentration. These have been defined as both lesbian ghettos and lesbian communities, albeit perhaps more 'alternative', 'underground' and/or less commercial than examples such as the Castro (Bell and Valentine, 1995a; Valentine, 2000, 2002; Browne and Ferreira, 2015). Examples include Adler and Brenner's (1992) unknown US city, Peake's (1993) study in Michigan, Rothenberg's (1995) work in Brooklyn's Park Slope (affectionately dubbed 'dyke slope' in Gieseking's later (2013) work) and Valentine's UK-based research (1993a, 1995). Whilst these locations may not visibly demonstrate their lesbian heritage as much as some of the more famous 'gay' districts around the world, their existence is known via word of mouth among women (Bell and Valentine, 1995a). Rothenberg (1995) has suggested that it is this social networking among lesbians that has successfully contributed to the growth of some of these areas. Geographical work focussing on lesbians, however, has also identified the place of private homes and/or temporary spaces within the concept of community (Johnston and Valentine, 1995; Valentine, 1993b, 1994). As Browne and Ferreira (2015: 15) summarise, "lesbian geographies contest traditional theories of urban space or 'territories' as continuous and visible areas. These spaces of lesbian conviviality are temporally specific spaces of resistance and can act as important reference points for the construction of lesbian identities". Some of the early lesbian and gay communities literature, however, has been criticised for talking about lesbians and gay men as if they were a 'pseudo-ethnic minority' (Davis, 1995).

Although no studies exist of specific locales where *only* LGBT people live in the UK, there are studies of those who identify as LGBT within areas where there is a high concentration of LGBT people and businesses. Examples include recent large-scale research within Brighton (Browne and Bakshi, 2013), and older work focussing on the Canal Street area (the 'Gay Village') of Manchester (e.g. Binnie and Skeggs, 2004; Whittle, 1994). Such studies will be discussed throughout this book.

## Cultural Communities and Practices

A second tradition draws on cultural sociology and anthropology in its focus on a search for belonging and/or the cultural construction of identities. May (2013: 3) defined belonging as "the process of creating a sense of identification with, or connection to, cultures, people, places and material objects". Delanty (2010) has noted that this tradition tends to focus on the self versus 'other', highlighting among others the work of Lash (1994, cited in Delanty, 2010: 154), who argued that "individuals are not placed into communities only by social forces . . . but they situate themselves in community". Similarly, Cohen (1987) argued that the boundaries between members and non-members are crucial to the construction of communities, as "*we*-ness [is] asserted in opposition to *them*" (Jenkins, 2014: 140, original emphasis). This distinction between 'insiders' and 'outsiders', or 'us' and 'them', is a theme that runs throughout this book.

The shift in emphasis away from social interaction embedded within specific localities towards symbolic meanings and identities has been related to the role of shared rituals in particular (Cohen, 1985). This will be returned to in Chapter 7, where I examine Pride events. Within this school of thought, the meaning of community is seen to be constructed by social actors (Delanty, 2010). These communities may be called 'elective communities' (Maffesoli, 1996), 'lifestyle communities' (Day, 2006) or 'interest communities' (Willmott, 1986), and can coincide with spatial communities. Despite the complexity of defining such 'communities of interest', they have been operationalised within public policy (within the Welsh 'Communities First' programme), in a context where much regeneration work has tended to focus on spatial communities (i.e. clearly defined areas) (Day, 2006).

Sociologically informed work has emphasised the importance of a sense of belonging and communities of identity, particularly for marginalised or stigmatised groups (Walkerdine and Studdert, 2011; Weeks, 1996; Weeks, Heaphy and Donovan, 2001), though this is not to suggest that these are entirely or necessarily distinct from spatial understandings/concentrations. One of the key examples of the use of interest communities in relation to sexuality was Weeks' (1996) article on the idea of a sexual community. The paper explored the concept of community and suggested that it could offer "a 'vocabulary of values' through which individuals construct their . . . sense of identity and belonging" (Weeks, 1996: 72). Weeks (1996) went on to argue that those groups whose existence is 'threatened' are most likely to construct a community of identity. Whilst pointing to the possible weakness of assuming similarity amongst lesbians and gay men due to differences, for example, of wealth, ethnicity, geography and political leanings, he also identified the potential for shared experiences of stigma, prejudice, inequality and oppression, giving rise to the need for a community of identity (Weeks, 1996). Such a community can then support activism and individual identity through shared ritual practices, such as Pride events, and a "sense of common purpose and solidarity represented by the term community" (Weeks, 1996: 76). According to Weeks (1996: 83), this "invented tradition" both "enables and empowers" by providing the context through which lesbian and gay lives are developed and social orders challenged. One might link the notion of 'cultural', and perhaps 'political', communities with broader social change, for instance the decriminalisation of sex between men, 'gay liberation' politics, activism and peer support in response to the emergence of HIV/AIDS and the campaign to repeal Section 28[1] (Kollman and Waites, 2011; Taylor, Kaminski and Dugan, 2002; Weeks, 2007). Indeed, 'community-based' responses to HIV/AIDS have been considered a form of social capital (Weeks, 1996). Political consciousness and collective action has been viewed as a basis for community (Delanty, 2010). Melluci (1996), for instance, identified community as being enacted through mobilisation processes involved in social movements, rather than being founded in any underlying 'reality'. Earlier research by Willmott (1986) also identified the role of collective action in constituting what he called 'communities of attachment', which he distinguished from interest communities (Crow and Allan, 1994). The role of collective action within LGBT life will be examined within Chapter 4, whilst the difficulties inherent in assuming and applying the concept of community in relation to LGBT people will be explored further within the following chapter.

## Imagined Communities and the 'Gay Imaginary'

A third view of communities was developed by Anderson (2006) in relation to nationalism. He argued that 'imagined communities' can exist where fellow members (of nation states) may never meet, know or hear of each other, but "in the minds of each lives the image of their communion" (Anderson, 2006: 6). This idea has subsequently been applied more broadly to many different imagined communities that exist outside of social interaction and/or 'lived' space (Delanty, 2010), where "people 'imagine' they share general beliefs, attitudes and recognise a collective . . . as having similar opinions and sentiments to their own" (Hague, 2011: 19). As Jenkins (2014: 143) argued, community can never be imaginary "even though it can never be anything other than imagined".

Anderson's (2006) notion of imagined communities has influenced a range of LGBT work. Bell and Valentine (1995a), for example, suggested that despite some examples of visible gay communities such as San Francisco, the majority of lesbians and gay men do not live or work in such 'gay spaces' and instead only belong to an imagined community with other LGB people. Weston (1995) also argued that lesbian and gay identity is bound up with constructions of 'we-ness' and finding other people 'like me', within what she referred to as a gay imaginary. Valentine and Skelton (2003) likened lesbian and gay youth's experience of the commercial scene to an imagined community, because whilst they did not know everyone there, participants felt a sense of belonging and shared identity. In an LGBT context the notion of an imagined community is often drawn on to suggest a 'bond', 'connection' or sense of solidarity, frequently based on the assumption of shared experiences of stigma, prejudice or discrimination (Weeks, 1996; Weeks, Heaphy and Donovan, 2001). A desired or assumed shared understanding of meanings and a 'vocabulary of values' (Weeks, 1996) is frequently perceived to negate the need for explanation, self-censorship or self-regulation (Simpson, 2015; Valentine, 1993c; Weeks, Heaphy and Donovan, 2001). Such imaginings within my research will be explored further within Chapter 8.

## Friendships and Personal Communities

Another view conceives of community as being based upon friendship and personal relationships. A key proponent of this idea is Pahl (2001), who has identified friendship as a form of flexible, non-spatial community. Pahl and Spencer (2004) later coined the term 'personal communities' to describe communities, based on choice and commitment, which "are personalized networks in the sense of being constituted out of personalized relationships consisting of families and friends" (Delanty, 2010: 115). Castells (2001) has also used the term 'personalized communities' to describe the "networks of interpersonal ties that provide sociability, support, information, a sense of belonging, and social identity" (Wellman, 2001: 127). These communities can be distinguished from other/spatial communities influenced by destiny or fate because they rely, at least to a certain extent, on choice. The degree to which personal taste and interests impact upon friendships means that these communities can overlap with communities of interest. This field was influenced by earlier work on social network analysis, which was developed in the 1950s and 1960s by Barnes (1954), Bott (1957) and others as a way to map personal ties that often transcend spatial boundaries (Crow and Allan, 1994). This work was seen to avoid the 'impressionistic' tone that was sometimes levelled as a criticism at earlier community studies by offering a way to measure 'connectedness', which was later renamed 'network density' (Crow and Allan, 1994). Wellman (1979: 1203) also argued that examining social linkages allows sociology to "free the study of community from normative and spatial predilections". It is worth noting, however, that the term 'network' has been critiqued. Smart (2007: 7) has argued that whilst the word allows for fluidity and does not tie significant relationships to a particular place, it "robs the concept of relationships of much of its emotional content and certainly does not invoke the special importance of connectedness, biography and memory in how people relate to one another".

In his 'classic' text *Gay men's friendships*, Nardi (1999) suggested that gay male friendships form 'invincible' communities. He proposed that participation in gay community organisations, such as bars, shops and political and social groups, contributes to 'gay identity achievement' (Nardi, 1999). In turn, gay identity leads to the creation and maintenance of communities, which provide the context for reproducing identity in newer generations looking for 'meaning and friendship' (Nardi, 1999). Over the years, friendships have also been identified as central to lesbian communities (Weinstock and Rothblum, 1996). The importance of these supportive friendships has led some scholars (and non-scholars) to compare lesbian and gay friendships to family, describing them as 'families of choice' or 'friendship families' (Holt, 2011; Weeks, Heaphy and Donovan, 2001; Weinstock and Rothblum, 1996; Weston, 1991). Weston (1991: 207) argued that "families we choose . . . have proved capable of . . . exchanges of material and emotional assistance, co-parenting arrangements, and support for persons with AIDS". In her research, families of choice resembled networks that crossed household lines, but often from the same gender, class, race and age, with a shared past often used to separate friendship family from other friendships (Weston, 1991). Weeks, Heaphy and Donovan (2001) later (re)affirmed the significance of families of choice for 'non-heterosexuals' in a UK context, highlighting the role of these relationships in asserting and supporting a positive individual, and collective, identity. This is important when individuals may be excluded from their 'families of origin' and/or broader communities (Weeks, Heaphy and Donovan, 2001). 'Communities of choice' and 'communities of need' (i.e. voluntary friendships and other elective relationships) have therefore been distinguished from communities of fate or origin that we are born into (Homfray, 2007; Howes, 2011; Weeks, Heaphy and Donovan, 2001).

These ideas have been the subject of much debate, however. Weinstock and Rothblum (1996), for instance, have suggested that whilst the comparison with family acknowledges the primacy of friendships for some people, it may reproduce the hegemony of the family. Heaphy (2011: 37), in calling for a sociology of relational displays, similarly argued that "we [can] reduce diverse and creative displays of care, love and commitment to family ones", which privileges the family and risks rendering alternative relations invisible. Gabb (2011: 45) has also noted that "some formative work in this [families of choice] area has been inclined to leave to one side those who do not feel 'at home' in this community-orientated versioning of intimacy", themes to which I will return throughout this book.

It is the separation of friendship and family that Pahl and Spencer (2004) have criticised, arguing that relationships are more blurred than this (though their work was not in an LGB-specific context). Instead, they propose distinctions between given and chosen relationships, and associated levels of commitment, which may be with family or friends. Bertone and Pallotta-Chiarolli (2014: 5) have also recently questioned the dichotomy between families of origin and families of choice, which they argue risks "losing sight of complexity and heterogeneity, both in GLBT and heterosexual experiences, which are actually highly differentiated, primarily on the basis of gender, but also of class and other structural and cultural dimensions". These arguments do not necessarily contradict the idea that some LGB friendships may be comparable to widespread beliefs about family, however, for example through the provision of care and support (Weeks, 2007; Weston, 1991; Woolwine, 2000). Pahl and Spencer's criticism that Weeks, Heaphy and Donovan (2001) were suggesting a replacement of (biological) family across the board may thus be a misunderstanding or overstatement. As Weston (1998: 398) clearly states, "laying claim to a gay family in no way depends upon a break with one's family of origin". I would also suggest that there are still concerns among some LGBT people that coming out to family may lead to the loss of family contact (which was the case for some of my participants). People comparing their friends to family in these circumstances may not be surprising, given a society that still promotes the primacy of (heteronormative) family. Smart (2007) concluded that it is important to recognise both chosen and given families as fluid, rather than one replacing the other. The emergence of personal communities as a concept thus broadens notions of families of choice to include family, colleagues and neighbours, as well as friends (Wilkinson et al., 2012). These committed personal relations can be described as offering solidarity, and therefore 'community-like properties' (Wilkinson et al., 2012). Friendships and personal communities amongst LGBT people will be explored further in Chapter 4.

## Virtual Communities and Cyberian Mailways

Another way of viewing communities has focussed on 'virtual communities' or 'ephemeral communities' (Castells, 1996). Here, the internet is seen as facilitating certain communities of interest that are enacted and supported online. As Day (2006: 227) noted, "electronic media promise a solution to the problem of mobility . . . Space is compressed almost to nothing, making it possible for individuals anywhere to establish contact with one another". Whilst some have viewed these communities as 'thin' networks (Calhoun, 1988), Castells (2001: 127) saw value in this virtual view of community as "de-emphasizing its cultural component, emphasizing its supportive role to individuals and families, and de-linking its social existence".

Virtual or online communities have also been discussed in previous LGBT research. Whittle (1998), for example, examined the use of cyberspace among trans people, dubbing it the 'trans-cyberian mail way', and emphasising its role in providing safe space and enabling friendships, expertise sharing and political activism. He commented, "cyberia has been a place where the trans community has been able to thrive, while the real world has often been a cold and unwelcoming place" (Whittle, 1998: 393). As trans people are likely to be geographically dispersed from one another, the internet has facilitated interaction across great distances (Whittle, 1998). Valentine (2008) also suggested that the internet offers the possibility of 'stretching intimacy' beyond the domestic home (and one could extend this argument to physical spaces more generally), enabling 'togetherness' whilst separate, and thus facilitating the sharing of knowledge, love and/or care. More recently, Ekins and King (2010: 37) have argued that the internet "has created critical mass and the formation of new virtual social worlds within which new trans identities, both 'virtual' and 'real', have emerged". These themes will be returned to in Chapter 5.

## Community Is Here to Stay?

However community is conceived, it is often understood to be positive, with beneficial impacts on individual health and/or happiness (Day, 2006). Nevertheless, there are those who also point to a reverse interpretation of community, and in particular the 'community outsiders' that are inevitably created. As Cornwell (1984: 53) suggested, "where there is belonging, there is also not belonging, and where there is in-clusion, there is also ex-clusion". This has recently been referred to as the 'darker' side of communities (Crow and Mah, 2012; Valentine and Skelton, 2003). It could be argued, therefore, that it is a divisive construct (Day, 2006). As Hines (2010) proposed, community suggests a universal, egalitarian conception at odds with (some) people's lived experience. Gay men in Woolwine's (2000) New York study felt that although they shared common experiences of alienation and marginalisation, they were too 'divided' to be a community. Similarly, in Holt's (2011) study in Sydney, some participants thought that the term 'gay community' implied a unity and uniformity that did not exist. Fraser's (2008: 252) participants, however, believed in 'a common thread' coexisting with diversity. Despite its strengths and weaknesses, "there is no sign that the term 'community' is going to go away, either from the everyday discourse of 'ordinary' people, or from the rhetoric of those who seek to govern and manage them" (Day, 2006: 233). Pahl (1996: 92) has asked the question "[why] does a dead idea refuse to lie down?". In Day's words (2006: 22), "the answer must be, because actually it is not deceased . . . it continues to fulfil a useful living purpose". In providing a useful way to speak of 'groupness', the concept is alluring, yet 'slippery', and "to be approached with extreme care" (Day, 2006: 2). However, in a more optimistic vein, Modood (2015) has argued that one can identify and study groupness without essentialising or othering. The extent to which LGBT people draw upon this notion of groupness is the crux of this book.

## The Research

The research on which this book draws took place throughout the UK in 2012 within the cross-research council 'Connected Communities' programme of work. The overall aim of the project was to explore understandings and experiences of 'LGBT communities' and assess implications for LGBT health and wellbeing. The phrase 'LGBT community' is frequently used in media, policy and practice arenas, as well as research, but often with little discussion of how and why it is being used. Whilst community has been interrogated more widely, the lack of explanation and/or critique about the notion of LGBT communities in particular has been noted previously (Keogh, Henderson and Dodds, 2004; McLean and O'Connor, 2003).

Throughout the research (and writing this book), I was informed by social constructionist and interactionist perspectives, and in particular Smart's (2007) 'connectedness thesis'. For her, "connectedness as a mindset encourages enquiry about all kinds of sociality and seeks to understand how association remains both possible and desirable, as well as how it may take different shapes at different times" (Smart, 2007: 189). I am also influenced by May (2013), who argued that the self is relational, and culturally and socially embedded. Sociology that centres on the 'doing' of, rather than 'being', family (Morgan, 1996) has also influenced work on 'displaying families' (Finch, 2007), 'displaying personal relationships' (Dermott and Seymour, 2011), and 'relational displays' (Heaphy, 2011), and I engage with this notion of display within the book. Drawing on the sociology of personal life (Smart, 2007; May, 2013), I am committed to documenting and trying to understand lived experience, because "any sociological investigation must begin in the day-to-day experiences of individuals" (May, 2013: 77). I also draw on the concept of intersectionality (Crenshaw, 1989; Yuval-Davis, 2011) in acknowledgment of the "importance of considering overlapping aspects of identity and how these complicate individual identities and interactional encounters" (Sanger and Taylor, 2013: 2).

The research utilised three methods of data collection: a short online survey to which there were 627 responses; an interactive project website to which people could post contributions, comments and/or upload files (documents or photographs); and a series of in-depth interviews and group discussions involving a total of 44 people (see appendix for further detail on methods and participants). Similar themes were explored in both the survey and in-depth methods. Question areas broadly centred on people's views on, and/or experiences of, communities currently, in the past, and in the future, but many participants also discussed their lives in a broader sense. This is important when trying to analyse people's understandings and experiences, and is therefore included within my analysis contained in the book. As such, I am mindful of Smart's (2007: 28) belief that "personal life is embedded in the social . . . the sociologist can map personal lives (revealed through the research process) into their social context and into their specific history or spatial location". The sociology of personal life, as May (2013: 66) suggests, "highlights the connectedness and social embeddedness of people's lives", where personal life is inevitably shaped by, and shapes, the 'public sphere'.

Overall, the project involved a range of participant ages, genders and sexualities. Amongst survey respondents, age ranges were relatively evenly spread between 25 and 54, though there were fewer responses from those aged 24 and under, and those aged 55 and over. An open question about gender identity produced 31 different responses, with an additional 241 individuals choosing not to disclose this information. With caution, I grouped these into the largest categories (all those with over five responses), which resulted in 189 female; 167 male; 12 trans; and 11 genderqueer, bigender, genderless or gender neutral respondents. It should be noted that these identities refer to current identities rather than genders assigned at birth. A sexual identity question was also open, and resulted in 44 different responses (and 245 people who said that they did not know or who did not answer this question). These were also, with caution, amalgamated into larger groups for all those over five responses. Hence, there were 177 gay; 114 lesbian; 48 bisexual, pansexual or polysexual; 24 queer; and 6 heterosexual/straight respondents. Of the 44 people who were involved in the in-depth stage of the research, 21 self-identified as female, 19 as male, and 4 did not identify as 'female' or 'male'. Of these 44 people, 21 also identified as gay, 12 as lesbian, 3 as bisexual, 2 as pansexual, 1 as straight, and 5 did not disclose their sexual identity. More detailed 'pen portraits' for these participants are contained within the appendix, and their relevant pseudonyms appear alongside quotes within the book. When I draw on survey respondents' data, brief biographical information is provided, using participants' own words. This offers some, albeit limited, context for their comments, and helps to distinguish survey respondents from one another. When I use the term 'participant' I am referring to those who were involved in any stage of the research, whilst I use 'survey respondent' or 'website contributor' to denote those who were involved in those specific aspects of the research.

Because the research sought to examine the construct of 'LGBT community', during the research process and throughout this book I also use the acronym LGBT to refer to people, but recognise that this is problematic because of the way it can appear to 'solidify' identities, and render some people's identities invisible. On the other hand, as Browne and Bakshi (2013: 215) suggest, understanding "the collective category LGBT . . . as solidarities, alliances and connections between LGBT people, can render this a viable category to both study and discuss". However, participants did identify in more various ways than the LGBT acronym suggests, and their views are included throughout the book. In addition, Chapter 2 explicitly explores views on this acronym, so I hope that my use of LGBT is not viewed as an uncritical acceptance. I also use the word 'trans' as a shorthand 'umbrella' term to refer to people whose gender identity differs from how they were assigned at birth. I therefore mean for the term to include a diverse range of gender identities and embodied experiences, and the complexities and fluidities with regard to identity within this broad grouping are illustrated throughout the book. The ways in which people conceptualised and referred to the 'opposite' of LGBT is problematic. I try to replicate participants' wording within my discussions, but sometimes when drawing these together I do use the terms 'heterosexual' and 'non-LGBT'. These do not sit comfortably but for clarification I mean for these to be understood as referring to cisgender heterosexual people who may commonly be placed outside of an LGBT community. I do not mean to imply or infer the exclusion of trans or any other gender or sexual minority by using these terms. However, the process of reproducing some authors' or participants' language that referred only to lesbians and/or gay men does at times unfortunately render bisexual and trans identities less visible.

Whilst this chapter has provided an overview of existing scholarship on community in general, and LGBT communities in particular, specific research is also examined within the subsequent chapters. This includes UK and international literature from a range of subject disciplines, including geography, health studies, history, psychology, and sociology, although my own sociological 'training' will inevitably have influenced my reading of this literature, and my research. This means, for example, that I do not try to assess 'community attachment', which is more commonly explored within psychological and public health research. Instead, I deliberately set out to examine and illustrate what LGBT community means to LGBT people. In doing so, I am interested in complicating this term as it has sometimes been under-explored within previous research that has assumed and defined 'the LGBT community' to be, essentially, groups of LGBT people (e.g. see Frost and Meyer, 2012). I therefore make no apology for the lack of measures and scales within my research or this book! Similarly, I use 'wellbeing' to refer to participants' own understandings of this term, rather than proposing any standardised usage. My purpose is to illustrate and explore *self-reported* impacts on health, wellbeing and 'quality of life', rather than measure these against any pre-existing criteria. Once again, I make no apology for this approach, but hope it proves useful in thinking about wider approaches towards constructions of both LGBT communities and LGBT wellbeing.

However, I acknowledge the weakness that much of the literature I engage with emanates from a 'Western' or Anglophone viewpoint, also noted elsewhere (May, 2013; Monro, 2015; Taylor and Addison, 2013). As Browne and Ferreira (2015) have observed, Anglo-American and Global North perspectives often dominate the field of geography, and I would suggest the same could be said more widely of the social sciences. For information, when referring to existing literature I have replicated the terms authors used (e.g. 'gay', 'lesbian and gay', LGB, LGBT). The term 'scene' is used to refer to areas of commercial venues that cater for a 'gay' or LGBT clientele. Though I do not suggest these areas are an entity in themselves, participants did at times talk about the scene as if it was a 'thing', rather than a site of interactions. As Browne and Bakshi (2013, 66) argue, scenes are "heterogeneous assemblages of emotions, meaning, cultures and materialities that are produced through an illusion of homogeneity". As such, like Browne and Ferreira (2015: 4), I see "place and space as something that we 'do', rather than something that simply 'is'".

## The Book

Although this book draws on UK-based research, it offers broader implications and is therefore of international relevance. Following this introductory chapter, the book is organised thematically around eight chapters, followed by a concluding chapter. With the exception of Chapter 2 that introduces how participants viewed the concept of LGBT community, the remaining substantive chapters each provide a brief introduction, an overview of existing literature in that area, a thematic analysis of my own research and a closing chapter summary.

The first three empirical chapters (Chapters 2–4) all explore understandings and experiences of LGBT communities. In Chapter 2, I focus on how participants understood and problematised the concept of LGBT community. This includes an analysis of language and 'labels' used by and about LGBT people. Following on from this, Chapter 3 examines whether, and how, difference was acknowledged within understandings of LGBT community. This chapter also illustrates experiences of inequalities and/or exclusions, often based on identity-based prejudice by LGBT people. Chapter 4 moves on to consider people's lived experiences of LGBT communities, exploring why some people engage with (the idea of) communities, looking particularly at friendships, safety and 'risk' and activism. In doing so, the chapter discusses practices of identity management and self-censorship in intimate relationships.

Space played a key role in participant understandings of community, and Chapters 5–7 each examine different forms of space. In Chapter 5 I explore geographical, temporary and online spaces. In doing so, the chapter looks at issues of visibility and support, as well as contrasts between 'public' and 'private' spaces, and urban and rural locations. Chapter 6 examines scene spaces in particular, and will show how, for some, the scene is experienced as an enjoyable space that can offer (at least the possibility of) friendship, feelings of comfort and safety and 'diversion' away from heteronormativity. However, I will also illustrate that scene spaces can undermine some people's identities because of the existence of norms and attitudes that can render those who are not seen to 'fit' as out of place, and therefore excluded. In Chapter 7 I focus on experiences and perceptions of Pride events, which were thought to be particularly significant for community by many participants.

Turning to an alternative view of communities, in Chapter 8 I discuss the notion of imagined LGBT communities, which is linked to a sense of belonging. This sense of belonging was often related to what participants saw as their similarities, together with a belief that this created mutual understanding. In the penultimate chapter, Chapter 9, I explore LGBT wellbeing linked to understandings and experiences of LGBT communities. Chapter 10 forms the conclusion to the book, and draws together my ideas on constructions and experiences of LGBT communities. I argue that use of the (singular) term LGBT community can risk minimising or misunderstanding diverse needs of LGBT people, both in terms of their everyday lives and in relation to service planning and provision. The idea of a plurality of LGBT communities is therefore more valuable, as it explicitly suggests that not all LGBT people (wish to) belong to one large homogenous, and ostensibly harmonious, group.

## Note

1  Section 28 of the Local Government Act 1988 was a controversial piece of legislation which stated that a local authority "shall not promote the teaching in any maintained school of the acceptability of homosexuality" (HMSO, 1988). After vigorous campaigning, it was repealed in Scotland in 2000 and in England and Wales in 2003.

## References

Adler, S. and Brenner, J. (1992) 'Gender and space: Lesbians and gay men in the city', *International Journal of Urban and Regional Research* 16(1): 24–34.

Anderson, B. (2006) *Imagined communities: Reflections on the origin and spread of nationalism.* London: Verso.

Barnes, J. (1954) 'Class and committees in a Norwegian island parish', *Human Relations* 7: 39–58.

Bell, D. and Valentine, G. (1995a) 'Introduction: Orientations' in Bell, D. and Valentine, G. (eds) *Mapping desire: Geographies of sexualities.* London: Routledge, pp. 1–27.

Bell, D. and Valentine, G. (1995b) 'Queer country: Rural lesbian and gay lives', *Journal of Rural Studies* 11(2): 113–122.

Bertone, C. and Pallotta-Chiarolli, M. (2014) 'Putting families of origin into the queer picture: Introducing this special issue', *Journal of GLBT Family Studies* 10(1–2): 1–14.

Binnie, J. (1995) 'Trading places: Consumption, sexuality and the production of queer space' in Bell, D. and Valentine, G. (eds) *Mapping desire: Geographies of sexualities.* London: Routledge, pp. 182–199.

Binnie, J. and Skeggs, B. (2004) 'Cosmopolitan knowledge and the production and consumption of sexualized space: Manchester's gay village', *The Sociological Review* 52(1): 39–61.

Bott, E. (1957) *Family and social network.* Cambridge: Tavistock Press.

Brown, M. (2014) 'Gender and sexuality II: There goes the gayborhood?', *Progress in Human Geography* 38(3): 457–465.

Browne, K. (2008) 'Imagining cities, living the other: Between the gay urban idyll and rural lesbian lives', *The Open Geography Journal* 1: 25–32.

Browne, K. and Bakshi, L. (2013) *Ordinary in Brighton: LGBT, activisms and the city.* Aldershot: Ashgate.

Browne, K. and Ferreira, E. (eds) (2015) *Lesbian geographies: Gender, place and power.* Farnham: Ashgate.

Calhoun, C. (1988) 'Populist politics, communications media, and large scale social integration', *Sociological Theory* 6(2): 219–241.

Casey, M.E. (2007) 'The queer unwanted and their undesirable "otherness"' in Browne, K., Lim, J. and Brown, G. (eds) *Geographies of sexualities: Theory, practices and politics*. Aldershot: Ashgate, pp. 125–136.

Castells, M. (1983) *The city and the grassroots: A cross cultural theory of urban social movements*. London: University of California Press.

Castells, M. (1996) *The information age, vol. 1: The rise of the network society*. Oxford: Blackwell.

Castells, M. (2001) *The internet galaxy: Reflections on the internet, business, and society*. Oxford: Oxford University Press.

Cohen, A.P. (1985) *The symbolic construction of community*. London: Tavistock.

Cohen, A.P. (1987) *Whalsay: Symbol, segment and boundary in a Shetland Island community*. Manchester: Manchester University Press.

Cornwell, J. (1984) *Hard-earned lives: Accounts of health and illness from East London*. London: Tavistock.

Crenshaw, K. (1989) 'Demarginalizing the intersection of race and sex: A black feminist critique of antidiscrimination doctrine, feminist theory and antiracist politics', *The University of Chicago Legal Forum* 140: 139–167.

Crow, G. (2012) 'Community re-studies: Lessons and prospects', *The Sociological Review* 60(3): 405–420.

Crow, G. and Allan, G. (1994) *Community life: An introduction to local social relationships*. New York: Harvester Wheatsheaf.

Crow, G. and Mah, A. (2012) *Conceptualisations and meanings of 'community': The theory and operationalisation of a contested concept*. Southampton: University of Southampton.

Davis, T. (1995) 'The diversity of queer politics and the redefinition of sexual identity and community in urban space' in Bell, D. and Valentine, G. (eds) *Mapping desire: Geographies of sexualities*. London: Routledge, pp. 284–303.

Day, G. (2006) *Community and everyday life*. New York: Routledge.

Delanty, G. (2010) *Community*. London: Routledge.

Dermott, E. and Seymour, J. (2011) *Displaying families: A new concept for the sociology of family life*. Basingstoke: Palgrave Macmillan.

Ekins, R. and King, D. (2010) 'The emergence of new transgendering identities in the age of the internet' in Hines, S. and Sanger, T. (eds) *Transgender identities: Towards a social analysis of gender diversity*. Abingdon: Routledge, pp. 25–42.

Finch, J. (2007) 'Displaying families', *Sociology* 41(1): 65–81.

Fraser, S. (2008) 'Getting out in the "real world": Young men, queer and theories of gay community', *Journal of Homosexuality* 55(2): 245–264.

Frost, D.M. and Meyer, I.H. (2012) 'Measuring community connectedness among diverse sexual minority populations', *Journal of Sex Research* 48(1): 36–49.

Gabb, J. (2011) 'Troubling displays: The affect of gender, sexuality and class' in Dermott, E. and Seymour, J. (eds) *Displaying families: A new concept for the sociology of family life*. Basingstoke: Palgrave Macmillan, pp. 38–57.

Ghaziani, A. (2014) *There goes the gayborhood?* Princeton: Princeton University Press.

Gieseking, J. (2013) 'Queering the meaning of "neighborhood": Reinterpreting the lesbian-queer experience of Park Slope, Brooklyn, 1983–2008' in Taylor, Y. and Addison, M. (eds) *Queer presences and absences*. New York: Palgrave Macmillan, pp. 178–200.

Government Equalities Office (2010) *Working for lesbian, gay, bisexual and transgender equality*. London: Government Equalities Office.

Hague, E. (2011) 'Benedict Anderson' in Hubbard, P. and Kitchin, R. (eds) *Key thinkers on space and place*. London: Sage, pp. 18–25.

Heaphy, B. (2011) 'Critical relational displays' in Dermott, E. and Seymour, J. (eds) *Displaying families: A new concept for the sociology of family life*. Basingstoke: Palgrave Macmillan, pp. 19–37.

Hines, S. (2007) 'Transgendering care: Practices of care within transgender communities', *Critical Social Policy* 27(4): 462–486.

Hines, S. (2010) 'Queerly situated: Exploring constraints and negotiations of trans queer subjectivities', *Gender, Place and Culture* 17(5): 597–613.

HMSO (Her Majesty's Stationery Office) (1988) *Local Government Act 1988*. London: HMSO.

Holt, M. (2011) 'Gay men and ambivalence about "gay community": From gay community attachment to personal communities', *Culture, Health and Sexuality* 13(8): 857–871.

Homfray, M. (2007) *Provincial queens: The gay and lesbian community in the North-West of England*. Bern: Peter Lang.

Howes, R. (2011) *Gay West: Civil society, community and LGBT history in Bristol and Bath, 1970 to 2010*. Bristol: SilverWood Books.

Jenkins, R. (2014) *Social identity*. Abingdon: Routledge.

Johnston, L. and Valentine, G. (1995) 'Wherever I lay my girlfriend, that's my home: The performance and surveillance of lesbian identities in domestic environments' in Bell, D. and Valentine, G. (eds) *Mapping desire: Geographies of sexualities*. London: Routledge, pp. 99–113.

Keogh, P., Henderson, L. and Dodds, C. (2004) *Ethnic minority gay men: Redefining community, restoring identity*. London: Sigma Research.

Knopp, L. (1995) 'Sexuality and urban space: A framework for analysis' in Bell, D. and Valentine, G. (eds) *Mapping desire: Geographies of sexualities*. London: Routledge, pp. 149–161.

Kollman, K. and Waites, M. (2011) 'United Kingdom: Changing political opportunity structures, policy success and continuing challenges for lesbian, gay and bisexual movements' in Tremblay, M., Paternotte, D. and Johnson, C. (eds) *The lesbian and gay movement and the state*. Farnham: Ashgate, pp. 181–196.

Levine, M.P. (1979) 'Gay ghetto', *Journal of Homosexuality* 4(4): 363–377.

Maffesoli, M. (1996) *The time of the tribes: The decline of individualism in mass society*. London: Sage.

Mallett, R. and Slater, J. (2014) 'Language' in Cameron, C. (ed) *Disability studies: A student's guide*. London: Sage, pp. 91–94.

May, V. (2013) *Connecting self to society: Belonging in a changing world*. New York: Palgrave Macmillan.

McLean, C. and O'Connor, W. (2003) *Sexual orientation research phase 2: The future of LGBT research*. Edinburgh: Scottish Executive.

Melucci, A. (1996) *The playing self: Person and meaning in the planetary society*. Cambridge: Cambridge University Press.

Modood, T. (2015) *Equality and group identity revisited*. Unpublished paper presented at European Sociological Association biennial conference, 25–28 August 2015, Prague.

Monk, D. (2011) 'Challenging homophobic bullying in schools: The politics of progress', *International Journal of Law in Context* 7(2): 181–207.

Monro, S. (2015) *Bisexuality: Identities, politics, and theories*. Basingstoke: Palgrave Macmillan.

Moran, L. and Skeggs, B. (2001) 'Property and propriety: Fear and safety in gay space', *Social and Cultural Geography* 2(4): 407–420.

Morgan, D. (1996) *Family connections: An introduction to family studies*. Cambridge: Polity Press.

Nardi, P.M. (1999) *Gay men's friendships*. Chicago: University of Chicago Press.

Pahl, R. (1996) 'Friendly society' in Kraemer, S. and Roberts, J. (eds) *The politics of attachment*. London: Free Association Books.

Pahl, R. (2001) *On friendship*. Cambridge: Polity Press.

Pahl, R. and Spencer, L. (2004) 'Personal communities: Not simply families of "fate" or "choice"', *Current Sociology* 24(2): 199–221.

Peake, L. (1993) '"Race" and sexuality: Challenging the patriarchal structuring of urban social space', *Environment and Planning D: Society and Space* 11(4): 415–432.

Phillipson, C. (2012) 'Community studies and re-studies in the 21st century: Methodological challenges and strategies for the future', *The Sociological Review* 60(3): 537–549.

Reiter, D.F. (2008) *Greetings from the gayborhood*. New York: Harry N. Abrams.

Rothblum, E. (2008) 'Finding a large and thriving lesbian and bisexual community: The costs and benefits of caring', *Gay and Lesbian Issues and Psychology Review* 4(2): 69–79.

Rothblum, E. (2010) 'Where is the "women's community?" Voices of lesbian, bisexual, and queer women and heterosexual sisters', *Feminism and Psychology* 20(4): 454–472.

Rothenberg, T. (1995) '"And she told two friends . . .": Lesbians creating urban social space' in Bell, D. and Valentine, G. (eds) *Mapping desire: Geographies of sexualities*. London: Routledge, pp. 165–181.

Sanger, T. and Taylor, Y. (2013) 'Introduction' in Sanger, T. and Taylor, Y. (eds) *Mapping intimacies: Relations, exchanges, affects*. Basingstoke: Palgrave Macmillan, pp. 1–14.

Simpson, P. (2015) *Middle-aged gay men, ageing and ageism: Over the rainbow?* Basingstoke: Palgrave Macmillan.

Smart, C. (2007) *Personal life*. Cambridge: Polity Press.

Smith, D.P. and Holt, L. (2005) '"Lesbian migrants in the gentrified valley" and "other" geographies of rural gentrification', *Journal of Rural Studies* 21(3): 313–322.

Taylor, V., Kaminski, E. and Dugan, K. (2002) 'From the Bowery to the Castro: Communities, identities and movements' in Richardson, D. and Seidman, S. (eds) *Handbook of lesbian and gay studies*. London: Sage, pp. 99–114.

Taylor, Y. and Addison, M. (2013) 'Queer presences and absences: An introduction' in Taylor, Y. and Addison, M. (eds) *Queer presences and absences*. New York: Palgrave Macmillan, pp. 1–10.

Valentine, G. (1993a) 'Desperately seeking Susan: A geography of lesbian friendships', *Area* 25(2): 109–116.

Valentine, G. (1993b) 'Negotiating and managing multiple sexual identities: Lesbian time-space strategies', *Transactions of the Institute of British Geographers* 18(2): 237–248.

Valentine, G. (1993c) '(Hetero)sexing space: Lesbian perceptions and experiences of everyday space', *Environment and Planning D: Society and Space* 11(4): 395–413.

Valentine, G. (1994) 'Toward a geography of the lesbian community', *Women and Environments* 14(1): 8–10.

Valentine, G. (1995) 'Out and about: Geographies of lesbian landscapes', *International Journal of Urban and Regional Research* 19(1): 96–111.

Valentine, G. (2000) 'Introduction: From nowhere to everywhere: Lesbian geographies', *Journal of Lesbian Studies* 4(1): 1–9.

Valentine, G. (2002) 'Queer bodies and the production of space' in Richardson, R. and Seidman, S (eds) *Handbook of lesbian and gay studies*. London: Sage, pp. 145–160.

Valentine, G. (2008) 'The ties that bind: Towards geographies of intimacy', *Geography Compass* 2(6): 2097–2110.

Valentine, G. and Skelton, T. (2003) 'Finding oneself, losing oneself: The lesbian and gay "scene" as a paradoxical space', *International Journal of Urban and Regional Research* 27(4): 849–866.

Walkerdine, V. and Studdert, D. (2011) *Concepts and meanings of community in the social sciences*. Swindon: Arts and Humanities Research Council.

Weeks, J. (1996) 'The idea of a sexual community', *Soundings* 2: 71–84.

Weeks, J. (2007) *The world we have won: The remaking of erotic and intimate life*. London: Routledge.

Weeks, J., Heaphy, B. and Donovan, C. (2001) *Same sex intimacies: Families of choice and other life experiments*. London: Routledge.

Weinstock, J.S. and Rothblum, E. (eds) (1996) *Lesbian friendships*. New York: New York University Press.

Wellman, B. (1979) 'The community question: The intimate networks of East Yorkers', *American Journal of Sociology* 84(5): 1201–1231.

Wellman, B. (2001) 'Physical place and cyberplace: The Rise of networked individualism', *International Journal of Urban and Regional Research* 25(2): 227–252.

Weston, K. (1991) *Families we choose: Lesbians, gays, kinship*. New York: Columbia University Press.

Weston, K. (1995) 'Get thee to a big city: Sexual imaginary and the great gay migration', *GLQ: A Journal of Lesbian and Gay Studies* 2(3): 253–277.

Weston, K. (1998) 'Families we choose' in Nardi, P.M. and Schneider, B.E. (eds) *Social perspectives in lesbian and gay studies: A reader*. London: Routledge, pp. 390–411.

Whittle, S. (1994) 'Consuming differences: The collaboration of the gay body with the cultural state' in Whittle, S. (ed) *The margins of the city: Gay men's urban lives*. Aldershot: Ashgate, pp. 27–41.

Whittle, S. (1998) 'The trans-cyberian mail way', *Social and Legal Studies* 7(3): 389–408.

Wilkinson, J., Bittman, M., Holt, M., Rawstorne, P., Kippax, S. and Worth, H. (2012) 'Solidarity beyond sexuality: The personal communities of gay men', *Sociology* 46(6): 1161–1177.

Willmott, P. (1986) *Social networks, informal care and public policy*. London: PSI.

Woolwine, D. (2000) 'Community in gay male experience and moral discourse', *Journal of Homosexuality* 38(4): 5–37.

Yuval-Davis, N. (2011) *The politics of belonging*. London: Sage.

# 2 'Owning' and Questioning LGBT Communities

"The idea of community is just a word, it does not stand up . . ."

(Bryn)

## Introduction

It has been suggested that "the emergence of distinctive sexual subcultures and communities is part of a wider process that has marked the modern world, and is becoming ever more characteristic of the era of late or post-modernity" (Weeks, 2003: 80). Building on Chapter 1 that introduced literature on how communities have been understood, this chapter explores participant understandings of community. In doing so, it looks at perspectives on language use by and about LGBT people, as well as strengths and weaknesses in adopting (or rejecting) recognisable identity 'labels', and/or the suggestion of a collective/community. Contrary to Weeks' (2003) suggestion, a tension clearly emerged in the research, with many people keen to question the assumption that LGBT people necessarily form or belong to distinct communities. There was also a level of anger that this presumption may be perpetuated by people identifying as heterosexual and cisgender. It was often the assumption of LGBT similarity or lack of diversity that was the reason the concept of community was critiqued. Yet there were also examples of people assuming that those who identify as LGBT do belong to, or form, LGBT communities. As Woodhead noted (1995: 236–237), "rhetoric of the 'lesbian and gay community' is easy to locate: published in the gay press, broadcast by other gay media . . . and, of course, talked about by many lesbians and gay men themselves". I would argue that LGBT people being able to 'own' this term is key, and I return to this below. The chapter explores these issues within the following five headings: The Acronym That 'Lumps Together', 'Managing' the Acronym, Ambivalence, Commonality and Agency.

## The Acronym That 'Lumps Together'

In this section I examine the acronym with which LGBT people are often referred, which participants frequently raised issues with in initial discussions about the concept of LGBT community. In doing so, language used to refer to people was linked with a lack of 'ownership' and/or agency:

> Frankly, we were given it [the LGBT acronym] . . . It's political, the minute you reduce people to an acronym you can label them, literally, and I think it serves its purpose for the system that gave it to us.
>
> (Bryn)

Another participant in the same discussion group disagreed that 'the system' was trying to label people:

> I disagree that LGBT is a label that has been imposed on us. It's one that has been invented by gay people, it started saying gay which was a reaction to being called queer, and then different identities wanted to be included, women were very strong to fight for lesbian . . . and then other identities came on. To their credit, the public bodies have latched onto that to see there is a group that they have to respond to.
>
> (Peter)

The suggestion of commonality or homogeneity that use of a combined acronym can imply was explicitly questioned by participants who drew attention to the diversity within and between groups of LGBT people:

> 'LGBT' has historically been a useful political concept but it suggests a homogeneity and communality which may not exist. It may also disguise or minimise differences within the extremely diverse groupings represented by each of the terms L, G, B and T.
>
> (Survey respondent 196: Gay man aged 65+)

A particular concern related to the relative visibility of different groups within the acronym. There were widespread doubts about the meaningfulness of grouping four identities together 'as one' when this may not necessarily be desired by those it includes:

> I am ambivalent about the lumping together of L&G with B&T and with Q whatever that means. For me T is a separate issue. The same importance, but squashing them all together just means all categories are diluted and ulti-mately misunderstood.
>
> (Survey respondent 75: Female lesbian aged 45–54)

Gemma raised the issue of differing histories and ideologies that complicate the ease with which identities can be 'lumped together' as a coherent group:

> Historically, LGBT communities have come together not always in the most easy and tension-free ways, and when we lump those four letters together we are almost side-stepping a whole lot of ideological issues that have manifested

over the years . . . We wouldn't expect it really of any other minority group, that we would lump a few kind of identities together and they would just get on.

(Gemma)

Participants questioned how alike people are within the LGBT acronym, with particular doubts voiced about whether joining LGB with T was positive, or realistic, particularly given the diversity of identities within 'trans' as an umbrella term:

> I think that the idea of LGBT community/communities has purchase but that more work needs to be done in terms of how trans fits in and indeed whether in relation to trans, transsexual and other transgendered people have sufficiently shared objectives as to be realistically considered as a community.
>
> (Survey respondent 586: Polysexual trans person aged 45–54)

> I have two trans friends who hate the idea of LGBT, because they feel the whole idea has been hijacked and stuck on the end like a tail.
>
> (Bryn)

The place of trans as a potential 'add-on' to LGB has been raised previously (Browne and Lim, 2010), and in this research was explicitly related to the difficulties of discussing gender and sexual identities together, and the potential for sexual orientation to dominate understandings:

> In terms of the T . . . we often have to appreciate that there are plenty of trans people who actually don't want to be LGBT because they'll say 'this is about my gender, it's not about my sexual orientation', and LGBT is always about sexual orientation. So I think that there's also a danger in just assuming that somebody wants to be in your gang.
>
> (Gemma)

> There is obviously a bit of a dissonance, especially if you include the I and Q, because you've got three things that are to do with sexuality, you've got something to do with gender identity . . . intersexuality is a physical embodiment question, which again I think I would say is slightly different from trans identity, and Q is a political identity.
>
> (Petra)

Echoing scholarship on the 'problem' of combining gender and sexual identities in one acronym (Richardson and Monro, 2012), people were sometimes open about their lack of knowledge about trans identities and how this fed into their uncertainty about the utility of a combined LGBT acronym:

> I know we do use the term LGBT all the time but I've always had an issue with the T bit . . . [I] see it as being a very, very different thing . . . I don't get the link at this point in my life.
>
> (Carl)

Nevertheless, perceived benefits of an overarching grouping were identified. As Browne and Lim (2010) have argued, trans people being part of a collective with LGB people can enable a greater sense of being listened to, empowered and/or having their needs met. For Rachel, meeting trans people was not always easy in the area where she lived, so she found some sense of a (metaphoric) 'collective' with LGB people:

> It's so you're not so alone, if you are in a group of other people like yourself . . . because being trans is predominantly, you are alone.
>
> (Rachel)

However, participant awareness of the potential for services to exclude B or T within LGBT was relatively common, though this is not to suggest that readers should, or that participants were, only seeing bisexual and trans identities through a lens of 'suffering' (Browne and Bakshi, 2013; Formby, 2015). Browne and Bakshi (2013) have argued that whilst presenting themselves as bi and trans inclusive, LGBT organisations, groups and individuals often perpetuate bi and trans exclusion. A number of participants identified particular groups or individuals as less visible, or provided for, within an LGBT community 'umbrella', within which lesbian and gay identities were often said to dominate:

> People will say they have consulted with the LGBT community when they have only consulted with a small aspect of that . . . it could mean they actually consulted with the LG part of that and not the B and the T.
>
> (Andrea)

Participants' experiences of such differences and potential misunderstandings are explored further in the following chapter, but it is important to note that the very suggestion of an LGBT grouping was questioned within the research. Some participants therefore suggested that separation of the acronym might be preferable, with some referring to the past when a combined acronym was not in use. Others, however, wished for less, or no, separation:

> It's divisive because you're separating. Those letters each individually say 'well those are the different parts of that community'. They're all split and we're giving people different names and different labels, whereas it's about inclusiveness, ultimately, allegedly.
>
> (Charlie)

The research therefore demonstrates how the concept of LGBT community was seen as problematic, at least in part, because the LGBT acronym itself was seen as problematic.

## 'Managing' the Acronym

I now turn to explore how participants managed complexities regarding the LGBT acronym. In discussions about the possibility of making the LGBT acronym more inclusive by adding more individual labels, such as queer, questioning and intersex, concerns were raised regarding 'manageability' of the term:

> When I first started coming out the phrase was very much the gay community . . . Groups were just starting then, the idea of people joining a group and meeting them and getting to know people. People had that idea that they were joining a community, and over the years gradually it splintered . . . I agree that people want to be included but it becomes unmanageable.
>
> (Peter)

Cronin and King (2010: 877) have suggested that "however unwieldy the use of such acronyms may feel on occasion, they represent a genuine attempt to move beyond the homogenous and essentialist assumptions that underpin the term 'gay community'". However, for a number of participants, a desire to be inclusive was often balanced with perceived 'usability', which meant that a longer acronym could be resisted as the 'cost' was seen to be too great. Similarly, the expansion of LGBT organisational names and foci as a response to internal and/or external critiques has been documented by Ghaziani (2011: 112) in the United States, who noted concerns about balancing recognition of diversity with the risk of becoming "alphabet soup". This concern and desire for inclusivity *and* understanding was expressed by some participants who worked in LGBT service provision, and who viewed a current lack of visibility of other identities such as pansexual and polysexual as problematic:

> It gets so unwieldy . . . but [without expansion] it leaves a massive gap for anyone whose gender identity or expression of sexuality doesn't fit . . . It doesn't allow you to identify yourself within the communities, but also it . . . limits any discussion of non-gender binary identities which is really restrictive in terms of engaging everybody . . . [but] if you start talking about pan or poly then . . . normal people, in inverted commas, have no idea what you're talking about.
>
> (Fiona)

> For me personally . . . although I would identify as a gay man . . . I think the idea that we've got these four boxes and there's a certain criteria that makes that box up and you've got to be part of that . . . excludes people who identify as queer, or intersex.
>
> (Ben)

There was also some recognition that people might use different labels at different times, or with different people, suggesting a need to acknowledge that such categorisations can be relative, and identities themselves fluid. Participants emphasised the complexities related to individual identities and labels at the same time as they recognised that current/more limited understandings might restrict discussion to homosexuality rather than sexuality more broadly:

> I think it [LGBT] is a useful term to the extent that people recognise what it represents. It's a useful term which may not be useful in the future if people's understanding develops . . . If you identify as transgender, as opposed to transsexual, and you're not male or female identified then it's difficult to identify as gay, isn't it, because it doesn't have much meaning . . . If you're not identifying as male or female it's impossible to have same-sex attraction, unless you're attracted to somebody else that doesn't, but you can't be sure that their non-identification is the same as yours . . . Once it becomes a discussion about sexuality rather than *homo*sexuality then I think it's probably healthier but . . . I don't know how we will arrive at that point.
>
> (Petra, original emphasis)

Echoing research by Coleman-Fountain (2014) that identified that people did not want to be defined by their sexuality, some participants had concerns about their sexual or gender identity being seen as more important than other aspects of their identity. Helen, for example, wanted to challenge the primacy of sexual and gender identities in some people's minds:

> I think what's really important is that we get rid of this idea of who LGBT people are, and we understand it as a part of an identity and not the whole thing, because I think you often have disabled people, LGBT people, people of colour or black people, and as a result black people can't be LGBT people . . . So we really need to break down these ideas.
>
> (Helen)

Similarly, Luce saw her sexuality as part of, but not necessarily core to, her identity:

> If you say 'I'm a cyclist. I belong to a group of cyclists', I imagine you perhaps after work go for a ride and perhaps at the weekend . . . but I don't think that it's you. And with LGBT it actually is your sexuality, but people see it as that's your life . . . Nobody thinks of motorists as a 100% person . . . it's a part of someone's life, but if you talk about gay and lesbians, then it's [the whole of] them.
>
> (Luce)

There was some agreement that multiple and complex identities are not easily encapsulated in an acronym that cannot take account of the nuances surrounding sexual desires, sexual practices, physical gendered bodies and political or personal identities. At the same time, there was also a desire by some for what Petra termed an "understandable narrative" with which to describe oneself. The importance of an 'understandable language' with which to describe herself to others was also identified by Julie:

I think sometimes it's a language and it's easy for people to understand because if there wasn't a word lesbian and I tried to explain to someone what I was, 'I sleep with women', I don't really want to say that. It [lesbian] is a quick word.

(Julie)

Julie wanted to be able to say how she was similar to some women (those who sleep with other women) and different to others (implicitly those who sleep with men) in an understandable 'quick' way, supporting May's (2013) suggestion that to 'have' an identity, and be a member of a group, we need to be recognised as such. Julie thus drew boundaries between herself (and implicitly other lesbians as 'us') and a heterosexual 'them', thus formulating, making sense of and strengthening her own identity (May, 2013).

The importance of language for understanding one's own identity was also raised. Petra, for instance, explained how they had identified as a gay man when they were younger because that was what was "available" then, but that over time they had begun to feel that this "wasn't the right label" for how they felt:

I think the narratives are more and more that there is a choice and you don't have to be male or female, so I think if that had been available to me when I was 14, 15, that might have made more sense of how I felt about myself, rather than going through my 20s having this real crisis, which I did, and trying very hard, 'well that woman thing didn't work, let's try a man thing', and that really didn't work.

(Petra)

Hines (2010: 603) has argued that "contemporary trans activism and discourse has opened up spaces and possibilities for trans identity construction and performance", and we can see these emerging possibilities in Petra's account. The advantages of an 'understandable' label or acronym, which can contribute to increased visibility and thereby improve (at least the possibility of) service provision, was also identified:

If you haven't got labels, you can't have groups, and you can't give grants. It cascades under a massive umbrella . . . I think that is a benefit of labels.

(Eva)

When we talk about LGBT, thinking about local governments . . . they need to be able to clump together in order to provide services . . . [and] in order to address, 'are we engaging with the LGBT community? What are their needs? Are we missing them?'

(Gerry)

However, there were clear differences as to whether people thought labels were necessary to identify LGBT people and/or provide services, which some participants connected to broader issues about personal identities and identity politics:

> You have the sets of personal politics about 'this is who I am as a person', but there's something about do you want to give up . . . identities and labels. So there's something about . . . how do you know who you are . . . Part of labels is about being able to define yourself and if you don't have anything to define yourself as then who am I?
>
> (Ben)

> A bunch of us have had several conversations . . . 'well in order for us to really get the kind of things that we're shouting for, we all need to give up our labels', and it's a catch 22 because we would have to all walk in here tomorrow and give up all of our labels for society to stop labelling us, but actually I don't want to give mine up because it's a really big part of me.
>
> (Gemma)

There are clearly complex issues connected with the use of acronyms and labels. Participants expressed a desire for language that they could use to understand themselves and describe themselves to others. However, they also felt there was a balance to be met in this language between extending the boundaries of inclusion and not losing too much usability and understanding.

## Ambivalence

In this section I move from discussion of the LGBT acronym to a focus on participants' views on use of the word community. Much of people's concern or discomfort related to who used, created or 'owned' the term. Participants held a variety of opinions relating to community, and were certainly not engaging with the term uncritically. In initial conversations, some people suggested that the word community has generally become more widely used to describe groups of people:

> As politicians and public bodies . . . became aware of LGBT people with needs and interests they had to find some way of referring to it, and so it's become communities. It's seen as an interest or needs group, it's part of a wider thing.
>
> (Peter)

However, there was scepticism about the value of assuming a particular group of people necessarily form a community:

> I do sometimes try and avoid the word community because I think it's overused when people just mean a group of people . . . I think it's too easy to label a group of people as a community.
>
> (Matt)

Whilst Matt tried to avoid the term, Tony identified the role of the 'marketing world' in creating a term by which they could define a group of people:

> I think there's a distinction to be drawn between the term community and group . . . I recognise the term LGBT community, but I think it's a term created by the marketing world . . . I don't think it's used correctly because I don't think there is such a thing as an LGBT community because that's saying here's a bunch of people and we're going to define them by that terminology.
>
> (Tony)

This ambivalence about the term community has also been raised in previous studies (Holt, 2011; Fraser, 2008; Woolwine, 2000), but in my research some participants explained that a degree of ambivalence about the concept of LGBT community was closely linked to their own identity and relationship with their sexuality, as well as the degree to which they felt they 'belonged'. For Shourjo, as he became more comfortable with his own identity and sexuality, he became more comfortable with feeling part of a wider community:

> I think I tried to disassociate myself from LGBT initially . . . Over the last three years maybe I haven't had any problems with using LGBT . . . It has always been an uncomfortable relationship with the whole LGBT community and my own ideas about what that might be based on . . . I was getting more and more comfortable in my own identity as a gay person but I was unsure about me being part of a wider [LGBT] community.
>
> (Shourjo)

Participants put forward a range of explanations for why people assume LGBT people belong to or share a community. Sometimes it was explained as homophobia on the part of heterosexual people, whilst Dilys thought it was a result of 'laziness' by heterosexual and LGBT people:

> I think certainly laziness has encouraged other people to adopt it [the term], and even ourselves, I mean there's quite a lot of LGBT people who refer to an LGBT community.
>
> (Dilys)

In critiquing other people's use of the term community, Jason demonstrated an understanding that community requires a physical connection or proximity. As this was lacking, he viewed community as an inaccurate, and possibly even homophobic, term:

> People put us in a group . . . homophobic heterosexual people . . . put us in a category where they mean a community but we're really not . . . We're not all together all the time so it's not really like a community.
>
> (Jason)

Some participants had specific concerns that in presenting LGBT people as a community, they are 'othered', and made to seem separate and/or different from those outside that community. Jackie appeared apprehensive about the creation of a group that can be labelled and then possibly 'disliked':

> I think for me there's a danger . . . We're creating groups and we're creating other . . . My concern is that especially with policy makers or people who are funding things that they create boundaries and by creating an LGBT community you're going to have a group of people who won't like that.
>
> (Jackie)

Luce was also concerned about expectations and assumptions that being assigned to a community can bring:

> I'm always very hesitant about the community thing . . . because I don't want people from outside that community, if you will, to say 'so that means you're part of that', and that means you're this, that or the other . . . I think from a society point of view a community's over there . . . it means 'not me', 'don't confuse me with them, that's their community' . . . so I think it [the term] is misused.
>
> (Luce)

Concern that use of the word community could contribute to stereotypes and/or social 'divisions' was shared by a large proportion of participants:

> Many years of political campaigning in non-LGBT related arenas has made me regard the idea of 'communities' whether based on gender, religion, ethnicity or something else, with great suspicion. In my experience they serve to entrench differences and promote hostility between the ins and the outs.
>
> (Survey respondent 194: Mostly female bisexual aged 45–54)

Sometimes this concern was about who has the right to speak for those who identify as LGBT:

> I automatically distrust people politically claiming to speak 'on behalf of LGBT people/the community' or act as 'community leaders' when they have no right or basis to make that claim, a point which too often goes unchallenged such is the ubiquity of [its] use.
>
> (Survey respondent 445: Gay man aged 25–34)

Steve thought that use of the term community by LGBT people formed a barrier to interactions with non-LGBT people, and held gay people responsible for establishing this 'barrier' between themselves and others:

> I actually think the term gay community stops one interacting outside of that and when you start saying gay community it keeps people out . . . By saying

it would be like a community you exclude people and it feels like there's another barrier.

(Steve)

By contrast, Jodi viewed the use of community as a form of 'ghettoisation' imposed by others:

It [LGBT community] doesn't exist. It's some kind of big myth. It'd be like saying there's a brown-eyed community or a blonde community and I think it's used to our detriment actually and we suffer from it being populated as a myth . . . it keeps us ghettoised.

(Jodi)

Whereas Jodi viewed what they saw as the imposition of ghettos negatively, Ruth looked back on them with a sense of nostalgia (see also Chapter 6):

The ghetto was a place where you could easily find your own.

(Ruth)

Traies (2015) has argued that community 'closeness', to an extent, relies on people being 'outsiders', and the more 'outside' people are, they more they need one another. As legislative 'gains' have been made that reduce this outsider status, some people, such as Ruth, feel they have 'lost' something at the same time.

Participants identified specific risks in providing services and/or advocacy based on the premise of community, as it could lead to the domination of certain groups of people, whilst others were neglected:

As a practitioner trying to engage with the LGBT community . . . you can find that sometimes you have to engage with social groups that exist but you are aware that they are often not the ones that need the help the most . . . I think the idea of LGBT community can really limit the services that are delivered or accessed or the way that information is disseminated.

(Andrea)

The idea of community could also make some people think that its members are all the same:

Through my work as a trainer around LGBT awareness, I think the idea of community tends to bring problems—people assume we're all the same!!
(Survey respondent 65: Gay man aged 55–64)

Despite her concerns, Andrea suggested that there were some advantages to the terms LGBT community or LGBT communities, as long as they were used with some awareness of the potential difficulties they posed:

It's problematic but for brevity and for the sake of pushing the conversation along for delivering services and dealing with people, you do need something like the term LGBT community or communities to have the conversation, but you also need to be questioning how you are using that language.

(Andrea)

Helen shared this sense of caution, arguing that the concept of community can heighten visibility, but also limit the range of provision:

> I think [use of the word community] is a mixed blessing. I think it's useful because at least they're addressing LGBT issues, and I think there are some core sort of shared issues and it forces people to acknowledge the existence of LGBT people, but I'm not sure that implying there's a homogenous community is always useful at the same time, because I think then you kind of try and do a 'one size fits all'.
>
> (Helen)

This notion of being a 'mixed blessing' was also raised by Ben, who thought that the idea of LGBT community helped bring people together and work toward shared goals. However, he also felt it could alienate or exclude others at the same time:

> I like at least in theory the idea that LGBT people come together as a, whether it's just as a community or whether it's as a social force for political change on gender politics, or sexual politics, but . . . I'm conscious that there are a lot of young people . . . that don't identify as LGBT, they don't necessarily feel that the LGB or T represents them, and I think that's important if you're working in the community.
>
> (Ben)

As we have seen, the concept of LGBT community is complex, with clear participant ambivalence about why LGBT people are assumed to form a community of many different people who may, or may not, share one facet of their identity, and an identity to which they may have, or attach, varying degrees of discomfort and importance. To assume that these people equate to a community was even read as homophobic by some, particularly given assumptions and stereotypes that can be associated with notions of (a) community.

## Commonality

This section moves beyond the idea of community to look more specifically at notions of commonality and similarity. The inferred suggestion of commonality within the concept of community was particularly problematic for some people who felt it was essentialist and/or might perpetuate stereotypes about LGBT people:

> I feel very uncomfortable with the use of 'community'/'communities' generally as they imply a commonality and familiarity which I don't think exists.

I have multiple identities as an individual and feel that talking about people in this context sometimes broaches on the absurd—and find anyone who uses this language dubious and with doubtful intention towards treating me as who I am—an individual rather than a generic/stereotypical 'type'.

(Survey respondent 445: Gay man aged 25–34)

Sometimes a lack of commonality was related to the relationships people formed, whether in explaining a lack of connection or in explaining specific connections:

Recently I joined an LBGT group which had been formed in my profession . . . political activism aside, I found the differences between us were greater than the commonalities, and eventually the group disintegrated.

(Survey respondent 196: Gay man aged 65+)

I have little in common with either lesbians or transsexuals, most of my mates tend to be either straight men and women or other gay men.

(Survey respondent 96: Male gay/faggot aged 35–44)

The lack of commonality between the individual components or 'teams' within LGBT was identified in critiques about the notion of a singular community:

It's a bit like saying all football players are part of a community, but there are ones who support this team and that team and you wouldn't necessarily put them together.

(Jodi)

A belief in problems associated with the concept of community was also identified in relation to providing services. Gemma, for example, felt that the concept of (a singular) community could lead to a lack of engagement with, or consideration of, varied needs and experiences:

Although we serve, from an organisational perspective, what we call the LGBT community, I think there is a danger in assuming that you know what that community is or what that community wants.

(Gemma)

Matt identified a particular danger in use of the word community and its suggestion of homogeneity, which he linked to oppression:

It's really dangerous because it homogenises people who aren't homogenous . . . that's the foundation for any kind of oppression is to homogenise your enemy . . . that's when a community can be dangerous, when it's used by bigots to homogenise people who aren't homogenous into one nice, easily oppressible package.

(Matt)

However, others clearly believed that LGBT people do have 'something' in common:

> With regards to LGBT, it [community] is definitely a group of like-minded people I would say, that all have something in common. That's not necessarily a community per se, but for us I would say it is.
>
> (Paula)

Others felt that the concept of community could be used strategically, especially when pushing for legislative or social change. Timothy, for example, suggested that the idea of community implies strength, size and credibility:

> The positive connotation of the word community for me suggests . . . mass, it's a mass of people and I think, you know, when we talk about the LGBT community it suggests there's a lot of us and therefore our needs cannot be ignored . . . whether it be for the government in terms of voting, or marketing . . . there's some credibility to that mass.
>
> (Timothy)

It was also seen as a useful term for organisations such as Stonewall (a UK LGBT charity) to use:

> It's useful to be able to say that we're a community because if you're Stonewall or somebody, you know, you use that word. It suggests a commonality of cause and a commonality of opinion.
>
> (Ruth)

Whilst Timothy and Ruth discussed a public or organisational 'suggestion' of community and commonality, Matt believed that there would be some shared concerns amongst LGBT people:

> The one thing where it's really useful to think of ourselves as a single community and be thought of as a community is as a lobbying force particularly on international issues . . . regardless of how young you are, where you fit on the gender spectrum and the sort of Kinsey scale, everyone there will tend to unite and condemn various atrocities around the world, and I think that's the greatest element of a singular community.
>
> (Matt)

As the research suggests, LGBT people have different identities, with different issues, and with different political interests, yet these are frequently not acknowledged within use of the term community that so often seems to assume commonality. However, there may be advantages in the strategic suggestion of community and/or commonality, with some (limited) basis for this in shared experiences of, or concern about, prejudice. In promoting the idea of shared experiences or collective strength and credibility, feelings of community can be fostered, albeit possibly in intangible ways (as Chapter 8 explores).

## Agency

In this final section I examine the role of agency within language use, and suggest how the concept of LGBT community might be drawn on in less problematic ways. As May (2013: 8) has observed, "most people experience a sense of connectedness to not one but several groups, places and cultures", and it was this diversity that people often wanted to be acknowledged within use of the word community. Whether it was about describing their identities, or their place within communities, a sense of agency was clearly important to people, especially in relation to being labelled in particular ways by other people:

> I'm not really a fan of labels to be honest with you. I mean I'm transsexual, but I don't see myself as transsexual. I see myself as female, because I see transsexual or whatever as being a label.
>
> (Louisa)

Being able to exercise agency was also important when it came to aligning oneself with a particular community, and/or resisting how others might assign people to communities:

> For the majority of people in this country you get lumped into communities whether you like it or not . . . so the ability to construct that community for yourself is very important. Society will assign a community to you I think . . . they'll lump you in with some people. So being able to have agency over that I think is very important, and that that community replicates something that you are happy to affiliate yourself with is very important.
>
> (Gemma)

> It [community] is such a broad term and it incorporates so many different people and I think that there's a certain amount of ownership in it but I think also a lot of people are lumped in to it that don't necessarily regard themselves as part of that.
>
> (Fiona)

Others were not negative about the term LGBT community, but stressed that they also wished to be included within other, broader conceptualisations of community:

> I am personally OK with the term [or] phrase LGBT community and feel fine about being included in this broad spectrum of individuals. I like the word community . . . I do however want to be included in the wider community without being labelled.
>
> (Paula)

For many, it was the concept of a universal, monolithic LGBT community that met with cynicism, and sometimes anger. A number of participants suggested that the term community should be used in the plural, to enable recognition of the diversity within and between LGBT people, for instance related to age, (dis)ability, ethnicity, geography, gender, political interests, social class and/or wealth. Whilst for some the diversity of LGBT people was clear, for others this came with age and experience:

> I definitely don't think there's one LGBT community and I think when I was a lot younger I probably would have got the idea that there was more of one, but as I got older . . . [and] more politically involved in LGBT things as well, and . . . just in myself kind of developed a more nuanced understanding of the world, and there's different groups of people, then perhaps I kind of came to realise that there was multiple communities and . . . I don't think you exclusively necessarily belong to [just] one.
>
> (Helen)

An awareness of their own intersecting identities and experiences led some to reject the idea of a single community in favour of acknowledging the plurality of available communities:

> You can be gay, and you can be Jewish, and you can be old, and you can be all these things, but you're not necessarily one. You can belong to more than one community in the same way . . . I think I tick all the boxes really, almost!
>
> (Steve)

Some suggested that links between people are forms of interlocking communities, which they described visually. In Peter's experience, these communities were not isolated:

> Communities interlock like circles. People don't know everyone in other communities but they know some people, so there is a link there . . . [but] I don't think there is one overall community anymore, or if there ever was.
>
> (Peter)

The presence of links between people and groups was often related to individual identities and social backgrounds, whereby communities might overlap whilst also being distinct from one another:

> A large proportion of the people I work and socialise with are gay men, and a lot of people who I know from different places then turn out to know each other. Therefore the use of the word 'community' makes sense. But the people I know tend to be male, identify as gay . . . are university educated, are comfortable dealing with the commercial scene on their own terms, aren't especially young or old, etc. etc. Therefore I don't feel part of a singular

LGBT community that would include everyone who is lesbian, gay, bisexual or transgender.

(Survey respondent 573: Gay man aged 35–44)

Issues of agency allied to use of the term LGBT community were evident, though weaknesses in the concept could be (seen to be) reduced when used by, rather than about, LGBT people. Use of communities in the plural was also viewed as a way to acknowledge the complexities and diversities inherent within the term.

## Chapter Summary

Despite the possibility of some shared experiences, the realities of diversities within and between LGBT individuals and/or groups were evident within the research. This contributed to critiques and sometimes anger about how the concept of community was applied to LGBT people. Some participants were clearly reticent to identify as part of a community, whilst others perceived (some) advantages in doing so. Within this, who was attributing community status to whom was considered significant. Diversities amongst LGBT people, and how these contribute to different life experiences, are the focus of the following chapter, but this diversity was not often thought to be captured within the common four letter acronym LGBT, nor in use of the word community, which is commonly understood as suggesting some form of commonality or shared perspective. Levels of discomfort with the phrase LGBT community tended to be reduced when it was used by LGBT people themselves, and/or when it was used in the plural, to at least suggest that not *all* LGBT people belong to one large group. However, singular use of LGBT community could be tactically deployed in activism and advocacy regarding LGBT rights. It was thus clear that the concept was used in critical, agentic, and strategic ways, yet these nuances were thought to be missed in much use of LGBT community within broader media, policy and practice arenas.

## References

Browne, K. and Bakshi, L. (2013) *Ordinary in Brighton: LGBT, activisms and the city.* Aldershot: Ashgate.

Browne, K. and Lim, J. (2010) 'Trans lives in the "gay capital of the UK"', *Gender, Place and Culture* 17(5): 615–633.

Coleman-Fountain, E. (2014) 'Lesbian and gay youth and the question of labels', *Sexualities* 17(7): 802–817.

Cronin, A. and King, A. (2010) 'Power, inequality and identification: Exploring diversity and intersectionality amongst older LGB adults', *Sociology* 44(5): 876–892.

Formby, E. (2015) 'Limitations of focussing on homophobic, biphobic and transphobic "bullying" to understand and address LGBT young people's experiences within and beyond school', *Sex Education* 15(6): 626–640.

Fraser, S. (2008) 'Getting out in the "real world": Young men, queer and theories of gay community', *Journal of Homosexuality* 55(2): 245–264.

Ghaziani, A. (2011) 'Post-gay collective identity construction', *Social Problems* 58(1): 99–125.

Hines, S. (2010) 'Queerly situated: Exploring constraints and negotiations of trans queer subjectivities', *Gender, Place and Culture* 17(5): 597–613.

Holt, M. (2011) 'Gay men and ambivalence about "gay community": From gay community attachment to personal communities', *Culture, Health and Sexuality* 13(8): 857–871.

May, V. (2013) *Connecting self to society: Belonging in a changing world*. New York: Palgrave Macmillan.

Richardson, D. and Monro, S. (2012) *Sexuality, equality and diversity*. Basingstoke: Palgrave Macmillan.

Traies, J. (2015) 'Old lesbians in the UK: Community and friendship', *Journal of Lesbian Studies* 19(1): 35–49.

Weeks, J. (2003) *Sexuality*. London: Routledge.

Woodhead, D. (1995) '"Surveillant gays": HIV, space and the constitution of identities' in Bell, D. and Valentine, G. (eds) *Mapping desire: Geographies of sexualities*. London: Routledge, pp. 231–244.

Woolwine, D. (2000) 'Community in gay male experience and moral discourse', *Journal of Homosexuality* 38(4): 5–37.

# 3    Diversity, Inequality and Prejudice Amongst LGBT People

## Introduction

Whilst community to many suggests commonality (Ghaziani, 2011; Guibernau, 2013), this research identified significant diversity amongst LGBT people. Previous research has also highlighted, for example, different experiences and positionings related to age, (dis)ability, ethnicity, gender, geography, political affiliation, social class and/or wealth (Heaphy, 2012; Hines, 2010; Taylor, 2007a; Weeks, 1996; Weeks, Heaphy and Donovan, 2001). The level to which these differences were acknowledged within my research varied. Whilst some participants argued that this diversity meant the application of the term community to (groups of) LGBT people was impossible or spurious, others stressed potential commonalities— such as shared experiences of stigma, prejudice, inequality or discrimination—as well as, or instead of, acknowledging difference. As Day (2006: 163–164) noted, "there are always going to be internal differences . . . between individuals and sub-groups", but people "join together to perpetuate the illusion that these are of secondary importance". Within my research, participants did not necessarily perpetuate an illusion that LGBT people are all alike, but some drew on the ideas of difference and sameness simultaneously to explain their acknowledgment of diversity at the same time as maintaining a sense of belonging, which might be described as solidarity without similarity. This view echoes Fraser's (2008: 260, original emphasis), who noted that "difference, disagreement and friction should not be permitted to defeat community . . . these elements are *necessary to* community" as community is about coming together where differences exist. Whilst the idea of sameness was linked to feelings of belonging, difference was present as a comparable (most often heterosexual) 'other'. However, when those deemed to be 'other' were excluded by LGBT people, the emotional component of not feeling a sense of belonging was most easily observed (May, 2013). Notions of sameness and belonging will be returned to in Chapter 8; here I focus on perceptions and experiences of difference.

This chapter examines multiple identities within conceptualisations of LGBT communities, demonstrating diverse experiences of sexuality, gender, age, (dis) ability, ethnicity, social class, wealth, faith and family. In doing so, the chapter illustrates contrasts between, and ambivalences about, individual diversities within and alongside an assumed collective identity. It also explores lived experiences of 'divisions', 'hierarchies', inequalities and exclusions, often based on identity-based prejudices amongst LGBT people. Understandings and expectations of normative behaviours and embodied identity practices that could make communities more or less appealing are also considered. Though there is some overlap with Chapter 6 which explores experiences of the scene specifically, in this chapter I focus on people's (lack of) awareness and experiences of difference more generally. These issues will be addressed within the following five headings: Diversity and Inequality, Identity-Based Prejudice, Faith and Religion, Parenting and (Non)conformity. First, I provide some context through an overview of exiting literature.

## Overview of Existing Literature

A broad range of research has evidenced different life experiences among LGBT people. Here I give an overview to show how notions of community may be complicated by levels of diversity, and the extent to which these are, or are not, acknowledged. An intersectional perspective explicitly acknowledges diversity in recognising that intersections of identities can result in exclusion and/or disadvantage. At the same time, individuals can be understood as belonging to multiple communities, "thanks to a range of embodied and imagined connections with other individuals" (Bertotti, Jamal and Harden, 2011). These connections and intersectional identities are understood to impact upon levels of 'community attachment' (Wilkinson et al., 2012), but other scholars have more explicitly acknowledged uneven power relations within recognition of diversity and intersectionality. Hines (2010: 606), for instance, indicated that trans communities can be "cut through with power relations and often fractious political positioning", whilst Heaphy (2012: 21) noted how 'diminished' resources significantly influence the "possibilities for lesbian and gay existence". Differing power relations and intersecting identities can thus manifest in lived experiences of significant inequality and/or pressures to conform to particular social norms, as I will go on to show. As Weeks (1996: 84) identified, "communities built around sexuality are no less likely than others to develop their own norms which may exclude as well as include". Similarly, Guibernau (2013) suggested that people are expected to conform and follow a community's rules as well as its hierarchies so that a feeling of solidarity can emerge. Whilst LGBT communities may not publish an explicit set of rules such as a country or church might, some participants experienced clear rules and problematic hierarchies amongst LGBT people, at the same time as others enjoyed a perception of solidarity. In an appraisal of group membership, conforming may be seen as less challenging or painful than the alternative—isolation (Guibernau, 2013), so the rewards of belonging outweigh the constraints of being 'obedient'. Throughout this book, such potential 'gains' and 'losses' are evident in people's (perceived) membership of LGBT communities.

Guibernau's (2013: 30–31) central argument on belonging focuses on choice, but she recognises that choices are not "free from constraints, which principally derive from social class, gender, ethnicity and religion". However, I would suggest that this list can, and should, be extended. With regard to LGBT communities, Browne and Bakshi (2013) amongst others have shown that bisexual and trans people can feel out of place within ostensibly LGBT spaces. A range of research has also identified biphobia among lesbian and gay people (Browne, 2010; Lehavot, Balsam and Ibrahim-Wells, 2009; Monro, 2015; Valentine and Skelton, 2003), with Barker et al. (2012) using the term 'double discrimination' to describe bisexual people's experiences of discrimination and/or 'suspicion' from both heterosexual *and* lesbian and gay people. In relation to trans identities, Hines (2010) has drawn attention to debates about gendered authenticity and surgical/bodily reconstruction, with some of her participants experiencing a hierarchy within trans community politics. This has implications for differences in feelings of community belonging, linked to broader (medicalised and discriminatory) discourses about the necessity for congruity between (gendered) body and identity (see Davy, 2011 for further discussion of 'authenticity' and trans people's embodiment and bodily aesthetics). Similar themes connected to hierarchies have been identified elsewhere, for example Simpson (2012, 2016) identified hierarchies related to gay men's looks and bodies, and Smit et al. (2012) identified a 'gay social hierarchy' linked to HIV-related stigma. As Hines (2007) has argued, subjective nuances make understanding community on the basis of shared identity problematic, but so too is understanding community on the basis of participation when levels of involvement vary. The complexities of trans identities and general limitations of a gender binary thus shed doubt on the notion of a (universal) trans community, whilst experiences of hierarchies and prejudices amongst LGBT people bring into question a (singular) LGBT community.

Bodies of research have identified prejudice within and on the scene, and amongst LGBT people more widely. Existing evidence, for example, has examined the impact of (older) age on experiences of community or specific scene spaces (Archibald, 2010; Cant, 2008; Casey, 2007; Cronin and King, 2010; Ellis, 2007; Heaphy, Yip and Thompson, 2003; MacKian and Goldring, 2010; Pugh, 2002; Taylor, 2008; Yip, 1996). Simpson's (2012, 2013a, 2013b) research identified issues about dress, appearance and ageism among gay men (both towards older and younger men), whilst Casey (2007) suggested that age can mark people out as 'undesirable others'. Brown (2008: 1225) argued that for older gay men and women, "metropolitan places can play a symbolic role in the affirmation of sexuality . . . [but] simultaneously be sites from which they feel marginalised and excluded". However, Simpson (2014: 154) has noted a tendency to describe gay men's experiences of ageing as dominated by loneliness and exclusion, which he argues overlooks the ambivalences involved in negotiating the scene, as well as the "multidirectional character of gay ageism". Cronin and King (2014) have argued that we should not overlook the socio-historical context in which older LGB people developed their identities, as this will influence their experiences later in life, as well as their access to, and participation in, networks and communities. There is also evidence of 'classism' (Browne and Bakshi, 2013; Lehavot, Balsam and Ibrahim-Wells, 2009), with Browne and Bakshi (2013) indicating that areas of social deprivation are sometimes seen as dangerous and linked to hate crime or a lack of acceptance, suggesting that working class areas and/or people are sometimes viewed as inherently 'anti-gay'. Moran et al. (2003) also found that when particular geographical areas or housing estates predominantly occupied by working class people were denigrated, lesbian and gay people living in those areas could feel 'othered'.

Racism and/or invisibility of black and minority ethnic (BME) people within particular LGB communities has also been documented in a range of research in the UK and beyond (Eisenstadt and Gatter, 1999; Holt, 2011; Lehavot, Balsam and Ibrahim-Wells, 2009; McKeown et al., 2010; Ridge, Hee and Minichiello, 1999; Yip, 2008). Rogers identified racism within gay spaces, which meant that for some people the phrase 'coming into' more accurately reflected their experiences than the more widely used 'coming out', i.e. to come into, as one participant described, racism, sexism and drug use. To not come into particular identities, communities and/or spaces was therefore not about being 'in the closet' or 'on the down low', but an active choice not to engage with certain spaces or communities (Rogers, 2012). Woolwine (2000: 16) concluded that his Hispanic and black participants (in America) either did not experience community, or experienced it "in a highly problematic fashion, namely, as a divided or racist community".

LGBT people's experiences of faith or religion have been discussed more fully elsewhere (Browne, Munt and Yip, 2010; Hunt, 2009; Yip, Keenan and Page, 2011; Yip and Keenan, 2009), with Yip (2008) suggesting that different religions and denominations have differing levels of 'tolerance', meaning that religious LGB people should not be viewed as a monolithic category who will all have the same experiences. However, research has suggested that religious LGBT people can experience prejudice towards their faith from other LGBT people (Valentine and Skelton, 2003). More recently, Taylor, Falconer and Snowdon (2014: 230) highlighted the "complex, multiple identities" of their participants, and questioned how religion, youth and non-heterosexuality have often been "characterised in opposition to each other".

A body of work has also drawn attention to the existence of norms and expectations on the scene, and elsewhere, which can result in exclusions and oppressions. Guibernau (2013) identified the role of dress codes within 'conditions' set by a group that people wish to join, and whilst her work largely focuses on nations and religious groupings, there are parallels with my research, and experiences of certain spaces and/or communities. Whilst dress codes might contribute to "a sense of sameness" (Valentine, 1996: 150), and operate as "a visual dimension of 'gaydar'" (Taylor, 2007b: 168), they might also lead to exclusion. Particular spaces or communities can therefore use visual signifiers such as dress to promote "conformity as a condition of belonging" (Tonkiss, 2003: 303), thus valuing and enforcing homogeneity (Young, 1990) via a 'disciplinary gaze' (Taylor, 2007b). Valentine and Skelton (2003) documented participants' accounts of feeling they had to conform to particular (gay male) identities in order to 'fit in' on the scene, which influenced their choice of clothes and music. Taylor (2007a, 2007b) also suggested that 'getting it wrong' often means 'not fitting in', so that failing to display gay signifiers correctly leads to being devalued or misrecognised (see also Skeggs, 1999). However, Simpson (2014) reminds us of the need to be cautious when discussing exclusions. He argues that middle-aged gay men are able to deploy 'ageing capital' to assert the value of a more 'natural' body and mode of 'dressing for comfort' (Simpson, 2014). Whilst this enabled self-acceptance and a capacity to resist social pressures, it did often involve reverse ageism by stereotyping younger gay men as self-obsessed and/or under-developed (Simpson, 2014). This usefully points to the multilevel complexities within individual identities and constructions of 'groupness'. Having described some of the multiple ways in which difference is present even within constructions of similarity, 'we-ness' and/or community, I now draw on my research to explore these issues further.

## Diversity and Inequality

Many participants acknowledged diversities within and between LGBT communities, such as those related to age, ethnicity, gender or social class. Some also recognised that LGBT people will have different interests and concerns:

> It's important not to see the LGBT community as a homogenous group of people . . . issues that are maybe quite important, say for gay men, may not be the same issues that are salient for lesbian women, or bisexual men or bisexual women, and then there's a debate about should the T go with the L, G and the B . . . [and] that's even before you talk about class and ethnicities and all of that.
>
> (Ben)

In acknowledging different life experiences, some participants demonstrated their own assumptions about other people's lives, which could be informed by wider stereotypes:

> I think that those who are less well educated and from more of a working class, BME or faith background may in many cases find it more difficult to be openly LGB because of pressure to conform from their family and community.
>
> (Survey respondent 290: Gay male aged 45–54)

A lack of awareness of, or understanding about, different life experiences might result from what May (2013) has referred to as 'social sorting', meaning that 'similar' people are more likely to meet and maintain ties. Ruth, for instance, suggested that there are fewer cross-class spaces now than there were in the past, because people have sorted themselves into groups of similar socio-economic backgrounds:

> One thing I remember about the lesbian community in the old days . . . I don't experience it as being so like that now, was that it was so cross-class . . . [but

now, groups] tend to have sorted themselves out and got rid of the ones they don't like and the ones that 'aren't like us, dear' . . . You'll go to one lesbian group and it's very middle class and you'll go to another group and it will be much more working class . . . and they don't tend to mix.

(Ruth)

Drawing on the title of Weeks' (2007) widely-cited book *The world we have won*, a number of writers have pointed out that 'we' are not all the same and therefore experience these 'wins' differently (McDermott, 2011; Taylor, 2011). Similarly, some participants acknowledged degrees of inequality within and between LGBT communities, despite wider social changes:

I think that we should recognise that things don't improve equally for everyone.

(Petra)

Some survey respondents also discussed their own intersecting identities, which had implications for their experiences of inequality:

My gender is as important as my sexuality—I identify as a lesbian feminist. Oppression, violence and discrimination as a woman is as impactful in my life as being queer is.

(Survey respondent 578: Female lesbian aged 55–64)

As this respondent suggested, gender can also inform life experiences and possible discrimination. Sometimes, it was inappropriate or inadequate facilities related to gender that participants identified as problematic, and which limited their use of space:

I also think with trans stuff, the gay community often doesn't include trans people just in terms of not having the [gender neutral] toilet provision, so it's just the same as them going somewhere else and it can reinforce the fact they're trans . . . I don't [identify as] trans, but I know a lot of people that do and I think that stops us going to some places.

(Helen)

Supporting scholarship elsewhere (Heaphy, 2012; Jennings, 2007; McDermott, 2011; Taylor, 2007a, 2009), social class was also perceived as significant within the research. Being from a working class or international background could make people feel that they did or should not 'sit' within a community because their (lack of) class did not 'fit':

Being from a working class background, I feel that you have to adjust your values to 'sit' within the gay community.

(Survey respondent 502: Gay man aged 35–44)

I've lived in Australia and California as well as the UK, and experiences can be very different. In the UK it is all about class. I don't fit in here.

(Survey respondent 598: Straight female aged 45–54)

By contrast, others acknowledged their privileged positions and how their social class (as well as education and ethnicity) had influenced their experiences of, and access to, community:

I know that it has been easier for me to create and participate in LGBT community as a result of the confidence gained by and the resources available to me as an educated, middle class, white person.

(Survey respondent 51: Female lesbian aged 55–64)

My LGBT community is mostly based around [a regional group for 'women who like women'] . . . the majority of the women I would say are middle class. I think that class is important in terms of giving me the confidence to contact the group in the first place.

(Survey respondent 513: Female lesbian aged 35–44)

Whilst social class could influence people's feelings of community, lack of financial resources could also act as a barrier. Laura, for example, linked (lack of) financial resources to varying experiences of rural living (which is explored further in Chapter 5). She identified the ways in which material deprivation and geographical location can intersect differently. Whilst living in a semi-rural location, Laura needed to monitor and manage the cost of petrol or public transport expenditure when accessing a gay choir and other LGBT-related events or spaces. In comparison, she was clearly aware that these considerations were not necessary for everybody:

It seemed to me in [the choir] . . . quite a few seemed to come from up [rural location] . . . and travel in to [the city] centre . . . and then travel out again . . . There was quite a division there between the haves and the have-nots which is part of the rural/urban thing which I hadn't realised before . . . It's kind of a bit segregated really . . . [because] it must be costly to do that.

(Laura)

Participants suggested that communities may or may not include a variety of different LGBT people, who may or may not 'mix' together. The research demonstrates how experiences of, and access to, forms of community are influenced by a range of inequalities. However, for some, resources allied to social class could make communities more accessible or appealing.

## Identity-Based Prejudice

Within the research, discrimination or exclusion within and from LGBT communities was often identified in relation to a number of specific issues. Personal experiences and/or perceptions of 'divisions' related to identity-based prejudice within LGBT communities are the focus of this section. Echoing themes in existing research (Hines, 2010; Simpson, 2012; Smit et al., 2012), one way in which prejudice was identified was in relation to hierarchies amongst LGBT people, which rendered some people less 'fitting' than others:

> In my experience just because people are queer/LGBT doesn't make them less discriminating in other ways, which means a lot of the same hierarchies and oppressive relationships exist also in queer communities, which generally don't make them safe spaces unless you 'fit in'.
>
> (Survey respondent 424: Queer/lesbian/bi/not sure [it depends on how I feel that day] female aged 25–34)

Hierarchies or "pecking orders" were often related to the individual groups perceived to make up an LGBT collective, with gay men viewed as "top of the heap", and trans people often viewed as the bottom. This made some identities less visible and/or 'validated' than others:

> I think that that's a problem that we see quite a lot . . . that the T is sidelined or marginalised . . . things that claim to be LGBT are really L and G . . . the B and the T [are] pretty invisible . . . and have often been kind of marginalised in the sense that their identity position isn't as valid and that has been definitely a hierarchical approach to what we consider to be LGBT.
>
> (Gemma)

Jo felt that there were separate and conflicting groupings within the LGBT acronym, which for her shed doubt on the possibility of safety, as well as a combined LGBT community:

> I think it's more LG, B standing alone, and then T standing alone possibly rather than LGBT together . . . that suggests that there's kind of conflict within itself. If that's supposed to be our safe haven, it's not because again there's oppression . . . because it's not a community.
>
> (Jo)

A survey respondent also identified the possibility of prejudice based on HIV status, suggesting that varied prejudice exists both within and without different communities:

> [I am] very 'out' about being gay and being [HIV] positive. I actually have more discrimination within the gay community about my HIV status than I do in the wider community about being gay.
>
> (Survey respondent 546: Gay man aged 35–44)

Reminiscent of Hines' (2010) research that evidenced hierarchies within trans politics, there were similar observations within this research about the necessity and divisiveness of trans community/politics:

Being part of the trans community is a political necessity. It also does your head in because it is so divisive.

(Survey respondent 598: Straight female aged 45–54)

However, the importance of shared principles was also identified, which some people thought could overcome differences related to identities and/or aspects of community that might otherwise have been experienced as problematic:

I have a really complicated relationship to my own sexuality, for various reasons, and at times this makes me feel really alienated from queer/LGBT communities where everything appears to be so focused around sex a lot of the time . . . [but] what I do like is queer approaches to identity, as long as this also incorporates race, class, disability, etc. Communities which are built around these principles can be really life affirming.

(Survey respondent 424: Queer/lesbian/bi/not sure [it depends on how I feel that day] female aged 25–34)

This participant recognised that differences could still lead to conflicts however:

I feel vaguely part of a queer community of activists, and at times these connections have been very important to me. At other times these have been very fraught and there have been conflicts which have exposed how this 'community' has never been truly inclusive and often cannot deal [with] intersecting oppressions such as racism.

(Survey respondent 424: Queer/lesbian/bi/not sure [it depends on how I feel that day] female aged 25–34)

Supporting existing evidence on biphobia among lesbian and gay people, this research identified bisexual people's poor experiences of inclusion, sometimes seen to result from a lack of understanding:

Lesbian and gay communities do not understand bisexuality, bi people or bi communities and discriminate against us, further excluding and isolating us, creating more hate crime and discrimination, and preventing bisexual people from being accepted and understood in society.

(Survey respondent 107: Bisexual cisgender female aged 25–34)

Participants suggested that they did not find it easy to be bisexual on the scene, sometimes stressing the misunderstandings and misperceptions that commonly revolve around themes of indecision, greed or 'falsity' that are often thought to influence relationships with bisexual people:

Within the [LGBT+] community there is also often friction, particularly with biphobia. I identify as polysexual but often use bi as there is less explaining, even in the LGBT+ community. My fiancé is a lesbian. There is still a belief that a bisexual and lesbian cannot have a happy, long-term relationship. We have been together for five years . . . That's as much proof as I need.

(Website contributor)

My personal experience of community as a bisexual woman has been fairly negative—very much dominated by the 'fake lesbian' thing (i.e. 'real' gay people being suspicious of bi's because so many girls were 'faking it').

(Survey respondent 454: Bisexual female aged 35–44)

Participants also identified "rejection", "resentment" and "misunderstanding" amongst LGB people towards trans people, which influenced their access to feelings of acceptance:

A lot of lesbian girls are really not accepting of trans women . . . You'd think that like a minority community would be accepting of a minority, but it doesn't work like that at all . . . Strangely it doesn't, which I felt really shocked at. Not everyone's like that, but . . . it still happens.

(Paula)

Many L and G people still find it hard to accept T people as friends, colleagues, campaigners or even possible lovers—some L, and a few G, people still refuse to work at all in any way with T people.

(Survey respondent 103: Bisexual trans man aged 55–64)

Whilst prejudice and discrimination were often linked to sexual or gender identity, other forms of discrimination were also identified, for example related to age, class and ethnicity. Ageism was one such form of discrimination that could lead to social isolation from and within LGBT communities, also linked to lack of physical mobility:

Ageism within the gay community forgets the campaign we started in the late sixties for equality, so we are pushed aside—it would be good to have some sort of buddy system similar to that for people with HIV/AIDS, befriending elderly gay people living alone and due to immobility are isolated.

(Survey respondent 319: Gay man aged 65+)

Difficulties related to physically accessing spaces and communities have been identified elsewhere (Cant, 2008), but in my research disablist attitudes were also identified as limiting inclusion for disabled LGBT people:

As a disabled lesbian I feel rejected and discriminated against in the 'LBGT community'.

(Survey respondent 604: Female lesbian aged 45–54)

Having disabilities and being treated for cancer and as a result having a reduced immune system has had an effect on how some LGBT people and straight people react with me. Some of the gay community regard me less favourably since becoming disabled.

(Survey respondent 165: Gay man aged 55–64)

Other forms of prejudice were also experienced. Gerry, for instance, recalled a racist incident when he was younger and had attended a gay night at a club in his home town. He remembered how excited he had felt to be going out initially, but how that had then been followed by criticism from his peers:

Feeling I suppose a form of racism or prejudice from peers, it was a horrible feeling. It did leave a knot in my tummy . . . To get this from, I suppose, other minorities, that was what was stark about it . . . They too were going to the club, they were white . . . It was a criticism of me, that's what it was. It did feel, you know, a community that is allowing you space to be yourself, to discover yourself . . . is actually being critical of you as well.

(Gerry)

By contrast, Gerry also recalled how interesting it was for him to hear (in connection with his job) "a niche diverse story from a South Indian [gay man] . . . which is beyond forced marriages [and] arranged marriages". This may indicate the extent to which he felt South Indian backgrounds are synonymised—in racist public perception—with particular forms of relationships.

As well as racism, there was also recognition of BME invisibility within LGBT communities:

When I have attended Pride events, almost everyone there has been white; this has changed somewhat this year, but not by much. Since I've become more educated in black activism, I have seen a significant amount of racism within the LGBT communities, and that puts me off.

(Survey respondent 158: Female bisexual [though I prefer pansexual as a term] aged 18–24)

Some also identified the possibility of experiences of multiple forms of discrimination, which they felt could be addressed within service delivery and broader advocacy work:

One of the things that we're kind of focusing on at the moment is kind of double or triple discrimination because you may have LGBT [trade union] members who are disabled and they're kind of ostracised from the LGBT community because they've got a disability and they're ostracised from the disability community because they're LGB or T . . . you can get this multiple discrimination where people are kind of pushed out and they don't feel as though they belong anywhere.

(Colin)

The research uncovered a variety of personal experiences of identity-based prejudice within LGBT communities. Often these were related to perceived hierarchies and/or forms of biphobia, transphobia, ageism, (dis)ableism and/or racism. That use of the phrase LGBT community tends to overlook these experiences is an important finding.

## Faith and Religion

Whilst some participants felt they were discriminated against or excluded based on aspects of their identities, others identified elements of their identities which contributed to their experiences and/or limited their involvement in communities. Spirituality or faith was one such example that was significant for some participants. Laura, for example, felt that she could not be as 'out' as she would like to be within her faith community, but at the same time did not wish to participate in, what was for her, a "shocking" scene-based LGBT community. This resulted in clear tensions between accessing particular spaces in the hopes of meeting somebody and the guilt that she experienced in going to those spaces:

> I can't keep going into the middle of [local city] . . . because it just, the guilt gets too much. I'm hoping to meet somebody who is coming from the faith angle like me.
>
> (Laura)

Her experiences led to a clear sense of isolation, and Laura found seeking a partner of similar faith particularly difficult. Yip (1996) has suggested that gay Christian groups such as the Lesbian and Gay Christian Movement (LGCM) offer safety and a place for 'honesty' and 'acceptance' for members to practice their sexuality and their Christianity. Laura was aware of the LGCM but it was not accessible to her for practical and financial reasons. Without this support, she found debates about 'gay marriage' that were prominent at the time of the research difficult to cope with, and the differences of opinion within Laura's evangelical church reinforced her feelings of isolation within the congregation:

> I'm a bit of a lone voice in my own church at the moment . . . It's been very confusing what's been going on . . . I think it is pretty heart-wrenching for everybody . . . I think I have been a bit of a thorn in their side.
>
> (Laura)

Laura was not the only one who struggled with reconciling what they thought were the beliefs of their God with their own views on gay marriage:

> It has been quite a rough couple of months for me at church . . . The faith in God that I was so certain about a year ago and the sexual identity that was so preciously defined by myself over the past forty odd years (lesbian at least) have been brought into question. Of course as a liberal politically I would go for gay marriage and not just blessings but my God appears to not be ready for this.
>
> (Website contributor)

Some LGBT professionals also identified impacts of particular faith doctrines on some of the people they worked with:

> I run a women's group and a lot of the women are religious . . . One of the ladies is coming out as gay and has been really connected with the church lifestyle but now they have kicked her to the curb and the impact that has had on her self esteem and confidence is ridiculous, it's really low. We are trying to build it back up for her and give her some options, there are churches out there that will accept LGBT people.
>
> (Julie)

In addition to the influence of religion in some people's lives, participants also identified prejudice from LGBT people towards religion, and sometimes religious LGBT people. This made some people feel silenced:

> Within the gay community, [my] religious beliefs, although not held strongly, are often open to ridicule, so I have learned that it is not appropriate to discuss them.
>
> (Survey respondent 502: Gay man aged 35–44)

For some, religion was just one of a list of identities that contributed to a sense of not belonging:

> There is so much racism, fatphobia, biphobia and hate towards people who follow a religion in various LGBT communities. I don't feel like I belong anywhere, and I won't unless I magically become a white, thin lesbian who's an atheist.
>
> (Survey respondent 535: Mostly female bisexual aged 35–44)

Ongoing impacts of growing up in a religious environment and/or Irish Catholic culture were also suggested as having an influence on identity:

> [I am] Irish, white and Catholic. Despite some of our progressiveness I know many of my fellow white Irish gay and lesbian friends still feel the 'hang ups' of being 'culturally Catholic'. We've discussed this amongst us at mind-numbingly tedious length.
>
> (Survey respondent 206: Gay man aged 25–34)

Having one's sexuality and faith understood was important, and for some this meant contacting people and establishing friendships with people with whom they shared a faith:

> The LGBT friends I feel most connected with are a number of people who share the same faith and who have known what it's like to battle to reconcile sexuality with Christianity. My coming out was delayed for many years

because my faith taught me homosexuality was 'sinful'. When I finally acknowledged that I am gay, the first people I sought out for support online were LGBT Christians.

(Survey respondent 206: Female lesbian aged 35–44)

Whilst supportive and understanding friends were significant, a number of participants also suggested that support received from designated gay Christian groups was important:

I have a faith, and am an ordained minister, and also receive mutual support from gay Christian groups, as well as socialising with and being supported by other LGBT groups.

(Survey respondent 78: Gay man aged 35–44)

As well as LGBT groups and networks, religious organisations were also identified as providing supportive spaces and attitudes:

I am a member of the Religious Society of Friends (Quakers) who have a firm commitment to equality and have bolstered my sense of worth within a faith context and provided a 'sub' LGBT community away from the pubs, clubs and the scene.

(Survey respondent 346: Gay man aged 45–54)

The role of religious organisations in supporting some people's 'coming out' was noted as unexpected:

Brought up practicing C of E [Church of England]—had concerns re coming out. I actually went on a Catholic retreat (run by Jesuits) which was a very positive experience and aided my 'coming out'.

(Survey respondent 304: Female gay woman/lesbian aged 45–54)

Religious LGBT people therefore had various experiences of/within LGBT communities. Whilst some found religion contributed to feelings of guilt or isolation, others found it was the attitudes of others towards religion that left them feeling isolated. However, sharing a faith and finding mutual support amongst others of faith could be a rewarding experience, once again illustrating complexities often un(der)acknowledged within representations of LGBT communities.

## Parenting

Becoming a parent was another aspect of identity that influenced people's life experiences, not only due to the parenting but also because of the ways in which it influenced their relationship with community. For some, this was in valuable ways as it led to new friendships and networks:

> [I am] happily married to my female partner . . . and was registered as my daughter's 'parent' on her birth certificate. Since becoming a family, we've found a community of (mostly) lesbian families, which is hugely valuable.
> (Survey respondent 627: Female lesbian aged 25–34)

Experiences such as this echo Ghaziani's (2014) research that suggested that gay parents may seek one another out in order to access support. He found that the importance of belonging and mutual understanding for queer families led to a 'clustering' in particular suburban areas (Ghaziani, 2014; see also Taylor, 2009 for further discussion of LGB parenting). However, within my research, not everyone was able to make such connections. Some parents suggested that they did not always find it easy to find a place (physical or otherwise) for themselves within local LGBT communities that were described by some as not child-friendly:

> When I first moved [here] . . . I was quite keen to meet other people, particularly other parents. There did not seem to be a lot of that about. A lot of the LGBT community seemed to be around hooking up and finding romantic or sexual encounters and I wasn't really looking for that . . . It would be nice if in the LGBT aspect there was a part for people who had children.
> (Liz)

Having children could therefore lead to a distancing from LGBT communities:

> I feel much less part of an LGBT community over the last 10 years and certainly this distance has increased since I've had children. Largely the scene locally is structured around men and alcohol/clubs. Neither of these hold a lot of interest for me as a lesbian parent in her 40s. I want my children to have a sense of their alternative heritage and the positives I have historically gained from the support of the lesbian community, however there is often a distance created as the child-centric world is still very straight and the gay world is still very non-child friendly.
> (Survey respondent 246: Female lesbian aged 35–44)

For Liz, trying to find other LGBT people with children was an important element of her parenting as it was through such connections that she could demonstrate to her child that her identity and relationship was 'healthy':

> One of the reasons I wanted to get in touch with people when I moved here was [for] my daughter's sake, so that she knew that there were other same-sex couples around and that it was OK and healthy before she was going to school.
> (Liz)

Whilst some, like Liz, felt able to be openly lesbian and introduce their children to other LGBT families, others took, or felt forced to take, a different approach to parenting. As a result, their interactions with other LGBT people were limited:

> I identified as lesbian later on in life and my 'physical' involvement in the LGBT community has been affected by my reluctance to 'come out' whilst my children are younger . . . The opportunities within my locality and a little further afield mean that I cannot visit the 'scene' or become involved in other groups, given that I would easily be 'outed' . . . This affects my development as an LGBT identified person which does feel restrictive.
>
> (Survey respondent 505: Female lesbian aged 45–54)

As people get older their life experiences inevitably alter, but becoming a parent could cause a sudden rupture with LGBT communities or spaces where these were deemed to not be child-friendly. However, parenting also led some people to find, or form, new communities with people with whom they could share their experiences.

## (Non)conformity

Guibernau (2013) has noted that belonging provides support and can contribute to self-esteem, but it can also be a source of anxiety when the benefits of belonging are outweighed by pressures to obey the norms of a particular group or community. This section focuses on experiences of inequality or prejudice resulting from people not conforming to certain norms and practices within particular communities, often related to image and appearance.

Some people chose to resist what they saw as stereotypes amongst LGBT people:

> The majority of LGBT communities surrounding where I live are very stereotypical due to LGBT people thinking they have to live up to a stereotype. That is not what I want to be part of, or want to portray to others.
>
> (Survey respondent 498: Gay man aged 25–34)

Where people shared an identity but not what they saw as stereotypical interests with other LGB people, they could feel isolated or judged:

> That sense of shared identity only extends so far . . . We do not have to buy into stereotypes if we do not wish to. For example, in my university days in the late 90s, I felt very disconnected from my LGB Society, as the focus there was on being trendy and fashionable and listening to pop music. I was interested in science fiction and role-playing and didn't give two hoots about fashion, and was therefore judged to be 'not properly gay'.
>
> (Survey respondent 380: Gay cis[gender] male aged 25–34)

It has been suggested that categorisations of people allow people to come to know and speak of themselves and others as certain types of people, and yet at the same time lead to expectations to which people must choose whether or not to conform (Mason, 2001). These might be understood as forms of group surveillance or regulation, which can be contrasted with self-surveillance and regulation discussed in Chapter 4. Within my research, there were concerns that expectations could be experienced as dictatorial so that people felt they had to present themselves in a certain way in order to belong to a community:

> With that label of community comes a danger that, yes, you are presenting a true way of doing something . . . that's the danger of community, that it becomes dictatorial in that sense.
>
> (Gemma)

> There are a lot of gay women . . . [who] try to change their role, the hair goes, the men's clothes come out . . . [but] I think you should be yourself and not conform to the LGBT norms.
>
> (Julie)

Fiona thought that norms and expectations about sexual desirability could limit how people presented or performed their identity in order to ensure that they conformed to certain looks:

> You have to be pretty, or you've got to be big and hairy or muscley, and those are your options . . . If I'm like that then that group of people will want to have sex with me . . . It narrows people's options a lot.
>
> (Fiona)

Fiona also drew attention to 'policing' by trans people that she felt continued around expectations of gender and gender expression:

> The policing that goes on with[in] the trans community is really high . . . I've got a friend who talks about how she would really like people to think that she was a butch lesbian . . . however her ability to present in that way is really diminished . . . [and] undermined by the trans community . . . you have to wear make-up, you have to have long hair, you have to wear skirts . . . I hear tremendously transphobic things coming out of trans people's mouths . . . from the person who you're meant to have this community bond with.
>
> (Fiona)

Elsewhere, however, Petra thought that things had improved with regard to 'authenticity' and gender expression, but nevertheless pointed to the diversity amongst trans people:

> I'm not sure that community is a very suitable word for such a diverse group of people . . . This dichotomy between . . . the normativity that some transsexual

people want to hold on to . . . as opposed to the queer studies ideals of trans as being inherently destabilising of binary gender . . . This idea of a hierarchy of trans . . . is an old fashioned idea, that the only authentic expression of trans must be transsexuality and anything else is somehow not as authentic . . . but nonetheless it has existed.

(Petra)

Fraser's (2008) participants saw community as 'oppressively normalising' in 'demanding conformity', and she therefore suggested that community could be interpreted as a 'regulatory myth'. However, both Helen and Gemma acknowledged a desire to balance their individual styles with being part of something, albeit something normative:

You eventually don't want to go there . . . and yet somehow you do go back, so there is some sort of draw there as well to be a part of that group and go to that place.

(Helen)

Similarly, when Gemma was younger, there was an appeal in scene spaces, if only because of a lack of visibility elsewhere:

For me at that time [when I was younger] . . . it did seem that you had to go there [the scene] to be part of it because . . . you can't see anything else.

(Gemma)

Laura exhibited a sense of acceptance or resignation about the need to fit in in order to reap the rewards of belonging or participation. She made numerous references to wanting to meet someone during the course of her interview, and noted how she consciously adapted her clothing in order to be recognised as a lesbian:

[If] you're looking for the right person . . . then you have to have places where people can meet . . . [where] there are identity codes like dress and things like that . . . I try to wear trousers all the time.

(Laura)

However, Laura was not the only woman who thought there was a need to conform to a 'lesbian look':

Gay women do it . . . you know, like you've got to have short hair and wear Timberland boots and things.

(Dilys)

Others felt less constrained and/or more able to resist norms as they got older, perhaps related to being more confident and 'established' in who they were, which might be described as developing ageing capital (Simpson, 2015). This means that for some people the disciplinary influence of normativities lessens over time:

> I suppose I felt under pressure in my early 20s to be maybe more someone who I wasn't, by going on the scene or something like that and, I don't know, that in itself is a bit less meaningful for me now.
>
> (Huw)

> As I get older . . . I feel that life choices (such as whether to marry or have children) are more eclectic within the LGBTQ community, and so I feel 'freer' to make choices that are right for me rather than having to conform.
>
> (Survey respondent 199: Lesbian in terms of relationship and who I have sex with [bisexual in terms of attraction] cisgender female aged 25–34)

Some people were happy to not fit in, though they recognised this might not be the case, or possible, for everybody. The notion of needing, or being able, to fit in made some people feel cynical about a community that was perceived to require people to fit in boxes in order to be included:

> Through years of battling within myself, I became stronger and more confident in myself. I am me and I don't quite fit in any of the boxes identified for lesbians. I don't care for fitting in completely, I have good gay and straight friends, but for others who don't fit in those boxes it would be extremely difficult to be themselves and fit in. This makes me cynical about the gay community.
>
> (Survey respondent 327: Female lesbian aged 25–34)

Gemma identified what she saw as a need to challenge (mis)perceptions about having to conform and fit in in order to access community. She therefore wanted youth work to promote a wider range of options and spaces to young people, in the hopes that this would help them resist or defy 'mainstream' norms:

> I really think it's quite important to signpost to young people that to be LGBT they don't have to go on the mainstream scene. There are other things there, they're just a bit harder to find . . . Young women and young men face these kind of pressures to conform . . . I hope that in our practice here we're careful to present options to young people that they can participate in their community in the way that they want to, that they don't have to change themselves to fit into a community, which I think a lot of LGBT people do feel.
>
> (Gemma)

Fiona and Ben similarly examined messages contained within professional teaching and youth work practice. Fiona, for example, was concerned that in attempts to address bullying in schools advocates were only presenting limited, normative ways to 'do' gay:

> A slightly concerning trend at the moment in terms of bullying work and homophobia work is that people are . . . getting these very masculine, conforming gay men to come and say 'look, I am 40 and I am in the army, I'm a policeman, I can do all of this stuff and I just happened to be gay', so it's alright to be gay if you fit into heteronormative structures but if you don't, if you're the boy at school who has long nails and a handbag it's like, 'well he's still weird, so carry on [bullying]'.
>
> (Fiona)

Ben also raised concerns about the promotion of binary identities in calling for spaces and language that enable more varied, including non-binary, identity options and expressions:

> I think that the community to some extent reinforces these narrow binary ideas and so having a space where people are able to have a few more options I think is something that I would want to see [in future practice] . . . how you're able to do your gender, do your sexual orientation, and that includes language, that includes ways of being, it includes spaces and discussions.
>
> (Ben)

Feelings of belonging to, or being a member of, particular communities were often thought to be conditional on conforming to certain norms or stereotypes associated with particular spaces or groups of people. Those who did not conform could feel isolated or obliged to alter their appearance, which was a cause for concern for those who worked with young LGBT people in particular. However, as people got older and accrued ageing capital (Simpson, 2015), this could facilitate growing confidence to resist or defy these norms.

## Chapter Summary

This chapter has shown how use of the term LGBT community often fails to acknowledge diversities, inequalities and prejudices amongst LGBT people. Where people had awareness and/or experience of these, this could make them sceptical about the value of such a term, and indeed the desirability of such a 'reality'. It was clear that community belonging is not a given even when people share a gender or sexual identity. Resources of ageing and social class could facilitate belonging and inclusion, for example, whilst being disabled, BME and/or lacking financial resources could lead to feelings of exclusion. Within the LGBT grouping, those who identified as bisexual and/or trans were more likely to experience discrimination from lesbian and gay people, which could make them criticise the idea of (a) community. Both having faith and becoming a parent could also lead to exclusions, or conversely new communities in which people could share their experiences. Often feelings of community belonging or membership were thought to be conditional on the basis of conforming to particular norms and/or fitting in other ways. This suggests that the notion of LGBT community is problematic to many, because of a suggestion that it requires similarity that was often felt to not exist, or be desirable. Despite some people feeling a sense of belonging with those with whom they shared a gender or sexual identity, I would suggest that it was when their identities were not alike in other ways, for example relating to age, ethnicity and/or social class, that tensions could arise. Overall, the research clearly shows that notions of community can overlook these issues of diversity and discrimination.

## References

Archibald, C. (2010) 'A path less travelled: Hearing the voices of older lesbians' in Jones, R.L. and Ward, R. (eds) *LGBT issues: Looking beyond categories*. Edinburgh: Dunedin Academic Press, pp. 30–41.

Barker, M., Richards, C., Jones, R., Bowes-Catton, H., Plowman, T., Yockney, J. and Morgan, M. (2012) *The bisexuality report: Bisexual inclusion in LGBT equality and diversity*. Milton Keynes: The Open University.

Bertotti, M., Jamal, F. and Harden, A. (2011) *A review of conceptualisations and meanings of 'community' within and across research traditions: A meta-narrative approach*. Swindon: Arts and Humanities Research Council.

Brown, G. (2008) 'Urban (homo)sexualities: Ordinary cities and ordinary sexualities', *Geography Compass* 2(4): 1215–1231.

Browne, K. (2010) 'Queer spiritual spaces: Conclusion' in Browne, K., Munt, S.R. and Yip, A.K.T. (eds) *Queer spiritual spaces: Sexuality and sacred places*. Farnham: Ashgate, pp. 231–246.

Browne, K. and Bakshi, L. (2013) *Ordinary in Brighton: LGBT, activisms and the city*. Aldershot: Ashgate.

Browne, K., Munt, S.R. and Yip, A.K.T. (2010) *Queer spiritual spaces: Sexuality and sacred places*. Farnham: Ashgate.

Cant, B. (2008) 'Gay men's narratives and the pursuit of wellbeing in healthcare settings: A London study', *Critical Public Health* 18(1): 41–50.

Casey, M.E. (2007) 'The queer unwanted and their undesirable "otherness"' in Browne, K., Lim, J. and Brown, G. (eds) *Geographies of sexualities: Theory, practices and politics*. Aldershot: Ashgate, pp. 125–136.

Cronin, A. and King, A. (2010) 'Power, inequality and identification: Exploring diversity and intersectionality amongst older LGB adults', *Sociology* 44(5): 876–892.

Cronin, A. and King, A. (2014) 'Only connect? Older lesbian, gay and bisexual (LGB) adults and social capital', *Ageing and Society* 34(2): 258–279.

Davy, Z. (2011) *Recognizing transsexuals: Personal, political and medicolegal embodiment*. Aldershot: Ashgate.

Day, G. (2006) *Community and everyday life*. New York: Routledge.

Eisenstadt, K. and Gatter, P. (1999) 'Coming together: Social networks of gay men and HIV prevention' in Aggleton, P., Hart, G. and Davies, P. (eds) *Families and communities responding to AIDS*. London: UCL Press, pp. 99–120.

Ellis, S.J. (2007) 'Homophobia, rights and community: Contemporary issues in the lives of LGB people in the UK' in Clarke, V. and Peel, E. (eds) *Out in psychology: Lesbian, gay, bisexual, trans and queer perspectives*. Chichester: John Wiley and Sons, pp. 291–310.

Fraser, S. (2008) 'Getting out in the "real world": Young men, queer and theories of gay community', *Journal of Homosexuality* 55(2): 245–264.

Ghaziani, A. (2011) 'Post-gay collective identity construction', *Social Problems* 58(1): 99–125.

Ghaziani, A. (2014) *There goes the gayborhood?* Princeton: Princeton University Press.

Guibernau, M. (2013) *Belonging: Solidarity and division in modern societies.* Cambridge: Polity Press.

Heaphy, B. (2012) 'Reflexive sexualities and reflexive sociology' in Hines, S. and Taylor, Y. (eds) *Sexualities: Past reflections, future directions.* Basingstoke: Palgrave Macmillan, pp. 15–31.

Heaphy, B., Yip, A.K.T. and Thompson, D. (2003) *Lesbian, gay and bisexual lives over 50.* Nottingham: York House Publications.

Hines, S. (2007) 'Transgendering care: Practices of care within transgender communities', *Critical Social Policy* 27(4): 462–486.

Hines, S. (2010) 'Queerly situated: Exploring constraints and negotiations of trans queer subjectivities', *Gender, Place and Culture* 17(5): 597–613.

Holt, M. (2011) 'Gay men and ambivalence about "gay community": From gay community attachment to personal communities', *Culture, Health and Sexuality* 13(8): 857–871.

Hunt, S. (ed) (2009) *Contemporary Christianity and LGBT sexualities.* Farnham: Ashgate.

Jennings, R. (2007) *A lesbian history of Britain: Love and sex between women since 1500.* Oxford: Greenwood World Publishing.

Lehavot, K., Balsam, K.F. and Ibrahim-Wells, G.D. (2009) 'Redefining the American quilt: Definitions and experiences of community among ethnically diverse lesbian and bisexual women', *Journal of Community Psychology* 37(4): 439–458.

MacKian, S. and Goldring, J.E. (2010) ' "What's he looking at me for?" Age, generation and categorisation for gay men's health promotion' in Jones, R.L. and Ward, R. (eds) *LGBT issues: Looking beyond categories.* Edinburgh: Dunedin Academic Press, pp. 16–29.

Mason, G. (2001) 'Body maps: Envisaging homophobia, violence and safety', *Social and Legal Studies* 10(1): 23–44.

May, V. (2013) *Connecting self to society: Belonging in a changing world.* New York: Palgrave Macmillan.

McDermott, E. (2011) 'The world *some* have won: Sexuality, class and inequality', *Sexualities* 14(1): 63–78.

McKeown, E., Nelson, S., Anderson, J., Low, N. and Elford, J. (2010) 'Disclosure, discrimination and desire: Experiences of Black and South Asian gay men in Britain', *Culture, Health and Sexuality* 10(7): 843–856.

Monro, S. (2015) *Bisexuality: Identities, politics, and theories.* Basingstoke: Palgrave Macmillan.

Moran, L., Skeggs, B., Tyrer, P. and Corteen, K. (2003) 'The formation of fear in gay space: The "straights" story', *Capital and Class* 27(2): 173–198.

Pugh, S. (2002) 'The forgotten: A community without a generation—Older lesbians and gay men' in Richardson, D. and Seidman, S. (eds) *Handbook of lesbian and gay studies.* London: Sage, pp. 161–181.

Ridge, D., Hee, A. and Minichiello, V. (1999) ' "Asian" men on the scene: Challenges to "gay communities" ', *Journal of Homosexuality* 36(3–4): 43–68.

Rogers, A. (2012) ' "In this our lives": Invisibility and black British gay identity' in Rivers, I. and Ward, R. (eds) *Out of the ordinary: Representations of LGBT lives.* Newcastle: Cambridge Scholars Publishing, pp. 43–60.

Simpson, P. (2012) 'Perils, precariousness and pleasures: Middle-aged gay men negotiating urban "heterospaces"', *Sociological Research Online* 17(3).

Simpson, P. (2013a) 'Alienation, ambivalence, agency: Middle-aged gay men and ageism in Manchester's gay village', *Sexualities* 16(3–4): 283–299.

Simpson, P. (2013b) 'Differentiating the self: The kinship practices of middle-aged gay men in Manchester', *Families, Relationships and Societies* 2(1): 97–113.

Simpson, P. (2014) 'Differentiating selves: Middle-aged gay men in Manchester's less visible "homospaces"', *The British Journal of Sociology* 65(1): 150–169.

Simpson, P. (2015) *Middle-aged gay men, ageing and ageism: Over the rainbow?* Basingstoke: Palgrave Macmillan.

Simpson, P. (2016) 'The resources of ageing? Middle-aged gay men's accounts of Manchester's gay voluntary organizations', *The Sociological Review* 64(2): 366–383.

Skeggs, B. (1999) 'Matter out of place: Visibility and sexualities in leisure spaces', *Leisure Studies* 18(3): 213–232.

Smit, P.J., Brady, M., Carter, M., Fernandes, R., Lamore, L., Meulbroek, M., Ohayon, M., Platteau, T., Rehberg, P., Rockstroh, J.K. and Thompson, M. (2012) 'HIV-related stigma within communities of gay men: A literature review', *AIDS Care* 24(4): 405–412.

Taylor, Y. (2007a) *Working-class lesbian life: Classed outsiders*. Basingstoke: Palgrave.

Taylor, Y. (2007b) '"If your face doesn't fit . . .": The misrecognition of working-class lesbians in scene space', *Leisure Studies* 26(2): 161–178.

Taylor, Y. (2008) '"That's not really my scene": Working-class lesbians in (and out of) place', *Sexualities* 11(5): 523–546.

Taylor, Y. (2009) *Lesbian and gay parenting: Securing social and educational capital.* Basingstoke: Palgrave Macmillan.

Taylor, Y. (2011) 'Queer presences and absences: Citizenship, community, diversity—or death', *Feminist Theory* 12(3): 335–341.

Taylor, Y., Falconer, E. and Snowdon, R. (2014) 'Sounding religious, sounding queer', *Ecclesial Practices* 1(2): 229–249.

Tonkiss, F. (2003) 'The ethics of indifference: Community and solitude in the city', *International Journal of Cultural Studies* 6(3): 297–311.

Valentine, G. (1996) '(Re)negotiating the "heterosexual street"' in Duncan, N. (ed) *Body-Space: Destabilising geographies of gender and sexuality.* London: Routledge, pp. 145–154.

Valentine, G. and Skelton, T. (2003) 'Finding oneself, losing oneself: The lesbian and gay "scene" as a paradoxical space', *International Journal of Urban and Regional Research* 27(4): 849–866.

Weeks, J. (1996) 'The idea of a sexual community', *Soundings* 2: 71–84.

Weeks, J. (2007) *The world we have won: The remaking of erotic and intimate life.* London: Routledge.

Weeks, J., Heaphy, B. and Donovan, C. (2001) *Same sex intimacies: Families of choice and other life experiments.* London: Routledge.

Wilkinson, J., Bittman, M., Holt, M., Rawstorne, P., Kippax, S. and Worth, H. (2012) 'Solidarity beyond sexuality: The personal communities of gay men', *Sociology* 46(6): 1161–1177.

Woolwine, D. (2000) 'Community in gay male experience and moral discourse', *Journal of Homosexuality* 38(4): 5–37.

Yip, A.K.T. (1996) 'Gay Christians and their participation in the gay subculture', *Deviant Behaviour* 17(3): 297–318.

Yip, A.K.T. (2008) 'Researching lesbian, gay, and bisexual Christians and Muslims: Some thematic reflections', *Sociological Research Online* 13(1).

Yip, A.K.T. and Keenan, M. (2009) 'Transgendering Christianity: Gender-variant Christians as visionaries' in Hunt, S. (ed) *Contemporary Christianity and LGBT sexualities.* Farnham: Ashgate, pp. 87–102.

Yip, A.K.T., Keenan, M. and Page, S.J. (2011) *Religion, youth and sexuality: Selected key findings from a multi-faith exploration.* Nottingham: University of Nottingham.

Young, I.M. (1990) *Justice and the politics of difference.* Princeton: Princeton University Press.

# 4    Lived Experience and 'Doing' Community

## Introduction

This chapter examines why people engage with (the idea of) communities, before subsequent chapters go on to look at specific aspects and experiences of communities. In focussing on lived experiences of community, or the 'doing' of community, the chapter builds on the previous one (which centred on the diversity of individual identities), and documents varied community practices. Primarily the chapter focuses on friendships, how and why people sought safety and attempted to avoid 'risk', and activism, though it also identifies changing engagements with, and experiences of, communities. In examining these interlinked areas, I explore how and why community is constructed by LGBT people themselves, not just used as an overarching 'label' by 'outsiders' (as Chapter 2 discussed). The chapter explores people's everyday lived experience of LGBT communities, which they often contrasted with perceptions and experiences of broader social contexts. In doing so, the chapter discusses practices of identity management and self-censorship in intimate relationships, and sets out how this relates to why some people choose to engage with the idea(l) of particular communities. Communities were thought to enable friendships, and thus the possibility of 'chosen families', as well as the opportunity to seek sex or intimacy. Often communities were understood as offering safety in numbers and/or safe spaces that enabled feelings of comfort and being relaxed, as well as physical demonstrations of intimacy and affection. Seeking safety was therefore identified as key to the development of and/or desire for LGBT communities, as was political activism. Essentially, meeting with other LGBT people and forming LGBT friendships was seen as a way of avoiding risk and ensuring safety, as well as offering the opportunity for political activism and potential social change. These issues are examined within the following seven headings: Socialising, Friendship and Seeking Intimacy; Friendship Families; Safety in Numbers; Accessing Safe Spaces; Self-Censorship; Activism; and Lived Experience Across the Life Course. First, I set the scene for my research with an overview of existing literature that focuses on the place of impressions management and self-regulation within human interaction, which forms the context for subsequent chapters, and indeed the foundation of this book.

## Overview of Existing Literature

Whilst I cannot summarise here all existing literature that has examined experiences of and within LGBT communities, I do show how research suggests they are important, and why. Friendships form one understanding of community, and Woolwine (2000) has proposed that gay friendships are among the most important elements of gay and lesbian lived experience. Holt (2011) has also suggested that families of choice and personal communities provide alternative ideas of community to those based on geography, or more narrowly, the scene. Earlier work has identified the importance of close friendships with people 'like me', which reduces the need for explanation, and means people can share experiences and feel relaxed (Rubin, 1985; Stanley, 1996; Weeks, Heaphy and Donovan, 2001; Woolwine, 2000). Whilst a great many (particularly gay men) lost friends as a result of the emergence of HIV/AIDS, it has also been suggested that it led to stronger bonds and/or new friendships (Cronin and King, 2014), as well as the renewal of former relationships following diagnosis (Weston, 1991). As Nardi (1999: 187) observed, whilst AIDS took a toll on "most gay men's friendship networks" it also opened up "possibilities of newer friends being made through grief and support", thus speeding up the process of friendship formation. Whilst a variety of themes have been explored in existing research, evidence suggests that friendships amongst LGBT people are important, and allied to notions of community.

One of the key ways that communities and friendships have been identified as important is in relation to feelings of safety and comfort. As Moran et al. (2004) discovered, people conceptualise a hierarchy of safety and danger from 'straights', and often use the word comfort to denote feelings of safety. 'Public'[1] spaces are therefore often the comparison against which LGBT communities, whether imagined or physical, are held up as having the ability, or potential, to facilitate people feeling comfortable, relaxed and at ease among other LGBT people. This is despite queer spaces that are often understood as safe spaces ironically being the most frequent sites of anti-gay violence because they become 'hunting grounds' used by homophobes (Myslik, 1996). We can see examples of this in the bombing of the Admiral Duncan pub in London in 1999, and the more recent mass shooting in the Pulse nightclub in Florida. However, safety is not just about the absence of violence; as Browne and Bakshi (2013: 135–136) have argued, it "is far more nebulous than this and relates to broader societal 'acceptances', feelings of safety, possibilities of enacting LGBT identities in taken for granted, indeed ordinary, ways". Guibernau (2013: 18) has emphasised the importance of 'significant others' in people's constructions of identity through social interaction, and specifically interpretations of how we think others will view us. I would argue, however, that her definition of significant others needs to be clearer to ascertain whether she means a 'common-sense' understanding of known/close others, because traditionally 'insignificant' (and sometimes arguably imagined) others can also have an influence on LGBT identity management and self-surveillance, though this is not to suggest that relationships and interactions with familiar others are insignificant. As Goffman (1959) argued, impressions management strategies are deployed in negotiations between people's self-image and public image, and I would argue these strategies are perhaps more conscious for some groups of people than others.

Mason (2001: 32) has argued that awareness of homophobic violence is a form of knowledge that "engenders a distinct tendency to monitor one's own body for signs of homosexuality". Stanko and Curry (1997) similarly identified a continuum of self-regulation, where the behaviours of homophobes become intertwined with self-imposed regulation within 'heterosexual' space. Knowledge of the threat of hostility, for example based on shared anecdotes or rumours, therefore leads to self-surveillance and the management of visible homosexuality, though this is not to suggest that self-surveillance is only influenced by the perceived threat of hostility or violence (Mason, 2001). Stanko and Curry (1997: 518, original emphasis) suggested that "gay and lesbian antiviolence projects have sponsored . . . the underlying message . . . that '*all* gays and lesbians—as well as anyone presumed to be gay or lesbian—are at risk at *all* times'". As such, violence or crime does not need to be experienced to be feared (Mason, 2001; Moran et al., 2003), with fear used here to refer to a sense of being unsafe and/or lacking control (Moran et al., 2003). The prevalence of Stonewall reports documenting hate crime and bullying indicate that Stanko and Curry's (1997) observation that activists highlight violence or discrimination in order to seek change is still true, and can (albeit unintentionally) feed into some people's fears or apprehension (Formby, 2015).

There is a long history of research documenting self-regulatory practices, such as people avoiding same-sex hand holding or kissing in public (Binnie, 1995; Browne, 2007, 2008; Mason, 2001; Moran et al., 2001; Valentine, 1993b, 1994; Weeks, Heaphy and Donovan, 2001). Myslik (1996: 160) argued that "adapting behaviour between gay and straight spaces . . . becomes natural and nearly unconscious". Whilst this comment is predicated on the assumption of clear 'gay' and 'straight' space that has been questioned elsewhere (Browne, 2008; Browne and Bakshi, 2011), more recent evidence of behaviour modification still exists, alongside improvements in legislative rights (Coleman-Fountain, 2014; Formby, 2013; Simpson, 2012). However, these arguments are complicated by the idea that space cannot be so easily defined as only 'heterosexual'. Browne and Bakshi (2011) have questioned the gay/straight space dichotomy by highlighting evidence of the heterosexualisation or 'degaying' of gay space, as well as straight space that is 'gayed' by its use by gay men. They also argue that 'mixed' spaces can be both 'straight' and 'gay' simultaneously, contesting assumptions that LGBT people can never feel comfortable in 'straight' venues (Browne and Bakshi, 2011). However, it should be noted that their observations are based on research in Brighton, which in my research was not viewed as a typical English town[2] (see Chapter 5). Elsewhere, Casey (2004: 457) has argued that whilst in theory mixed bars challenge gay/straight binaries, in practice in cities with a small scene, such as Newcastle, "such mixing and diluting of spaces threatens to heterosexualise once queered sites". Browne and Bakshi's (2013) research does however point to the importance of context when examining LGBT experiences, indicating that 'straight' spaces can be experienced as safe, influenced by geography, gender and class, amongst a host of other issues. However, my research shows that beliefs surrounding communities are often predicated on dichotomous notions of safety and comfort amongst LGBT people, and a lack thereof elsewhere.

Building on this evidence but turning more specifically to the notion of 'display' now (see Chapter 1), we can see that UK civil partnerships and more recent 'equal' marriage may be a way of displaying relationship 'status'. At the same time, however, affection within relationships may not always be so 'easily' or safely displayed to unknown others. An early Stonewall (1996) report documented that 88% of survey respondents always or sometimes avoided kissing or holding hands in public, also documented in much more recent Stonewall research, though without parallel statistical information (Guasp, Gammon and Ellison, 2013). In 2015, a 'freedom to kiss' campaign was launched in London that drew attention to people's fears or discomfort, demonstrating that social attitudes are perceived to not always be in step with legislation (Buchanan, 2015). Similarly, in 2016, Pride in London launched their '#nofilter' campaign, calling on people to 'celebrate authenticity' and not filter or self-censor their behaviour (see http://prideinlondon.org/campaigns/nofilter). Supporting Heaphy's (2011: 32) notion of "display as temporally and spatially located interaction", and Finch's (2011: 201) observation about "the significance of particular audiences", this suggests that some people perceive that they can only display their relationships in certain places (see Chapters 5 and 6), or at certain times/ during certain events (see Chapter 7). Those who do display their relationship, for instance by holding hands whilst food shopping, may be chastised, as in the recent UK example of a gay couple being told by a supermarket security guard that their behaviour was 'inappropriate' (BBC, 2016). Needless to say, I am not aware of any heterosexual couples receiving such a warning. It is precisely intimate relationships being understood as such that prevents some people from being affectionate in public, hence avoiding 'tie signs' (Goffman, 1971) that suggest a significant/intimate relationship. Campaigns about kissing and not filtering encourage people to be 'open' and cease their self-regulatory behaviour, yet I argue LGBT communities are often constructed and imagined as not requiring this conscious 'unfiltering', because for some people 'filtering' has become their usual way of being.

## Socialising, Friendship and Seeking Intimacy

I now look at the importance of friendship and socialising within experiences and perceptions, or the 'doing', of community. In total, 73% of survey respondents felt 'somewhat' (48%) or 'strongly' (25%) part of one or more LGBT communities; conversely, a total of 27% 'did not really' (17%), 'definitely did not' (8%) or did not know (2%). When asked to order a number of options, survey respondents ranked 'desire to meet/interact with other LGBT people (physically or online)' as the second most 'true' explanation for the existence of LGBT communities. Echoing findings from Ellis (2007), who identified the role of community during times of 'crisis' or changing circumstance, participants stressed the importance of communities in relation to making a new start, such as moving to a new geographical area or following a relationship breakdown:

> Recently when I moved to [city] I wanted to just kind of socialise more with people like I'd met in [other city] . . . so I ended up joining various sort of odd little societies and things . . . to find people . . . searching kind of for the familiar I guess . . . I think it's those points where you're . . . first coming out, or if it falls apart, so you split up with your long-term partner or that social group falls apart, or you move . . .
>
> (Helen)

Community was therefore viewed as an access point for forming new friendships:

> I came back [to Britain] in 2001, 2002, and I had to find a trans community and I was very, very pleased that there was one . . . I'd been living in [the Middle East], as you can imagine there's not much going on there . . . so I had to get used to my own self again . . . I think that it's a very useful thing that there is a trans community and of course . . . after a while you make friends . . . so you begin to pick and choose.
>
> (Petra)

Ruth referred to finding more similar people amongst LGBT people with whom she could then develop friendships:

> When I was young we used to go down the Gateways club[3] and it was years before we said to each other, 'actually we don't have anything else in common with most of those people' . . . in my late life I've come to live [here] where there are so many queer people that you actually can meet someone that you've got something in common with as well so that's really nice.
>
> (Ruth)

Participants suggested that engaging with particular communities in the form of specific scenes or social groups enabled them to more easily meet and/or socialise with other LGBT people. Like Petra and Ruth, some participants made initial connections through shared gender and/or sexual identities, and then chose their (closer) friends from within these connections.

Sometimes communities were viewed as consisting of friends and broader groups of people that enabled social and sexual encounters:

> My 'communities' are my close gay friends where I live, and secondly, wider group(s) of men in London and elsewhere where I can socialise and have sex.
>
> (Survey respondent 480: Gay man aged 55–64)

There was a widespread assumption that most people want to find a partner or relationship that would initially necessitate meeting other LGBT people:

> There is always the inescapable demographic need to find, some way or somehow, whether it's online, whether it's kind of ridiculous things like hanky codes, or it's through going to a bar or a club . . . other people who have the same sexual orientation as you . . . Most people live in monogamous relationships and you've got to find them somehow.
>
> (Matt)

That this search often involved bars and clubs was not always seen as a good thing:

> I wanted to pull as well . . . There's this thing about being attracted to people and wanting to find people to date and I think that's kind of a unique part of the LGBT community . . . If we could move it away from just being bars and clubs to being more broad in society, then I think people would feel less like they have to go out there [on the scene] . . . otherwise they're going to be single forever.
>
> (Helen)

Some also sought out LGBT people because they felt they enabled discussions about relationships and intimacy that they felt they could not have with straight friends:

> The reason why I enjoy lesbians' company, gay men's company, trans individuals' company, I really enjoy it, because I've got straight friends and I love them all to bits, but I still don't sit there and talk about my relationship or my sex life with them. I can't because they've grown up in a society where that's not normal.
>
> (Julie)

A perceived benefit of having friendships with other LGBT people was therefore often related to an assumed mutual understanding, and/or the potential for mutual support (see also Chapters 8 and 9). However, some participants did not think that communities had facilitated friendships, because in their view communities *were* friendships, whether or not they were with other LGBT people:

> You probably have a circle of friends who are also gay so isn't that in itself a community which you're part of . . . [but] it's a different community to the gay scene community.
>
> (Fin)

> Communities that mean more in the sense of LGBT community, as well as in a more general sense, seem to be networks of friends, networks of people who genuinely get to know you and not just as an identity.
>
> (Charlie)

For some, the idea of a community of friends, or personal community, was explicitly drawn on because of the lack of appeal or accessibility of scene-based forms of community (see Chapter 6 for further detail). Others identified the importance of heterosexual allies within their LGBT community:

> I also consider 'straight' friends who are part of my life, to be part of my/the LGBT community . . . so everyone who came to my wedding, is to me, part of my LGBT community, as there was 'no issue'—it was not a scene thing, or an old school 'ghetto-isation'.
> (Survey respondent 38: Female lesbian aged 35–44)

> [I] strongly believe that these safe spaces and communities should involve heterosexual allies—I have many in my life, and my life is much richer for them.
> (Survey respondent 380: Gay cis[gender] male aged 25–34)

Despite different views on the composition of LGBT communities, the research shows that people often thought they enable and/or encompass friendships, as well as the opportunity to seek sex and/or intimacy. The doing of community was therefore linked to being with (other) LGBT people.

## Friendship Families

Previous research that has identified families we choose (Weston, 1991) and friendship families (Simpson, 2015) among lesbian and gay friendship networks is also relevant to the concept of community. In the UK, the importance of supportive friendships and families of choice (Jones-Wild, 2012; Traies, 2015), particularly when family of origin relationships may have been weakened or lost altogether, was highlighted by Weeks, Heaphy and Donovan (2001). Illustrating this idea, some participants suggested that particular friendships become akin to family:

> My friends are my family, similar to how a lot of LGBT [people] feel.
> (Survey respondent 38: Female lesbian aged 35–44)

Some also linked chosen family to feelings of community:

> Many people my age and older consider their close LGBTQI friends 'family' and this is their primary source of community.
> (Survey respondent 489: Outwardly I am most often male, inwardly I feel more akin to the notion of 'two spirit', gay aged 25–34)

However, Colin thought that chosen family was a status 'beyond' community:

> You've got different levels . . . ultimately when you get something like this [group] it goes beyond community and it does become family.
> (Colin)

Families of choice were identified as particularly important at specific times of the year. As Helen commented:

> A lot of people are closer than other friendship groups and I think that's because a lot of people maybe don't have that link, at least for a period of the time . . . with their families . . . I know friends . . . and they have 'gay Christmas' because they can't go home, or at least some of their friends can't go home, so they do something to really support each other in that way. So there is something in that bond that's perhaps needed to be a little bit stronger than . . . with other groups of friends because of family difficulties . . . it was much more than a 'house Christmas'.
>
> (Helen)

In a US context, Woolwine (2000: 23) similarly identified the significance of friends spending Thanksgiving together, suggesting that whilst his participants did not necessarily use the family metaphor, their "relationships, and the functions performed by friends . . . were strikingly similar". However, in Nardi's (1999) study, there was a greater mix of men choosing to spend significant events such as Christmas or Thanksgiving with friends *and* family, family only or friends only. Whilst Helen's time at university was relatively recent, Ruth recalled a similar desire to establish close friendships, which she identified was particularly important at a time when lesbianism was largely invisible. Referring to the establishment of a group of friends via a small advert in *Arena Three*,[4] Ruth commented:

> [Meeting] the first other people like us we ever knew, because it was very isolating when we were young . . . it was just wonderful, it was like the first time in your whole life there was a band of people there you could be completely open with . . . It's hard to describe now because it was all so different. It was very, very important.
>
> (Ruth)

In discussing her formative years, Ruth suggested that sharing experiences helped develop and maintain family-like relationships, including with ex-partners, echoing previous research that has suggested that lesbians are more likely to keep ex-lovers as friends so as not to isolate each other from particular communities or networks (Traies, 2015; Valentine, 1993a, 1994, 1995). Families of choice may therefore be particularly significant for older lesbians (Traies, 2015), and by implication older gay men, as evidenced by Ruth:

> We're still friends 45 years later, well I suppose more like family to each other because we've had that close sharing at a time when we couldn't share with anyone else . . . We all joke about how lesbians stay in touch with their exes and you find a way of making your ex into family, and I think . . . we

need that because we need that person who has shared that oppression, who understands, even if we're no longer their partner any more.

(Ruth)

It should be noted, however, that experiences of 'distance' from families of origin do not occur evenly across differing cultural groups or intersecting identities (Bertone and Pallotta-Chiarolli, 2014; Heaphy, Smart and Einarsdottir, 2013; Yip, 2008), which may have implications for variability in people's engagement with chosen family discourses. Nevertheless, my research demonstrates that some people do use family as a metaphor against which friendships and/or communities are compared.

## Safety in Numbers

This section turns to notions of safety and feeling comfortable with other LGBT people, which are important in helping us understand how people experience and conceptualise community. For some participants, a sense of constant 'otherness' was palpable, to the extent that they thought they might be 'judged' by every single new person they met:

Surely every straight person out there when they meet somebody new doesn't think, 'oh I hope nobody's going to judge me on who I sleep with'?

(Jackie)

This concern with "how we think others perceive us; how we imagine they judge us on the basis of this" (Cooley, 1902: 152) is particularly stark. However, I am not suggesting that people thought that judgement would always happen, but that there was an ongoing sense, if not of fear, of unease, or a perception of the need to be 'careful' (Guasp, Gammon and Ellison, 2013) and to monitor and minimise 'visible manifestations' of sexuality (Mason, 2001). A strong theme running throughout the research was therefore the presumption or experience of heterosexism and homophobia in society, which meant that many participants desired spaces of safety. This desire for safety and somewhere they could feel comfortable was often used to explain why LGBT people 'magnetise' towards each other, which was understood as a 'natural' response to (external) oppression:

There's a natural tendency, it's almost like being a magnet, you know, you're drawn to each other.

(Gerry)

I just think we naturally flock to people who are like us . . . If we stopped having as much LGBT oppression, then we probably would stop having such strong LGBT communities.

(Helen)

Similarly, participants drew on the idea of safety in numbers to explain why LGBT people (wish to) group together:

> Doesn't it come down to just like a basic instinct in nature generally, not just with humans . . . this whole concept of safety in numbers? If you can associate yourself with a group of people you feel more comfortable . . . [and] feel that we're safe with one another.
>
> (Timothy)

> At a party, the gays tend to gather . . . and that's safety in numbers . . . sort of, 'I'll talk to you because I know you're gay', and I've done that . . . because you've got a common interest and if you don't know people at the party you've at least got something.
>
> (Graham)

The notion of safety in numbers is not necessarily only physical, but can also relate to emotional and psychological safety (Myslik, 1996), and the creation of 'majorities' (Browne and Bakshi, 2013) in particular spaces (see Chapter 5 for further discussion). Participants identified feeling at home or more relaxed with other LGBT people, which was contrasted with feeling less at ease, or more anxious, elsewhere:

> That sense of being comfortable and being yourself with your partner and not feeling overly self-conscious about how you come across.
>
> (Liz)

This feeling of comfort has been interpreted by Woolwine (2000: 26) and others as being able to express a 'true' or " 'whole self' that the heterosexual world insists not be entirely expressed", though the notion of a 'true' or 'whole' self has been questioned (Hall, 1996; Woodiwiss, 2013). However, the doing of community was related to safety (in numbers) because being with other LGBT people was thought to offer a feeling of home, which can facilitate feelings of comfort and ease.

## Accessing 'Safe' Spaces

Moving on from feelings of comfort and safety with particular people or groups, it was clear that participants also thought certain (geographical, commercial and/or temporary) spaces could offer or provide feelings of comfort and safety that they did not always experience elsewhere. A broader social context that was assumed to be negative was implicitly and explicitly the reason that people chose to engage with particular communities. The importance of space, and specifically the scene, is explored in more detail within Chapters 5 and 6, but here I want to show how decisions about socialising were related to feeling comfortable, for example an identified need or want to go out on the scene was explicitly linked to being able to show physical affection. Fiona and Ben, for instance, both talked about the advantage of being able to hold hands, kiss and dance with their partners at ease. However, spaces thought to be safe or 'LGBT-friendly' were not limited to the scene. Other forms of 'LGBT space' were also linked to feeling safe and able to relax:

> LGBT spaces allow me to relax a bit and not feel so different all the time . . . there is a sense of relief.
>
> (Survey respondent 448: Mostly identify as cis[gender]
> female queer aged 18–24)

Formal groups were thought to enable a feeling of comfort, whether in youth or work-based settings:

> I don't have to feel conscious here [at a youth group] about what I say . . . When I'm with my straight friends, if I'm like, 'oh that boy's nice' . . . they're like, 'why did you just say that to me?'
>
> (Jason)

> [This work group] is a more comfortable environment where you're not having to second guess people's thoughts.
>
> (Adam)

These extracts illustrate how some participants felt a sense of difference in their daily lives, which meant they sought out spaces where they would feel relief, and not have to 'second guess' people's thoughts. Whilst specific groups and venues were identified as safe by many participants, whole geographical areas such as Brighton were also identified as safe (see Chapter 5), and therefore not requiring forms of self-regulation. Whilst for some this might be where they lived, for others these were places they visited, or in some cases imagined:

> Places like Brighton, or you go to San Francisco, you feel as though you can walk down the street holding whoever's hand you want to hold because there's other people doing it and you can identify with those people . . . I don't have to think, 'oh I can't say that'.
>
> (Jackie)

> Yeah, or 'what will they think?', or 'how will they interpret it?', or 'how do we have to package it to make it a bit palatable?'
>
> (Luce)

For those who did not live in areas that were thought to be more 'accepting', they were aware of their self-regulation practices in (avoiding) other non-scene spaces:

> You come from a big city, so you know your wallet, you don't put it in your outer pockets, you know that, it's ingrained, and I realise that . . . I don't go to

certain places. I'm very aware of that . . . perhaps this kind of ingrained sixth sense that you develop over the years.

(Luce)

This 'sixth sense' can be conceptualised as a 'safety map' that is personalised, but can be shared (Mason, 2001). In constructing these maps, people draw on previous experiences and popular understandings of risk associated with particular areas, 'types' of people and/or times of day, which they believe make them more or less vulnerable (Mason, 2001). These beliefs may be informed by lesbian and gay 'community knowledges' (Weeks, Heaphy and Donovan, 2001), but can also intersect with and be informed by, for example, class (see Chapter 3) and/or gender. Moran et al. (2003), for instance, noted how gay men can see straight men as more frightening than straight women, illustrating how fear can be gendered, with 'straights' differently constructed as both dangerous and safe. Valentine (1996) similarly identified gender differences in suggesting that gay men are more likely to be victimised in 'gay-identified neighbourhoods', whilst lesbians are more likely to report violent encounters in the 'heterosexual street'. Despite these differences, it is clear that communities and spaces, whether commercial, geographical or organised groups, were believed to generate feelings of safety and provide the opportunity to express physical affection. By comparison, self-regulation practices were employed elsewhere in order to minimise perceived risks. Community was therefore 'done' in relation to particular spaces, as well as particular (LGBT) people.

## Self-Censorship

In discussing their feelings of safety and comfort when with certain people and/ or in particular spaces, participants drew attention to their identity management and/or lack of relationship display practices elsewhere. Whilst participants did not explicitly discuss self-censorship, they talked about self-surveillance practices in numerous ways. Gerry, for example, talked about "editing" himself in the past:

Often being gay, you're sort of having to survive in a heterosexual world, you learn to not get noticed, to fit in, especially in situations where you might feel vulnerable . . . imagining how other people might react . . . [and] taking responsibility for other people's reactions.

(Gerry)

By contrast, more recently he and his partner had been consciously trying to become more accustomed to showing physical affection in public:

Us being able to be tactile in public has increased over time I think.

(Gerry)

Though evidence suggests that self-surveillance practices may vary, for example by gender, age and ethnic background (Mason, 2001), choosing not to hold hands with their partner was a commonly cited example of behaviour modification. This was discussed in relation to current and historic social contexts, with the inference that some people have got used to not holding their partner's hand, even though they would like to:

> I appreciate the fight for 'marriage' but more than this I want to be able to walk down the street holding my partner's hand without feeling this is a brave act or something that marks me out as 'different'.
>
> (Website contributor)

> I know what you mean about walking down the street holding your partner's hand. To me it's the most important barometer of social acceptance. Even in London or Manchester it's rare to see this going on outside a few choice streets. I wonder if this is something the community has simply gotten used to doing?
>
> (Website reply to above post)

> I fear it's too late for me, I would never feel comfortable walking down a street holding my partner's hand. I have missed out on so much of my life by having to hide a big part of myself during my formative years.
>
> (Website reply to above posts)

This exchange alludes to tensions between social attitudes and campaigns for 'equal marriage' that were prominent at the time of the research. Charlie also made reference to broader social contexts, which they identified as variable:

> I think we're in a very confusing and unpredictable time at the moment because we're making steps towards acceptance but we're not there, so you don't know whether you're going to be completely accepted or going to be spat at, and I've experienced both.
>
> (Charlie)

Perhaps because of these tensions and changeable social contexts, hand holding had been used as an educational exercise by one participant:

> On training I have challenged people to go out and hold hands with someone of the same gender and walk down the street and see what happens.
>
> (Liz)

For some people, censorship was linked to not being 'out':

> I spent the first 30 years of my life avoiding chat about my emotions, desires etc. for fear of outing myself. People used to compliment me on being such a good listener; in truth I was just a silenced talker.
>
> (Website contributor)

For others who regarded themselves as 'out', censorship could be seen as a form of self-protection or 'self-care' (Mason, 2001):

> Not wanting to offend people, make them uncomfortable, or bring on hostilities from people.
>
> (Liz)

In this way, self-surveillance can be viewed as a form of resisting the surveillance of others, so that "attempts to camouflage homosexuality represent both an oppressive silencing and a resistance to the trap of visibility" (Mason, 2001: 35). Taking responsibility for other people's reactions, developing a sixth sense, and getting used to avoiding hand holding can therefore be regarded as self-management (Mason, 2001) or identity management practices designed to avoid hostility or discomfort (Formby, 2013). This perspective signals the agency involved in these actions, as participants literally control the 'visibility' of their sexualities (Mason, 2001), though levels or times of being 'out' do not only relate to habit or personal 'choice', which is inevitably mediated by personal circumstances. Petra, for example, commented on their experiences of being an undergraduate student, when they had felt free to express their gender identity as they wished. They contrasted this with when they were looking for employment and had felt their possibilities for 'freedom' were limited until they returned to being a (postgraduate) student later in life:

> [Whilst I was an undergraduate student] I didn't have to make any compromises for work or anything and [I] always have had to do that before . . . but I didn't take it [my gender transition] any further because I thought . . . I would be out on the job market again . . . I thought, 'oh fuck . . . I'm going to have to be careful about what I do and how much I change my body and God I'll have to buy different clothes again' . . . It [gender transition] has never been possible before . . . [as] I've had to support children . . . [but now] I've actually got the freedom to live exactly as I want.
>
> (Petra)

As I have shown, embodied self-censorship practices outside of LGBT communities or spaces are enacted for a variety of reasons, including a combination of fear or apprehension, self-protection, habit and/or practical responses to employment and family responsibilities. Lived experience of, or within, LGBT communities was often described in contrast to these practices of self-censorship.

## Activism

In this section I focus on the place of political activism in people's understandings and experiences of community. In doing so, I show how activism was understood as driving community development and engagement, or the 'doing' of community. Survey respondents ranked 'developments in "gay rights" or "gay liberation" political activism' as the fourth highest option (out of eleven) in explaining the development of historic communities. In addition, 'coming together as part of community/political activism (e.g. for repeal of Section 28, for "gay marriage")' was the third highest ranked option (out of nine) to explain the existence of current communities. Responses to both questions therefore suggest that activism is seen as contributing to community development, both historically and currently. Other participant contributions also identified the importance of activism, which for some was fundamentally linked to what they thought was the purpose of communities. The Stonewall 'riots' in New York and grassroots/activist responses to the onset of HIV/AIDS were common historical examples cited, with more recent UK examples often including the campaign to repeal Section 28, and the campaign for 'equal' marriage. Involvement in political issues was thought to have brought people together and contributed to the growth of communities:

> For me it has always been important . . . to be part of something bigger that can help move things forward in a political sense . . . I think it [community] arose from political activism . . . that's why people come together, because they feel oppressed.
>
> (Liz)

> In the past you had to have some sort of community to put forward a united front to fight for equal rights and human rights, so I think it organically grew.
>
> (Dilys)

Laura similarly talked about how feeling part of something contributed to a sense of community, whilst acknowledging diverse opinions within such a grouping:

> There are moments when you think you're really caught up in something and feel part of things . . . working together really to make change, and I think that's been a real positive, what the LGBT community has managed to do historically . . . I think it's important we all stay together but within our community we will have quite different shades, varying interests or standpoints where we're coming from.
>
> (Laura)

The potential role of visible community in informing public opinion was also identified as important:

> Just because I bring in a piece of legislation midnight tonight doesn't mean people wake up with different hearts and minds tomorrow. Community is what influences hearts and minds, not legislation . . . Having that community visible keeps us in a position where we are influencing hearts and minds of ourselves, and also of wider society.
>
> (Gemma)

For some, social isolation did not detract from feeling part of a wider community capable of political activism and contributing to social reform:

> Disability and living a very solitary life disconnect me from physical interaction with my lesbian friends who live in a different part of the country. However my lesbian identity and understanding is important to me and I would consider myself part of a wider community particularly where social reform and political activism are concerned.
>
> (Survey respondent 432: Lesbian woman aged 55–64)

Some respondents linked their own life experiences to historical activism, for which they were grateful:

> I am aware that the ease of my coming out has been as a result of those who have stood up and been counted over the years. I am very grateful to my community.
>
> (Survey respondent 97: Female lesbian aged 45–54)

It was recognised that not everyone is interested in politics, which was a cause of lament for some, though Gemma felt that ultimately she had been able to find political (sub)communities:

> A lot of people don't really care, they just want to go to the pub, and that was quite a disappointing realisation for me, that gay clubs are not full of politically mobilised people . . . but you find your people and then you find your people within the people I suppose . . . communities within communities I guess.
>
> (Gemma)

In one particular group discussion (in Group 1), participants did not want LGBT people to 'settle' for less than they thought they should and become 'apathetic' or 'complacent'. They argued that 'less obvious' oppression was still oppression, with some citing as an example school teacher disinterest and/or lack of confidence in supporting pupils' sexualities. As a result, group members suggested that whilst Section 28 may have gone, experiences for some young people have not vastly improved. Elsewhere, other participants suggested that they were more interested in activism than their peers, but without identifying this as problematic:

> While I feel a close connectedness with my peers who are LGBTQ*, I tend to be more invested in the academic and activist aspects of the LGBTQ* community, which some of my peers are not. I am generally not interested in the kinds of LGBTQ* social clubbing/drinking spaces they are. This is not a bad thing, but it's just not (and never has been) the kind of space I want to spend my time in.
>
> (Survey respondent 486: Trans*, masculine gay queer
> attracted to masculinity, aged 25–34)

Guibernau (2013) has suggested that feelings of nationalism or community can lay dormant until a threat is perceived. However, participants in this research explicitly talked about communities as important sites of vigilance or 'readiness' for resistance and lobbying, so that people could mobilise if or when necessary. As this suggests, for some, feelings of community or activism were never entirely dormant:

> For me, the concept of community is really important because for marginal communities to be able to mobilise they have to have a community; you can't mobilise one person . . . If you let go of your identity and your culture . . . you're not ready to mobilise when somebody comes to shut you down again . . . To be able to access others when the shit hits the fan, not to put too fine a point on it, is important.
>
> (Gemma)

Fin, on the other hand, said that she had spent many years involved in pushing for disability and/or LGBT rights, but felt it was now down to the next generation to "progress further":

> You get to a point where you think, I'm fed up with it, you know, let somebody else do the support for LGBT, and I don't mean that in a negative way, I just think I've done my bit.
>
> (Fin)

Fin identified the importance of recognising how levels of activism, and lived experience more generally, can vary across the life course, which I explore below. Overall, it is clear that activism was seen as a purpose of, and contributing factor to, (doing) communities. A lack of activism was a cause for lament for some, linked to a feeling that LGBT people need to be ready to mobilise if and when their rights are challenged.

## Lived Experience Across the Life Course

Whilst Chapter 3 identified varied experiences of community among diverse groups of people, here I wish to discuss how ageing and changes across their life course also influence people's engagement with, and experiences of, doing communities. Participants identified, for example, that particular aspects of their identities played out differently at different times in their lives. For those who had enjoyed access to the scene, this could lose its appeal as they got older, bored with it or developed relationships where they were less likely to go out:

> For my sins, I used to [go out on the scene] quite a lot. I can't stand it now, I'm sick to death of it . . . I used to really enjoy it [but] I'm getting a bit bored of it now.
>
> (Matt)

This echoes themes within Browne and Bakshi's (2011) research that found less 'need' for the scene as people's friendships and relationships were established. Simpson (2013) has also suggested that 'growing out of' the scene is linked to a transition of socialising within domestic spaces, typically understood as a 'natural' part of ageing that enables people to escape concerns associated with the scene, such as ageism and alcohol (see Chapter 5 for further discussion of domestic spaces). Some suggested that as they were in a long-term relationship they socialised, and therefore engaged with communities, less than they used to:

> I'm at a stage of life where I socialise less and am in a long-term partnership of 13 years duration so am less involved in gay communities than when I was in my 20s and 30s.
>
> (Survey respondent 12: Gay man aged 45–54)

Others suggested that their sexual identity had become less central to their life:

> My answers would have been different at different stages of life . . . Being a lesbian in a small working class mining community meant I had to leave at that time. Now being a parent is most important, alongside my gender and being a carer, being disabled less so.
>
> (Survey respondent 5: Female lesbian aged 35–44)

Participants therefore illustrated how their sense, or experiences, of communities changed over time, informed by other changes in their lives. Most often this was in relation to decreasing involvement in communities, though this was not always by choice:

> From 1980–1990 when I was a founder member of a local gay switchboard I felt a huge sense of gay community . . . Since then almost everyone I knew . . . has died . . . As no-one really wants to hear about my experiences now, I feel almost totally disconnected from any gay community.
>
> (Survey respondent 576: Gay man aged 45–54)

We can see similarities here with Holt's (2011) research that identified that older gay men felt a greater sense of community in the past, when they were involved in greater levels of gay activism and/or collective responses to HIV. Some older participants also located their changing experiences within evolving social contexts, and how this impacted upon their current sense or perception of a shared history with particular people:

> I was born into a world where I could have gone to prison because my name was in someone's address book. Now I have laws to protect my rights. I am one of a generation of men who has had this transition in life, from shame to visibility. I sometimes envy younger men and wish I too were young. But

I also know and relish my story, my past and what I have in common with other men and women of my age.

(Survey respondent 480: Gay man aged 55–64)

Getting 'old' not only impacted on participants' involvement in communities, but could also be a source of fear if it involved people having to 'come out' in the context of accessing care services (see Heaphy, Yip and Thompson, 2003 for further discussion). However, some also felt they had gained in confidence as they got older, which Simpson (2015) might regard as a form of ageing capital:

I have more confidence [now] and care less about what other people think of me . . . I feel I have had the best of both worlds, having lived a heterosexual life and had children, before living life as 'me' with a loving long-term partner.

(Survey respondent 547: Female lesbian aged 65+)

Alongside ageing, participants also identified specific lifestyle changes, such as those related to employment, which could lead to lower levels of engagement in and with communities through choice:

Have previously been more involved within LGBT communities. Living in the countryside and being busy with a career and personal business owned by myself and partner has meant less involvement in communities than previously, through choice.

(Survey respondent 233: Gay man aged 25–34)

Parenting was another factor that people identified linked to their age and changing social practices that impacted upon their perceptions and experiences of community:

The sense of LGBT community I now gain is largely from self-organised rainbow families meetings, and the occasional Pride or activism event. This relationship feels quite two dimensional from where it used to be a key part of my social outlet and identity.

(Survey respondent 246: Female lesbian aged 35–44)

However, events for 'rainbow families' could offer new and different forms of community:

While in my 20s going out to gay bars and going to Pride were very prominent in my life. That was my sense of community then. And online dating. Now I am in my 40s, settled down with my partner, and we are about to become parents. I still go and support Pride but my gay life now will be about rainbow families' picnics with other gay families.

(Survey respondent 253: Female lesbian aged 35–44)

Experiences of communities can also vary as some people choose to distance themselves following gender transition, which can lead to heated debates about 'assimilation' (Hines, 2007a, 2007b). Illustrating such complexities about access to and/or desire for community, a survey respondent felt that:

> As an intersex and trans person seeking medical treatment I faded out of any communities after I'd got my body sorted.
> (Survey respondent 612: Heterosexual male aged 45–54)

It is therefore clear that ageing and other changes across their life course influence people's lived experience of, and engagement with, (doing) communities, particularly with regard to patterns of socialising.

## Chapter Summary

As I have shown, LGBT communities are thought to enable and/or encompass friendships, as well as opportunities to seek sexual and/or intimate encounters. The metaphor of family is used by some as a comparator against which friendships and communities are compared. Communities were also linked to notions of safety and feeling comfortable, as it was believed that certain spaces or being among particular people enabled displays of same-sex affection that were not always possible, or safe, elsewhere. Seeking out other LGBT people was therefore linked to looking for safety and avoiding risk. Some people maintained self-regulatory practices in other, non-LGBT contexts in order to minimise perceived risks. These practices can be understood as forms of self-protection or (hate) crime prevention, though it was suggested that degrees of habit and/or concern for other people's feelings were also contributing factors, as were practical considerations surrounding employment opportunities and family commitments. I am not suggesting that all LGBT people filter, edit or regulate their behaviour, but that a notable way in which communities were understood and portrayed was in their ability to allow people to escape such practices. LGBT communities could therefore be constructed in opposition to other communities because participants did not feel the need to self-censor in them. Even for those who did hold hands or kiss in public, some still thought that certain scenes, groups and events enable other people to not worry about their actions. However, as noted in Chapter 3, we should remember that the idea(l) or 'reality' of LGBT communities is that they are not (equally) safe for all.

An alternative focus for people's desire for, or understanding of, communities related to activism, which was seen as a strong reason for people to come together as a grouping, both historically and in the recent past. Seeking out and being with other LGBT people was therefore linked to the possibility of social change. Some believed that communities had to be visible and ready to deal with ongoing and/ or future rights-based issues. However, it was clear that ageing and other changes to people's circumstances could influence their experiences and engagement with communities, particularly with regard to patterns of socialising in different spaces. In examining the interlinked areas of friendship, risk and activism, I have demonstrated that as much as it may be used as a convenient label by 'outsiders', LGBT community is also actively constructed by LGBT people themselves. The doing of community was linked to being with LGBT people, and wanting safety. LGBT communities were therefore 'done' in relation to specific spaces and particular people, and these themes will flow throughout the rest of this book.

## Notes

1  Though I use the term 'public' space here, I recognise that the public/private dichotomy has been critiqued, for example by Duncan (1996) who stressed that spaces are heterogeneous and not always clearly 'public' or 'private'.
2  Brighton is a seaside resort in the South of England known for having a large LGBT population, leading to it sometimes being known as the 'gay capital of the UK'.
3  The Gateways was a lesbian nightclub in London that opened in the 1930s and closed down in 1985.
4  *Arena Three* was a British monthly magazine written by and for lesbians in the early 1960s to early 1970s.

## References

BBC (2016) *Gay couple's fury at Sainsbury's hand-hold complaint*. [Online] Available at: www.bbc.co.uk/news/uk-england-london-37034082 [accessed 31.10.2016].

Bertone, C. and Pallotta-Chiarolli, M. (2014) 'Putting families of origin into the queer picture: Introducing this special issue', *Journal of GLBT Family Studies* 10(1–2): 1–14.

Binnie, J. (1995) 'Trading places: Consumption, sexuality and the production of queer space' in Bell, D. and Valentine, G. (eds) *Mapping desire: Geographies of sexualities*. London: Routledge, pp. 182–199.

Browne, K. (2007) 'A party with politics? (Re)making LGBTQ Pride spaces in Dublin and Brighton', *Social and Cultural Geography* 8(1): 63–87.

Browne, K. (2008) 'Imagining cities, living the other: Between the gay urban idyll and rural lesbian lives', *The Open Geography Journal* 1: 25–32.

Browne, K. and Bakshi, L. (2011) 'We are here to party? Lesbian, gay, bisexual and trans leisurescapes beyond commercial gay scenes', *Leisure Studies* 30(2): 179–196.

Browne, K. and Bakshi, L. (2013) *Ordinary in Brighton: LGBT, activisms and the city.* Aldershot: Ashgate.

Buchanan, R.T. (2015) *Valentine's Day public 'kiss-in' marks start of LGBT 'Freedom to kiss' campaign*. [Online] Available at: www.independent.co.uk/news/uk/britains-first-public-kissin-marks-start-of-lgbt-freedom-to-kiss-campaign-10046441.html [accessed 31.10.2016].

Casey, M.E. (2004) 'De-dyking queer space(s): Heterosexual female visibility in gay and lesbian spaces', *Sexualities* 7(4): 446–461.

Coleman-Fountain, E. (2014) 'Lesbian and gay youth and the question of labels', *Sexualities* 17(7): 802–817.

Cooley, C.H. (1902) *Human nature and the social order*. New York: Charles Scribner's Sons.

Cronin, A. and King, A. (2014) 'Only connect? Older lesbian, gay and bisexual (LGB) adults and social capital', *Ageing and Society* 34(2): 258–279.

Duncan, N. (1996) 'Introduction' in Duncan, N. (ed) *BodySpace: Destabilising geographies of gender and sexuality.* London: Routledge, pp. 1–12.

Ellis, S.J. (2007) 'Community in the 21st century: Issues arising from a study of British lesbians and gay men' in Peel, E., Clarke, V. and Drescher, J. (eds) *British lesbian, gay, and bisexual psychologies: Theory, research, and practice.* Binghamton: The Haworth Medical Press.

Finch, J. (2011) 'Exploring the concept of display in family relationships' in Dermott, E. and Seymour, J. (eds) *Displaying families: A new concept for the sociology of family life.* Basingstoke: Palgrave Macmillan, pp. 197–205.

Formby, E. (2013) 'Understanding and responding to homophobia and bullying: Contrasting staff and young people's views within community settings in England', *Sexuality Research and Social Policy* 10(4): 302–316.

Formby, E. (2015) 'Limitations of focussing on homophobic, biphobic and transphobic "bullying" to understand and address LGBT young people's experiences within and beyond school', *Sex Education* 15(6): 626–640.

Goffman, E. (1959) *The presentation of self in everyday life.* New York: Doubleday Anchor Books.

Goffman, E. (1971) *Relations in public: Microstudies of the public order.* London: Allen Lane.

Guasp, A., Gammon, A. and Ellison, G. (2013) *Homophobic hate crime: The gay British crime survey 2013.* London: Stonewall.

Guibernau, M. (2013) *Belonging: Solidarity and division in modern societies.* Cambridge: Polity Press.

Hall, S. (1996) 'Introduction: Who needs identity?' in Hall, S. and du Gay, P. (eds) *Questions of cultural identity.* London: Sage, pp. 1–17.

Heaphy, B. (2011) 'Critical relational displays' in Dermott, E. and Seymour, J. (eds) *Displaying families: A new concept for the sociology of family life.* Basingstoke: Palgrave Macmillan, pp. 19–37.

Heaphy, B., Smart, C. and Einarsdottir, A. (2013) *Same sex marriages: New generations, new relationships.* Basingstoke: Palgrave Macmillan.

Heaphy, B., Yip, A.K.T. and Thompson, D. (2003) *Lesbian, gay and bisexual lives over 50.* Nottingham: York House Publications.

Hines, S. (2007a) 'Transgendering care: Practices of care within transgender communities', *Critical Social Policy* 27(4): 462–486.

Hines, S. (2007b) '(Trans)forming gender: Social change and transgender citizenship', *Sociological Research Online* 12(1).

Holt, M. (2011) 'Gay men and ambivalence about "gay community": From gay community attachment to personal communities', *Culture, Health and Sexuality* 13(8): 857–871.

Jones-Wild, R. (2012) 'Reimagining families of choice' in Hines, S. and Taylor, Y. (eds) *Sexualities: Past reflections, future directions.* Basingstoke: Palgrave Macmillan, pp. 149–167.

Mason, G. (2001) 'Body maps: Envisaging homophobia, violence and safety', *Social and Legal Studies* 10(1): 23–44.

Moran, L. and Skeggs, B. (2001) 'Property and propriety: Fear and safety in gay space', *Social and Cultural Geography* 2(4): 407–420.

Moran, L., Skeggs, B., Tyrer, P. and Corteen, K. (2003) 'The formation of fear in gay space: The "straights" story', *Capital and Class* 27(2): 173–198.

Moran, L., Skeggs, B., Tyrer, P. and Corteen, K. (2004) *Sexuality and the politics of violence and safety.* London: Routledge.

Myslik, W.D. (1996) 'Renegotiating the social/sexual identities of places' in Duncan, N. (ed) *BodySpace: Destabilising geographies of gender and sexuality*. London: Routledge, pp. 155–168.

Nardi, P.M. (1999) *Gay men's friendships*. Chicago: University of Chicago Press.

Rubin, L. (1985) *Just friends: The role of friendship in our lives*. New York: Harper and Row.

Simpson, P. (2012) 'Perils, precariousness and pleasures: Middle-aged gay men negotiating urban "heterospaces"', *Sociological Research Online* 17(3).

Simpson, P. (2013) 'Differentiating the self: The kinship practices of middle-aged gay men in Manchester', *Families, Relationships and Societies* 2(1): 97–113.

Simpson, P. (2015) *Middle-aged gay men, ageing and ageism: Over the rainbow?* Basingstoke: Palgrave Macmillan.

Stanko, E.A. and Curry, P. (1997) 'Homophobic violence and the self "at risk": Interrogating the boundaries', *Social and Legal Studies* 6(4): 513–532.

Stanley, J.L. (1996) 'The lesbian's experience of friendship' in Weinstock, J.S. and Rothblum. E. (eds) *Lesbian friendships*. New York: New York University Press, pp. 39–59.

Stonewall (1996) *Violence survey*. London: Stonewall.

Traies, J. (2015) 'Old lesbians in the UK: Community and friendship', *Journal of Lesbian Studies* 19(1): 35–49.

Valentine, G. (1993a) 'Desperately seeking Susan: A geography of lesbian friendships', *Area* 25(2): 109–116.

Valentine, G. (1993b) '(Hetero)sexing space: Lesbian perceptions and experiences of everyday space', *Environment and Planning D: Society and Space* 11(4): 395–413.

Valentine, G. (1994) 'Toward a geography of the lesbian community', *Women and Environments* 14(1): 8–10.

Valentine, G. (1995) 'Out and about: Geographies of lesbian landscapes', *International Journal of Urban and Regional Research* 19(1): 96–111.

Valentine, G. (1996) '(Re)negotiating the "heterosexual street"' in Duncan, N. (ed) *BodySpace: Destabilising geographies of gender and sexuality*. London: Routledge, pp. 145–154.

Weeks, J., Heaphy, B. and Donovan, C. (2001) *Same sex intimacies: Families of choice and other life experiments*. London: Routledge.

Weston, K. (1991) *Families we choose: Lesbians, gays, kinship*. New York: Columbia University Press.

Woodiwiss, J. (2013) 'Bridging the gap between past and present: Childhood sexual abuse, recovery and the contradictory self', *Women's Studies International Forum* 38: 135–146.

Woolwine, D. (2000) 'Community in gay male experience and moral discourse', *Journal of Homosexuality* 38(4): 5–37.

Yip, A.K.T. (2008) 'Researching lesbian, gay, and bisexual Christians and Muslims: Some thematic reflections', *Sociological Research Online* 13(1).

# 5   Relationships to, Within and Beyond Physical Spaces

## Introduction

It is clear from preceding chapters that space plays a key role in conceptualisations of community, including how LGBT communities were understood within the research, whether participants' emphases were on physical, virtual or symbolic spaces, or a combination of these. This chapter examines a range of experiences and perceptions of different geographical, temporary and online spaces, which were often thought to facilitate (access to) community and/or friendship. In doing so, I will examine themes related to safety, visibility, support and access to financial resources, alongside the occupation of 'public' and 'private' spaces. Contrasts between experiences and perceptions of urbanity and rurality will also be explored. In discussing people's decisions about places of home and travel linked to their gender and sexual identities, I will outline perceptions about places to both seek out and avoid. In addition, I will look at access to virtual spaces and communities. In particular, I will identify the value of web-based information and interaction for those experiencing physical isolation, particularly young and/or trans people. Overall, the chapter will demonstrate a tendency for 'LGBT space' to be identified, homogenised and constructed in contrast or opposition to (often monolithic) 'non-LGBT space'. These issues will be addressed under the following six headings: Physical Space and Geographical Areas, Relocation, Rural Living, Travel and Tourism, Groups and Services and Online Spaces and Virtual Communities.

## Overview of Existing Literature

Before I examine my own research, I outline here previous research that has explored various spaces in relation to LGBT lives, with a focus on geographical areas and relocation, travel and tourism, organised groups and services, private homes and online spaces.

First, I want to say a few words on the concept of space, and in particular how I see it as socially produced (Lefebvre, 1991) and "constituted through interactions" (Massey, 2005: 9). As Soja (1996: 10, original emphasis) outlined, Lefebvre (1991) believed that space can be conceptualised as "the *perceived* space of materialized Spatial Practice; the *conceived* space . . . defined as Representations of Space; and the *lived* Spaces of Representation". Drawing on Lefebvre, Soja (1996: 6, original emphasis) also theorised space in three ways: Firstspace, "the 'real' material world" (Lefebvre's perceived space); Secondspace, the "'imagined' representations of spatiality" (Lefebvre's conceived space); and Thirdspace, the "multiplicity of *real-and-imagined* places" (Lefebvre's lived space). Space and place can be interchangeable concepts; as Cresswell (2004: 10) suggests, space "in many ways, plays the same role as place", since place is also "a way of seeing, knowing and understanding the world" (Cresswell, 2004: 11). I therefore use both terms but mean for neither to be understood as exclusively physical or virtual coordinates. In what follows, I do refer to geographical locations, but I also use space in a much broader way, and even when I do refer to physical locations, these places (such as Brighton) are not read as 'real', being partly constructed, imagined or animated through social practices.

Guibernau (2013) has suggested that a feeling of belonging often includes attachment to a particular landscape: the white cliffs of Dover, the Statue of Liberty, the Great Wall of China and so on. As May (2013: 9–10) argues, people have connections and relationships with places as well as people, which "help create our sense of self". These ideas can be illustrated with reference to certain places that have significance in the popular imaginary of LGBT people, for example Brighton in the UK and San Francisco in America. Weeks, Heaphy and Donovan (2001) have suggested that for those who live in particular areas, a sense of lesbian and gay community can be felt geographically. However, geographical understandings of community are complicated as places can be imagined as well as experienced based on short-term—or sometimes no—visits. Browne and Bakshi (2013) suggest that Brighton is such a place that is often imagined, because marketing and perceptions of the city may not relate to its boundaries. A sense of community can be imagined or visited by those not from Brighton, but is not always experienced by those who live in Brighton. As such, migration or relocation to Brighton based on idealistic imaginings can result in disappointment (Browne and Bakshi, 2013). Though Brighton may be viewed as a utopia by some, to others who live there, it can be experienced as "just a seaside town with a big gay scene" (Browne and Bakshi, 2013: 45). Perhaps influenced by their imaginings of certain places, a body of research has identified people 'escaping' their familial or geographical home environments (Cant, 1997; Scourfield, Roen and McDermott, 2008; Valentine, 1993c; Valentine, Skelton and Butler, 2003). Migration has been documented in moves towards desired environments, as well as away from hostile ones (Formby, 2015b; Howes, 2011; Smith and Holt, 2005), and in relation to moving towards more urban rather than rural areas, because of their assumed greater anonymity, safety and/or LGB population size (Browne, 2008; Valentine, 1993a, 1993c; Valentine and Skelton, 2003). As Browne and Bakshi (2013: 52) suggest, "rural to urban migrations have long been the focus of [gay and lesbian] studies . . . setting up urban utopias that contrast with apparently repressive ruralities".

Weston (1995) has explored the place of what she called the 'great gay migration' to 'the urban' within the gay imaginary, illustrated by a focus on the growth of a gay population in San Francisco. She questioned the popularised urban/rural dichotomy, despite a common assumption that gay people need to move to an urban area in order to find their 'proper place' and be gay (Weston, 1995). At the same time, she recognised that for some the 'dream' of being gay required an urban location, to the extent that collective 'gayness' itself was based around a symbolic urban/rural dichotomy (Weston, 1995). The notion of ready-made LGB communities in urban areas has also been questioned, as research has illustrated the possibility of isolation or exclusion in relatively large cities (Ellis, 2007). The frequent assumption of greater safety in urban environments has also been challenged by evidence of anti-gay violence in areas of greater gay visibility (Myslik, 1996; Weston, 1995). People can therefore have variable experiences and perceptions of the same space. In Moran et al.'s (2003, 2004) research, for example, gay men living in, near or making regular visits to Manchester's Village reported lower levels of safety than out of town visitors who reported higher levels of safety.

Brown (2008) has argued that previous (geographical) research has tended to focus on cities with clusters of commercial gay venues, meaning that suburbs and 'ordinary' towns have been overlooked, and assumptions about gay migration to larger cities perpetuated. Taylor and Falconer (2015) have also recently questioned the dominant 'metro-centric' assumption that lesbian and gay people should migrate to the 'big city'. As Brown (2012: 1069, 1070) proposed, instead of focussing on exceptional metropolitan gay lives we should research "ordinary homosexualities as they are lived and understood in ordinary cities and other locations", because the "pressures and pleasures of gay life are not the same in Leicester as they are in London". However, existing literature has examined rural gay and lesbian geographies (e.g. see Bell and Valentine, 1995; Browne, 2008; Taylor, 2008), suggesting that they can pose a barrier to people accessing a scene. For others, moving to a rural location was thought to offer an escape from 'man-made' cities, and thus the possibility of a feminist utopia as well as a rural one (Bell and Valentine, 1995; Browne and Ferreira, 2015). Bell and Valentine (1995) drew attention to their participants' desires for facilities and services in which to socialise, though they also acknowledged telephone helplines, chatlines and sexlines that could overcome rural isolation. Since then, the growth of the internet has increased people's ability to connect with other LGBT people from whom they may be geographically dispersed (Lehavot, Balsam and Ibrahim-Wells, 2009). The assumed association between anonymity and safety in cities has been questioned in research in semi-rural Hebden Bridge,[1] where lesbians argued that visibility through living and trading amongst people meant people had the chance to get to know them, thus heightening their safety (Smith and Holt, 2005). Bell and Valentine (1995: 120) concluded that for some, "the countryside offers nothing but isolation and loathing", whilst for others, "the rural can be a place of fantasy and utopia, a place for living an idyllic 'gay' life". Living in nonmetropolitan areas can therefore pose constraints as well as opportunities (Oswald and Lazarevic, 2011).

'Choices' about where to live may be financially constrained, as scholars have pointed to risks in assuming that the so-called pink pound affords everyone the ability to choose their home (Browne, 2008; Mason, 2001). Taylor (2007) has argued that middle class lesbians may be able to protect themselves from discrimination by moving to more liberal, 'trendy' areas. However, moving to Brighton, which might be viewed as such a liberal, trendy area, may not afford everyone freedom from discrimination if they do not have access to housing, and where housing support is evaluated on the basis of local connections rather than LGBT imaginings of a cultural home (Browne and Bakshi, 2013). Such experiences do not necessarily diminish imaginings of an 'LGBTQ haven', however, as American research suggests that Park Slope in New York "retains its place in the lesbian-queer geographical imagination as a lesbian-queer neighbourhood even though it does not offer all lesbians and queer women equal refuge or promise" (Gieseking, 2013: 188).

Moving on to examine travel and tourism, it has been argued that tourism can enhance identity through the creation of 'homelands'. Queer tourists leave home, where they may not be accepted, in order to visit a homeland or community where they are accepted (Howe, 2001). Queer spaces such as San Francisco therefore have cultural and emotional significance, even for those who do not live or make the 'pilgrimage' there (Myslik, 1996). In the gay imaginary, homelands and gay meccas are constructed as sites of origin and visibility that are able to offer 'sanctuary' from homophobia and a feeling of coming home (Waitt and Markwell, 2006). Hughes (2006: 200) has suggested that the push of discrimination and disapproval stimulates a desire to get away and be oneself, but getting away may not always prove free from homophobia, as tourists still face the risk of discrimination and what he calls 'discomfort risk' related to "feeling uncomfortable in the presence of apparently disapproving heterosexuals". Decisions about where to go are therefore constrained, and large parts of the world can be discarded due to perceptions of anti-gay legislation or cultural disapproval (Hughes, 2006). In examining gay men's travel to destinations thought to be 'tolerant', Casey (2010) has identified the cultural and economic capital required to 'know', and be able to afford, the 'right' holidays to take. Whilst such liminal experiences can be revitalising to some, Casey (2010) suggests that for some men living on a low income, holidays are not escapism but literally a break that makes life bearable.

Alternative spaces that can also make life 'bearable' are organised groups and services. Existing research has suggested that organisations and groups can be experienced as community (Woolwine, 2000), and Brown (2009: 1505) has argued that "community organisations . . . and social and support groups . . . are the backbone of lesbian and gay social networks", particularly for those excluded or alienated from the scene. Cronin and King (2014: 275) have proposed that adults who belong to such groups "enjoy high levels of social support and bonding social capital, thus . . . may be better placed to face the challenges of later life than their heterosexual counterparts". Other research has also documented the importance of particular social/support groups for young LGBT people and for trans people, particularly when they are unable to draw on more informal friendship networks and/or access to the scene is restricted or undesired (Formby, 2013, 2015a; Hines, 2010). Valentine and Skelton (2003) have suggested that support groups offer young people information and advice, and access to LGB peers, which may facilitate heightened confidence and self-esteem. They suggest that these groups can be particularly important for young people who do not have access to university environments that may offer more tolerant and supportive settings (Valentine and Skelton, 2003), though research has also documented unsupportive higher education contexts for LGBT students and staff (Formby, 2015b; Valentine, Wood and Plummer, 2009). Browne and Bakshi (2013) are cautious about viewing social groups as 'saviours', as some people can also experience them as marginalising. Simpson (2016) has explored middle-aged gay men's complex experiences of gay voluntary organisations and has suggested that whilst enabling feelings of self-empowerment and belonging, interactions within them can also reproduce relations of ageing and ageism often associated with the commercial scene. Though these spaces can operate as (somewhat limited) 'communities of understanding', they can also perpetuate habitual social distance between younger and older gay men (Simpson, 2016). For older lesbians, Traies (2015: 40) has found that groups are often highly organised via newsletters, e-mail groups and social media, with women frequently interconnected by belonging to more than one group, thus challenging previous assertions that lesbians lack networks.

In areas where services and/or public spaces might be lacking, private homes may offer temporary LGBT spaces and/or communities, whether through choice or perceived necessity due to lack of other space. This has been said to particularly be the case for black gay men, lesbians, older gay men, young people, and those with less financial resources to go out (Bell and Valentine, 1995; Brown, 2008; Homfray, 2007; Johnston and Valentine, 1995; Taylor, Kaminski and Dugan, 2002; Valentine, 1993b, 1994). Parties and other gatherings in people's homes can thus blur the distinction between 'private' and 'public' (Brown, 2008). Whilst Simpson (2013, 2015) identified middle-aged gay men's use of domestic homes within a developing pattern of socialising away from issues they associated with the scene, such as ageism or alcohol, he also observed exclusions of gay men living on a low income who were less able to participate in dinner party or barbeque social circuits. Socio-economic circumstances can therefore lengthen some people's 'dependence' on the scene for socialising (Simpson, 2013), but contrasts are evident between the perceived safety of domestic spaces and the possibility of homophobia from neighbours (Simpson, 2015). Casey (2013) has shown how privacy of the home is contested by concerns about neighbours overhearing conversations held in gardens, on balconies or even inside if windows are open. For young people, homes are often regulated by parents or guardians, meaning that they can feel out of place or vulnerable even on 'home territory' (Choi, 2013; Formby, 2015a). Casey (2013: 149) has argued that home "needs to be addressed as a multi-layered phenomena that intersects with the identities of its inhabitants (and I would argue, with the identities and lives of neighbours as well)". Home thus offers "multiple and contradictory experiences of safety and danger" (Moran et al., 2004: 85), and this is particularly the case for those who experience domestic violence and abuse in LGBT relationships (Donovan and Hester, 2014).

Finally, I want to examine online space. It has been argued that online/virtual gay communities are now larger than offline/physical communities, leading to decreased visibility of gay people 'on the streets' (Rosser, West and Weinmeyer, 2008). Research has also suggested that the anonymity of the internet can offer a space for exploring identities that may be distinct from offline social worlds, but can lead to changes in offline practices and/or identities (O'Riordan and White, 2010). For trans people specifically, online spaces can facilitate digital gendered embodiment that differs from physical embodiment (O'Riordan and White, 2010). As Whittle (1998: 400) noted, "Cyberspace has presented a safe area where body image and presentation are not among the initial aspects of personal judgement and social hierarchy within the transgender community". Craig and McInroy (2014) identified how new media enabled their young participants to access resources, explore identity, find likeness, digitally come out and potentially expand online identities into offline life. They argued that online activities were an important part of their participants' 'coming out process', by offering the chance to safely and anonymously explore, develop, rehearse and adapt identities online prior to offline (Craig and McInroy, 2014). This contrasts with common understandings of the internet as posing (only) risk to young people. Taylor, Falconer and Snowdon (2014b) also explored the importance of 'online embodiment' in experiences of coming out, which in their view muddles the distinction between online and face-to-face interactions. In their research, participants deliberately chose to use social media as a more 'controlled' way of coming out, in order to delay unintended responses and avoid "difficult embodied emotions" in face-to-face encounters (Taylor, Falconer and Snowdon, 2014b: 1148).

The internet also provides social opportunities. For women who adopt a lesbian lifestyle later in life, the internet can provide "an important access point to lesbian networks" that might be physically lacking due to their inability to move because of lack of financial resources and/or existing family ties (Cronin and King, 2014: 265). Whilst the internet may offer new opportunities, this does not mean that virtual communities lack 'differential treatment', for example in relation to ethnicity (Wakeford, 2002). Simpson (2014, 2015) has suggested that what he terms the online gay scene can be experienced as ageist, 'looksist' and racist. Though enabling cyber-cruising/sex, and non-sexual chat/interaction, it has been described as a constrained or risky space for middle-aged gay men, because of the ways it can legitimate ageist objectification that reduces men to their age and/or body parts (Simpson, 2014). In his study of gayborhoods, Ghaziani (2014: 58) reflected on whether networking apps such as Grindr were "the cause of gay bars closing", but argued instead that they can creatively recreate community by supplementing rather than supplanting bar attendance. He argued that the internet has enabled virtual community in non-physical ways that has fostered flexibility in where people can live, concluding that the internet "adds to, and builds on, other forms of communication and community" (Ghaziani, 2014: 126).

## Physical Space and Geographical Areas

Turning to participant reflections on physical and geographical spaces now, a key, and often the initial, way in which community was conceptualised was as physical space, sometimes referred to as visual communities. This is not surprising given the long history of community being understood in geographical terms (Homfray, 2007; Walkerdine and Studdert, 2011). However, within spatial understandings there were still differences: some people referred to specific geographical areas such as Brighton, whilst others mentioned commercial scenes more generally (see the following chapter for further detail), and sometimes people talked about specific LGBT groups or events as temporary spatial communities. When asked to identify the type or types of community (if any) they felt part of,[2] just over half (53%) of survey respondents identified that they felt part of a community or communities that were 'physical and near where I live', and just under half (48%) felt part of a community or communities that were 'virtual/online'. Equally, 48% felt part of a community or communities that were 'a feeling'; 34% felt community was 'physical but not near where I live'; and 24% felt it or they were 'physical and based where I work'. These multiple, overlapping senses of community were also evident in open text survey data:

> Based on all of the above: I feel it at work, with LGBT colleagues, friends from across the world, driven by my interests, i.e. lesbian football team, lesbian camping, LGBT film festival, etc.
> (Survey respondent 475: Gay/lesbian female aged 25–34)

However, because physical understandings of community were dominant, some people only felt part of a community when in particular spaces or places:

> In terms of my everyday life, I wouldn't say that I feel like I belong to the gay community because I suppose . . . [I see] that as being a physical community, and the only time I'd feel that was if I was out, if I'd gone to a gay bar or a gay club, or I'd gone to a Pride event.
> (Carl)

In terms of geography, certain areas were seen to constitute or possess LGBT community, with Brighton in particular having enviable, if not legendary, status within a gay imaginary:

> When I go to places like Brighton I actually feel there's a good LGBT community . . . it's got a really nice vibe about the fact that it's not just centred around the bars . . . people are just walking in and out of the shops and it's obvious that they're in a same-sex relationship, but they're just enjoying life, you know, they're sitting in the park, they're going to the beach, and that for me is a real sense of community . . . It's people just living their lives in an area where it's very obvious that there's a high visibility of lesbian and gay people.
> (Timothy)

Timothy's sense that community in Brighton was not just centred around the bars echoes Browne and Bakshi's (2013) suggestion that it is the 'dispersed' LGBT community that is key to Brighton's extraordinariness.

Ruth lived within a city with a large, visible LGBT population, evidenced for example by the numbers of rainbow flags flying in the area. Partly because of this visibility, she had a feeling that "these are my tribe, this is where I belong", but at the same time she also thought that it was not really 'real life':

> It's a right on bubble. It's not real life . . . it's a peculiar place.
>
> (Ruth)

Manchester was another area specifically discussed within the research, whether or not participants lived there. Whilst it was noted that the city offered a range of LGBT provision, this was not always thought to constitute community:

> I live in Manchester where there are a range of accessible LGBT focussed services/businesses/bars, clubs etc., however I don't feel that this necessarily constitutes a community.
>
> (Survey respondent 95: Female lesbian aged 35–44)

For Jason and some others, however, Manchester was thought to offer legendary opportunities to meet other young gay men, but for the time being at least, the city was unreachable for Jason as a teenager living elsewhere.

London was an area that attracted mixed views. Some felt that it had less of a clearly defined locus of attention or 'sociable' atmosphere than other locations perceived to be gay-friendly:

> The idea of community in London is misleading in that there's no LGBT centre in London, all we have that's shared is the commercial, youth and beauty, and male-orientated gay scene.
>
> (Survey respondent 546: Gay man aged 35–44)

> I'm more drawn to acknowledged 'gay-friendly' environments than purely gay venues, which tend to be less sociable, perhaps particularly in London.
>
> (Survey respondent 128: Gay man aged 25–34)

Others, however, thought London was an example of strong community:

> I've just come back from London and obviously there's a really strong trans community and gay community there . . . I know lots of people there and it's very accepting . . . there's definitely a strong community there.
>
> (Paula)

It was noticeable that London was thought to have more options by those who did not live there, whereas those who did were often less complimentary, reminiscent of Cant's (2008: 45) participants who felt that London did not have a community, but a "street with pubs in it".

A minority of participants voiced concerns about the extent to which LGBT communities were, or could be seen as, separated from other people when they were concentrated in particular geographical areas or commercial spaces:

> There's a push and pull as well between wanting sanctuary and wanting to huddle together in the LGBT community, 'right, we shall stay and we'll be safe here', and needing to integrate and educate.
>
> (Charlie)

> I can't imagine ever living in a place where you don't really engage with wider society . . . I've been with people before who may never go into straight bars and I find that really weird . . . they're only comfortable going into gay places . . . I just don't get that because that to me is just so narrow.
>
> (Gerry)

However, some identified separateness as a good thing:

> I think people can take it [LGBT community] one way or the other. They can see it as, 'OK, it's excluding us from everyone, it's setting us off into our own like little group, sub-culture sort of thing' . . . [but] I see that as a really positive thing.
>
> (Julie)

Some people aspired to move away from the notion of LGBT community to community more generally including LGBT people. This would necessarily move away from the idea of certain areas being associated with LGBT people:

> I actually like the idea of living in a little market town where I know my neighbours know and we're OK. That to me is being part of the community, and ultimately that's got to be the overall goal. We don't need an LGBT community because we are the community.
>
> (Timothy)

Others suggested that 'allowing' people into LGBT communities (which here were understood as scene spaces) could facilitate understanding and/or equality:

> I have a lot of straight friends who just love coming out [with me] . . . it's just nice to allow people to come into our community and it opens up their eyes too. I think when people don't allow that to happen that is where the problem lies because you have this divide, but if you just keep it open and equal for everyone then it works.
>
> (Julie)

Overall, it was clear that communities are frequently conceptualised spatially, and often in relation to particular geographical areas. These findings partially support Weston's (1995) research, which is not to suggest that gay or LGBT people *should* get themselves to a big city, but that there still appears to be an imaginary that holds up certain areas (often other than those where they live) as bigger and better. These exceptional spaces were frequently the comparator against which their 'ordinary' homes were imagined and judged. They offered, at least symbolically, the possibility of a physical LGBT community where they may have only had access to imagined or virtual forms of LGBT community.

## Relocation

In this section I look at relocation, or migration, as the desire for safety and/or visible LGBT space meant that some people's choices about where to live were influenced by their gender or sexual identities. In drawing on Brown's (2008) call to examine 'ordinary' lives, I wish to highlight how those participants living in small towns and cities in between the rural idyll and the urban utopia often imagined and constructed other/larger urban areas as better for LGBT people. At the same time, they did not necessarily choose to live there, though of course this decision may have been constrained by limited financial resources (Browne, 2008; Mason, 2001; Taylor, 2007). Despite academic acknowledgment of a false 'urban-tolerance/rural-intolerance' dichotomy (Browne and Ferreira, 2015), participants' constructions of urban as better point to the prevalence of Weston's (1995) earlier ideas, which some LGBT practitioners observed amongst the young people they worked with:

> A lot of young people in general in [this city] have migrated from rural areas . . . we hear again and again, 'there is absolutely no way that I would have come out where I live, my life would be absolute hell', so then they come to [this city] or [another city] where they have no money, they have nowhere to live, and that makes young people so much more vulnerable.
>
> (Fiona)

Many participants drew on the idea that people leave more rural areas to move to London or other large cities in Britain, thus perpetuating assumptions of urban as better:

> Most of the people in rural Wales will move out because of the lack of support, because of the lack of understanding, and they will move to the bigger cities.
>
> (Dilys)

> [In] the LGBT community we know that people migrate to the cities, like that historically has been the case . . . just that massive population gives you opportunities . . . it's no wonder that people still do migrate to the cities.
>
> (Gemma)

People also made decisions about where to live themselves, and in doing so prioritised their sexuality and what they saw as measures to prevent social isolation over and above other factors:

> I feel the need to be part of an LGBT community more outweighs the other needs in my life regarding community and where I live. This has meant that I feel I need to stay in Manchester rather than move closer to friends and family. I feel this struggle continually and worry that not being close to a large LGBT community could isolate me and my husband.
>
> (Survey respondent 100: Gay man aged 25–34)

Some did not rule out relocating in the future, believing that certain cities 'allow' practices that others perhaps do not:

> If you're able to live as open as you are able to be at an event like Pride . . . there was a different freedom. If a city or a certain part of a city allows that to happen . . . there may be some appeal in that.
>
> (Gerry)

Some participants illustrated how "social relations of class are embodied in housing 'choices'" (Taylor, 2007: 122), with Megan believing that she needed to move from a 'dodgy' to more cosmopolitan area in order to be together with her partner:

> My partner and I live in [an area] which is quite a dodgy area really. We can't be together in that we can't hold hands, so I'm looking to move, or we're looking to move, to [a different area], because it's a far more cosmopolitan area . . . it's only like five miles down the road, but it's a totally different culture there.
>
> (Megan)

Megan thus shows how notions of cosmopolitanism can be 'classed', because the area which she views as dodgy may itself be home to working class lesbians also wishing to be together (Taylor, 2007).

Other participants had not necessarily left the area, but left their family home. Ben felt that in order to "sort his own head" prior to coming out, he had to leave the "traditional working class masculine environment" that was his family home. For Gemma, both where she lived and where she worked had been influenced by her identity:

> It's not a terrible place I come from, but it doesn't have a gay scene, so I moved to [this city] and I guess made use of the scene at that time . . . definitely the work that I've done . . . has been completely driven by my identity . . . I've made a career out of being a lesbian.
>
> (Gemma)

Echoing research by Hughes (2006) and Pritchard et al. (2000) that suggests lesbians and gay men avoid certain countries where being gay is illegal or 'a problem', Fiona and Helen had thought about their relationships and sexual identities in relation to decisions about living and studying abroad, believing that their options or freedoms might be more limited than others':

> From being in a relationship with a man to going in to a relationship with a woman, my options on where I can live have totally changed.
>
> (Fiona)

> I did a semester abroad and I deliberately didn't pick a country where it was illegal to be gay because I thought . . . that would be quite oppressive . . . As a result I looked at America and I picked [a state] and one of the factors in picking that was that it was a more liberal state and I'd previously worked in [a different state] where you can lose your job for being gay . . . [and] I just kind of didn't want to put myself through that for a term . . . I was like not willing to risk going to prison for a semester abroad when there's other places I can go . . . you don't quite get the same freedom as other people.
>
> (Helen)

Perceptions of safety and opportunities as an LGBT person meant that some people made decisions about where to live informed by their sexual or gender identity, whether in moving towards places associated with community or away from places associated with danger or repression.

## Rural Living

I now turn to examine experiences of rurality. Brown (2008) has critiqued research that focuses on gay ghettos for continuing to see and label certain cities as 'gay' or 'gay-friendly', leading to other, often more rural, areas being viewed as less so. Browne and Ferreira (2015) have also questioned the simplistic view that rural spaces equate with marginalisation whilst urban spaces equate with freedom, and the homophobic/gay-friendly dichotomy that these assumptions are often based on. Nevertheless, some participants identified that rurality and semi-rurality can prove a challenge to accessing visible forms of LGBT community. A sense of invisibility and/or inaccessibility was thus linked to notions of community, and *Little Britain*'s[3] catchphrase 'the only gay in the village' appeared in a number of responses:

> When I think of myself and communities the phrase 'the only gay in the village' pops to mind. The only sense of any form of gay community in my town is the one gay bar and Pride in the summer. Other than that, we seem almost invisible. It also doesn't help that I do live almost 10 miles from town and so can feel very isolated. Chances are I am not the only one in the village. But it's how to find them.
>
> (Website contributor)

> For me the 'community' needs to be where I live. I would have to travel about an hour to get to a lesbian pub. I cannot afford to do that. There are other 'gays in the village' according to my GP but she cannot tell me who they are so I cannot find them. They might be 'friends in waiting'. There is a gay parenting group about 45 minutes away but they meet . . . [at a time] when my kids are with their Dad.
>
> (Survey respondent 550: Female lesbian aged 35–44)

Others living in villages or country areas had different experiences, however:

> I live in a village and you very quickly get to know who is gay and who is out, just sharing a smile with someone. When you are a single parent with a gay partner living in a white middle class area it can raise eyebrows unfortunately.
>
> (Liz)

Whilst the above quote illustrates that there was more than one gay person in the village to share a smile with, it nevertheless suggests that this level of visibility was perceived to be worthy of some people raising their eyebrows. Supporting Heaphy's (2011: 28) suggestion that "Lesbian, gay and queer families tend to be highly conscious of how they do and display family, especially where children are involved", others avoided the raising of eyebrows, or worse, by minimising or concealing aspects of their lives for the sake of their children:

> Living in a large rural village we are careful about being too open because we do not want to cause our children any problems at school.
>
> (Survey respondent 550: Female lesbian aged 35–44)

> It really is a very small world and connections are easily made. In order to have some measure of control, I therefore keep more hidden . . . My partner and I will be able to be more free in a few years' time [when my children go to university], where we will not be so hidden and more free to join groups, visit 'gay places' and socialise with others so developing our network.
>
> (Survey respondent 505: Female lesbian aged 45–54)

Ruth discussed her mixed experiences of rural living, commenting that:

> I think we were pleasantly surprised when we moved to the deep country, we thought it would be terribly homophobic and it wasn't.
>
> (Ruth)

However, she later suggested that:

> [A pub] is quite a dangerous place but if you live in a village and that's the only place to go out in the evening . . . you have to kind of make it yours . . . it's very difficult.
>
> (Ruth)

Feeling welcome was important to Ruth, and there were times when she and her partner travelled a long way to a gay-owned place in order to feel safe:

> When we lived in the country . . . if we'd heard a pub had been taken over by some gay boys or some girls we would travel a long way to go to it because it's sort of become our space. I remember going to one pub . . . semi-rural, and we heard it had been taken over by a couple of lesbians. They hadn't made it into a lesbian pub because obviously . . . you couldn't live just on the lesbians in that area . . . [but] I remember going into it and thinking, 'oh my god, this feels like a safe space' . . . I mean it was actually not a gay pub but there was just something about it and it was because you knew the people behind the bar were on your side. I just thought, 'oh, this really feels like a nice space'.
>
> (Ruth)

It was not only in villages and other rural locations that people suggested they had limited spaces in which to find or enact LGBT communities:

> To be honest, in [this town] . . . we don't have much of a community in terms of places . . . we don't have any gay venues really. We have one LGBT night, that to be fair, is only for the scene people . . . So all of us guys kind of get left off the side because we don't like all that type of environment.
>
> (Julie)

Echoing previous research, this small town environment was also criticised in relation to gossip, and what have been termed 'incestuous' (Valentine, 1993a, 1995; Weston, 1995) networks:

> You just want to go to a place where, you know, your friends haven't slept with your girlfriend, and that's what it's like . . . if you've had any sort of connection with anyone in this town . . . I can guarantee if I walked in there [to a specific venue] it would be, 'she's sleeping with so and so, she slept with so and so'.
>
> (Julie)

Gemma contrasted densely populated urban areas with less populated, more rural areas. As she said:

> We've got two Scotlands. We've got central belt Scotland which is populated, it has a reasonable transport infrastructure, it has resources, it has services, it has all these things, and it has a pretty dense population. And then we have the other Scotland, which is everywhere North and South of the central belt, which is a huge part of the country.
>
> (Gemma)

She also related this diversity to the provision of services:

> When you're talking about . . . service provision you have to take this into account . . . you can't even tell them [people] to go on the internet because

sometimes they don't have it . . . that is really a pressing point for isolated parts of Scotland . . . It's a shame that people feel they can't stay where they were born if they want to.

(Gemma)

As Gemma suggests, LGBT services should take into consideration rural isolation, particularly as experiences of rural living may be informed by lack of access to financial resources. Laura, for example, had to juggle wanting to access LGBT groups and services with managing her budget to cover public transport or petrol and car parking fees.

Overall, those living in rural locations did tend to think that urban experiences would be better for LGBT people, with associated beliefs about greater visibility, though this is not to suggest that experiences of rural living were only negative.

## Travel and Tourism

This section focuses on travel and tourism, which was identified as an important issue for some participants. This was sometimes explained as 'checking out' or wanting to experience other cultures or spaces that were associated with 'enlightenment' or feeling comfortable:

When I go to Thailand we can be together everywhere. The guard comes completely down . . . the only homophobic experience that we've had there was from a European tourist . . . it's just embedded within the culture there that men can hold hands, kiss in the street, whatever . . . that is very enlightening as an experience to go there.

(Timothy)

If I go on holiday, yeah, I definitely will check out the gay scene in that place. We went to New York, we checked out a couple of places; when I was in San Francisco, I checked out some places . . . I'm interested to see what scenes are like, and it's a place where I would feel comfortable to go as a tourist because I'd feel it was safer.

(Gemma)

Although the situation regarding attitudes towards homosexuality in Thailand might be more complicated than Timothy believes (see Sanders, 2002; Waitt and Markwell, 2006), it is clear that different cultures and spaces can be experienced as safer than experiences or perceptions of the UK. As such, participants suggested that some LGBT people make decisions about holiday destinations based on seeking comfort or safety, and wanting to avoid self-censorship:

[Our] holiday destinations tend to be places where I know there is a bit of a scene so that if we want to go out at night and hold hands, then we can do that . . . I've always struggled myself about why I have this need to go to holiday destinations where I can feel safe because I know many people just go anywhere . . . but I did that one year, against my better judgement, I went to Mexico and it was horrendous . . . my boyfriend got picked on so much. One of them [another tourist] even put hot soup in the restaurant in his lap . . . we're never going anywhere again where we cannot be together at a time when we should be enjoying ourselves and being able to be ourselves.

(Timothy)

Ben also described an experience on holiday where he had oppressed his identity because he did not feel able to be 'out'. In Pritchard et al.'s (2000) research, lesbians wanted to feel safe, welcome and able to show an 'emotional connection' such as holding hands whilst on holiday. Similarly, on future holidays, both Timothy and Ben wanted to feel safe and able to be themselves:

I had to oppress part of my personal identity and my life, so for that reason I probably won't go back [there] . . . It wasn't until after that I realised that actually I need to . . . go somewhere I feel comfortable being me. That's maybe not something that heterosexual people think about and so I can understand why lots of people go to Lesbos and Gran Canaria and Ibiza, because it's safe . . . You can kiss in the street, hold hands . . .

(Ben)

As Hughes (2006) suggested, holidays may be a time when people particularly do not want to face the prospect of disapproval or discrimination. As a result, people's sexual and gender identity can inform their decision-making about travel destinations, both in terms of wanting to visit places associated with LGBT safety and visibility, and in terms of avoiding other places associated with discrimination and disadvantage. Holidays were also identified as particularly important as they gave some people the opportunity to experience forms of community that they otherwise might not.

## Groups and Services

In this penultimate section I focus on experiences of organised groups and services, which were an alternative way in which community was spatially understood. Groups and services were often thought to operate as temporary spaces or (sub)communities that were experienced as welcoming. Where people lived in areas that did not have visible forms of LGBT space, and sometimes even where they did, specific groups often provided an opportunity to meet other LGBT people, share experiences, and access mutual support:

When I first came out . . . I was very involved in the LGBT society . . . I remember going around the freshers' fair and finding the LGBT stall and walking past it three times and eventually going up to it . . . [It was] clear

I wanted to be a part of something. I wanted other people that shared that experience.

(Helen)

Sometimes, participation in organised social or support groups was thought to facilitate community:

I threw myself in [to the LGBT committee] as a student because it was something I desperately wanted to do . . . if there wasn't a society or a committee to facilitate stuff then there wouldn't be a community.

(Matt)

Sense of community can come from joining organised groups. These were generally started by committed individuals working together.

(Peter)

Having a group to belong to for a sense of mutual support and/or credibility was suggested to be important, and was often identified in relation to work-based groups or communities:

This [work] group for me is an enabler for us to have a credible position in the community, so for example me alone wanting to take part in Pride, I wouldn't do it, but by being part of this group I feel comfortable that we as a collective group can go and represent [our employer] in the community.

(Timothy)

In realising that I was bisexual I found a desire to connect with others to be able to talk about what this decision would mean for me and my future relationships. It has led to a completely new community with whom I share my life. This has been within my workplace and through LGBT professional groups.

(Survey respondent 132: Bisexual female aged 45–54)

For those at university, student or university-based LGBT groups were also valuable, particularly when relocating to a new city:

My fiancée was the chair of a university LGBT group when we met so our relationship has always been heavily connected to the importance of LGBT community. We have both attended several universities in new cities. The university LGBT group is always the first group we go to and [they] are always hugely welcoming. We tend to become well known quickly in a community. Without the LGBT community in a city we both feel quite isolated and unhappy.

(Survey respondent 552: Polysexual [or bisexual depending on the person asking] female aged 25–34)

For some, being comfortable and feeling accepted, which they experienced within LGBT groups, were particularly important given the isolation they experienced from family members. As Louisa said of attending a women's group:

> I come here because of acceptance, I mean all my family don't want to know me. I've lost all family completely because of who I am.
>
> (Louisa)

Louisa described how the group she attended offered support, contrasting this with society at large:

> It [this group] is a place of support . . . where you can sort of be yourself without the constraints of society . . . society hasn't accepted, fully like, well certainly not people like myself . . . I think we are kind of a community because of that.
>
> (Louisa)

Sometimes it was suggested that specific groups were more worthy of the term community than other, commercial, spaces:

> LGB communities where they exist do tend to focus on institutions, on organisations, because I know if you go to [a particular street], LGB community as a single entity doesn't really exist [but] I'm thinking of the [city's] gay choir which forms a nucleus where you get an LGBT community worthy of the name, but outside of those institutions I guess it's slightly looser.
>
> (Paul)

Paul was not the only one to mention choirs, which played a large part in some people's lives:

> [I] am part of an LGBT choir, and this has had a massive part to play in my life.
>
> (Survey respondent 32: Female lesbian aged 25–34)

However, joining something already established could be off-putting to some:

> The [gay] choir which I've been to recently . . . I just found everybody there was very established in relationships and things.
>
> (Laura)

It has been argued that UK bisexual communities are less likely to be "found in commercial scenes in the way that lesbian/gay communities often are", but identified through networks of groups, events, online spaces and a national magazine (Barker et al., 2012: 17). In Browne and Bakshi's (2013) research, some of their participants fantasised about discrete bi(sexual) communities that could come into being at specific events such as BiFest or BiCon, which were also dubbed 'BiTopia'. Similarly, survey respondents found the company and validation of other bisexual people valuable:

> My life changed radically for the better once I discovered and attended BiCon and found other bisexuals to interact with online and in person. It was the first time my identity was validated and I was over 40 at the time . . . I still love to meet up with bi friends every year at BiCon and can easily interact with bi people online.
>
> (Survey respondent 511: Bisexual, polyamorous, submissive female aged 55–64)

Some young people in my research suggested that they found it hard to meet other young LGBT people in the area where they lived, and this was a key reason why they attended specific LGBT groups or events. Jason, for example, wanted "to cast [his] net wider", and meet other young people willing to be 'out'. He said that the group was his only option because accessing the (local) scene was not possible at his age.

As well as groups and services, specific events were also viewed as temporary space. Pride events were identified as particularly important by many, and for this reason form their own chapter (see Chapter 7). For areas, even cities, with no permanent LGBT spaces, Ruth cited the significance of other specific events creating temporary safe spaces, such as a lesbian arts festival that had run for many years:

> It was very important because one of the sort of missions of the whole thing was to make [that city] a more gay-friendly place for the people who lived there, because we felt when we first went there that life was pretty hard for lesbians in [that city] because there wasn't any scene or anything . . . [so] we kind of set up a . . . temporary lesbian space in the middle of [the city] . . . every year.
>
> (Ruth)

Many people desired greater numbers of non-scene LGBT community spaces that they hoped would be more accessible and welcoming:

> The [LGBT centre] closed down and now a lot of the community don't have places to go. People who don't have a lot of money, people who don't feel able to access the gay scene because they don't fit the bill . . . and the trans community have spent a long time trying to find appropriate meeting places for their group . . . but they've had so many hotels slam the door in their face because they think it's weird, and the gay scene's not interested because they don't make enough money out of it . . . it would be nice just to have

a community space . . . that wasn't money driven and . . . wasn't all about alcohol and clubbing.

(Gemma)

For Matt, it was the presence of alcohol and loud music in commercial spaces that made non-scene spaces more appealing and appropriate to build or sustain community:

> I think it's disgraceful that the only way essentially you can get out and meet other . . . I'd like to say LGBT but it's mostly G [people], is by going to some-where where you consume alcohol, there's almost invariably loud music . . . I don't mind getting drunk and dancing around like an idiot, but that's not the basis for a community . . . I can't think of any other social group which some people would claim to have its community concreted through a bar or a club . . . what I think we need is more non-commercial spaces . . . a kind of non-commercial, non-alcoholic, daytime sort of space.

(Matt)

Participants also felt that particular LGBT social groups or spaces tended to appeal to different ages, meaning that people of different ages were unlikely to socialise together. This could be, as Simpson's (2016) research suggests, due to their desire to socialise only with people who had shared similar experiences and/or historical contexts. Others also suggested a need for different services or spaces according to age or people's interests:

> I have recently joined an over-50s LGBT group. I feel that there should be more groups like this for older LGBT people. Most of the groups centre around socialising in gay pubs and clubs. The community should cater for all ages, not just 20–30 age group[s].

(Survey respondent 172: Bisexual female aged 55–64)

> It would be good to have coffee bars or wine bars or book shops that were LGBT-friendly, it needs to be different things for different groups of people.

(Liz)

In particular, Laura wanted more women-only groups or spaces where she said she would feel safer:

> Men are very . . . exuberant . . . I suppose it comes down to the nightclub cul-ture . . . a little bit of that is OK, but not a huge amount . . . I suppose it [my ideal] would be to have a separate women's [space] . . . because I think within that you can feel safer . . . you do find that the men kind of dominate . . . in the community . . . and can be overbearing.

(Laura)

Supporting previous research (Brown, 2008; Valentine, 1993b, 1994), some participants suggested that organised groups sometimes met in private homes:

> I think there's a lot of that [meeting in each other's homes], and that's why you have to make sure that the group is safe, and that only certain people can come into it, because you're going to open your home to them.
>
> (Ruth)

It was clear that when trying to think about an improved, or idealised, future, specific spaces were still important, but some people clearly wanted these to be focussed away from the commercial scene, which raises the question of how to fund and support non-commercial ventures, particularly within the current climate of 'austerity' in the UK. Overall, organised groups and services were clearly understood as forms of temporary space and/or community that could enable friendships and peer support.

## Online Spaces and Virtual Communities

This final section examines online spaces and virtual communities that were understood to provide safe spaces for LGBT people to meet and/or interact. Online forums and other websites were thought to support LGBT communities in two key ways: by facilitating connections between LGBT people, particularly for those who might be less physically connected, and by increasing access to LGBT-related news and information. The assumption that the internet was used as a way of finding others with similar interests or identities was widely shared, though opinions differed as to whether this *constituted* community or merely *supported* community through facilitating communication. As Matt commented on his use of a particular social media site:

> That is how I chat to lots of my friends, and lots of my friends are LGBT . . . I wouldn't say that Facebook is my LGBT community, but it's a way to interact with my LGBT community.
>
> (Matt)

Matt's use of social media to some extent illustrates Delanty's (2010: 149) suggestion that online spaces do not necessarily create new communities, but add to existing ones, and can therefore be viewed as 'communication communities' that have made "belonging more communicative".

Wakeford (2002: 128) has identified a common assumption in what she terms cyberqueer studies "that communication in online spaces is a replacement for 'community' elsewhere". This assumption was not borne out within my research, however, as online spaces were thought to contribute to and/or enhance, but not necessarily replace, offline communities. Participants suggested that the internet was a personal and political communication tool that contributed to the development of both online and offline communities, and which had the potential to bring about social change:

Because of the politics I'm involved in . . . I tend to talk to people through the internet and arrange things and organise events . . . I don't see why the internet can't be a part of that [building a community], and it's definitely a tool for making that happen.

(Helen)

Online content has been very influential, not just from the UK, but especially so in countries like India because people access information and get experience. You can just read about things, see pictures, see videos, and get live information from all over the world. One of the reasons there's so much change that has happened in India over a short period of time is I think because there's easy access to information.

(Shourjo)

A number of participants felt that the internet could support connections between people, particularly when much of their time might be spent with people or in places that were assumed to be 'straight':

Communities on the internet definitely exist . . . whether it's a dating type community or whether it's just a sort of friends type community, but there's a huge number of them.

(Tony)

I feel more part of an online gay community now . . . by kind of meeting people over Twitter that have got similar kind of beliefs, outlooks . . . in that respect I feel like I've connected with a lot of people that are similar to me that happen to be gay . . . it's a very virtual community . . . which you can dip in and out of when you want to.

(Carl)

Many suggested that online spaces could also develop new communities, rather than just support or extend existing ones. The value of web-based interactions in supporting people experiencing isolation in their physical lives was often emphasised in relation to young people:

For young LGBT people . . . it's very important . . . I think that in terms of making a safe space for people to meet it's really important, in terms of making a practical space for people to meet who might be quite geographically isolated.

(Gemma)

Whilst some people identified risks associated with online spaces, for example the possibility of online networking sites and apps being used to target people for hate crime, younger participants thought that online dangers were exaggerated or over-emphasised. For them, a focus on risk did not acknowledge the potential for happiness or safety via online communication, particularly for isolated LGBT young people:

> It's not all 'this person met on the internet and . . . ended up in a ditch' . . . We don't get told the good stuff . . . you don't get told this person met this person and lived happily ever after.
>
> (Kerry)

> It's just as easy to get thrown in a ditch if you meet them in person.
>
> (Jason)

A number of participants also stressed the importance of online forums within trans communities, echoing earlier work by Whittle (1998). Fiona, for example, felt that:

> [The internet has] allowed people to talk to people, to communicate, to build communities [in areas] where it's absolutely impossible to make any physical communities.
>
> (Fiona)

Others commented on the usefulness of online spaces for facilitating identity explorations, peer communication and mutual support:

> Trans communities online are so important . . . online worlds have provided safe spaces to try things out, safe spaces to meet others, and practical ways to meet others, and an international trans community has been able to mobilise in that way.
>
> (Gemma)

> I know my trans friends find great support through various trans communities and even places you wouldn't expect it like Facebook and Tumblr . . . I've heard there's a huge trans community on Tumblr.
>
> (Matt)

Rachel identified advantages in accessing information via the internet:

> For the online community for trans people it is predominantly a means of finding out information on medication.
>
> (Rachel)

However, Rachel also felt that the presence of online communities could reduce the possibilities for 'real', offline trans communities:

> Although there is a so-called trans community the majority is online and it's difficult to get people to come from behind their computers and deal with

things in the real world . . . I don't feel there is a community offline for trans people.

(Rachel)

Nevertheless, some people felt that online spaces would enable more trans people to access information and make decisions about their identities in ways that had not been as possible for trans people in the past:

[There are] quite a lot of older people transitioning now, including me . . . I think the reason for that is that these things weren't available to people when they were younger and so I think that you will see . . . much more people making these decisions about themselves a lot earlier because the information is much, much more available.

(Petra)

Online spaces were also particularly discussed in relation to dating, and a number of participants had themselves, or knew of people who had, met their partner this way. Research has suggested that the internet has because the most common way for gay men to meet each other (Holt, 2011). As Shourjo commented:

We met online . . . there's definitely an online community.

(Shourjo)

A second common assumption within cyberqueer studies that Wakeford (2002: 128) identified was that "groups of users interacting electronically . . . are assumed to have already achieved some kind of community simply through having this communication". This was not borne out in participant data, where people did not necessarily view online communication as a form of community. Dilys, for instance, was doubtful about thinking of online spaces as communities:

I wouldn't say there was any kind of community structure on the internet. I mean forums are great, but I wouldn't think of them as communities at all.

(Dilys)

Although some participants imagined that they would have used the internet more as a young person had it been available then, they did not necessarily think virtual communities were as good:

We didn't have that online community that people have these days, but I can imagine that if we did that's probably what I would have done, I probably would have come out online first, maybe to people that I didn't particularly know, just to . . . get some kind of support.

(Carl)

If I didn't go to uni I would never have found any of this community stuff . . . god knows what I would have done. Probably focus on online stuff, maybe find some kind of community group, but it just wouldn't be as good.

(Matt)

For some people, online spaces or communities were implicitly, if not explicitly, seen as somehow lesser than physical spaces or communities, which were sometimes described as more real:

I think that cyberspace only is relevant when it's sort of mapped onto real spaces . . . Maybe cyberspace therefore is where you go when you can't find a real space; it's like a substitute . . . I would definitely think of the online stuff as a substitute . . . even though we're in the digital age and all that, nothing beats [physically] meeting people.

(Matt)

However, Matt did recognise some, albeit limited, potential for community online:

Stuff like Grindr fascinates me . . . maybe that's a community [but] it's not a great one.

(Matt)

Matt's comments echo Lehavot, Balsam and Ibrahim-Wells' (2009) findings that some of their participants missed the physicality of meetings, whilst also finding online interactions useful.

For some, online developments were thought to contribute to looser and/or more fragmented communities:

While the internet means there is greater support for a wider range of people, online forums means the community feels much looser than it may have done in the past.

(Survey respondent 265: Female lesbian aged 25–34)

I don't think there is an LGBT community. There is a gay community, there is a lesbian community, there is a bi community and you get more specialist communities within that as well . . . that is more acute in the online community.

(Shourjo)

Traies' (2015) research suggested that as younger lesbians 'assimilate' into 'mainstream' society the less they may need lesbian social groups and supportive communities. Echoing these themes, and in thinking about the future, Peter wondered to what extent physical spaces would feature within community:

I think there is a great divide and it will be interesting to see what happens . . . my generation where the online thing came after you had formed your experiences, it's something you do but it's not something I naturally take to, but for people who have grown up with it I think it's their first port of call and the question is whether they will want to go to physical community groups or if their whole lives will be spent on the online environment.

(Peter)

Recent research has identified significant internet use by older LGB people, however (Knocker, 2012), so the divide identified by Peter and some others is not universal. Some participants knew of older friends who frequently communicated with other (LGBT) people online, who then became friends, which was particularly valuable given their lack of mobility or hearing:

Once you become less mobile or deaf or whatever it's jolly useful to be able to email people . . . That's a really important sort of social life for some people.

(Ruth)

Not everyone with a disability found online spaces conducive to communication, however:

I am dyslexic and this may mean I have less connection with online communities as I tend only to talk to people I know online due to my writing.
(Survey respondent 388: Queer, pansexual, lesbian cis[gender] woman aged 18–24, spelling corrected)

On the whole, online spaces were sometimes understood as online or virtual communities that supported information exchange and identity explorations of particular importance to those planning or in the process of 'coming out', at any age, whether as LGB or trans. The internet was also viewed as an important source of communication that could bolster community ties, political activism and personal/intimate relationships.

## Chapter Summary

It was clear that communities are frequently conceptualised spatially, whether in regard to particular geographical areas or more temporally-specific spaces, such as organised groups and services. These spaces can be seen as illustrations of Lefebvre's (1991) 'lived' spaces and Soja's (1996) 'Thirdspace' (i.e. 'real' and 'imagined'). Linked to notions of safety and visibility, people's gender and sexual identities could inform decision-making about places of home and travel, though these decisions could also be influenced by financial resources. There were strong views about places perceived to be better for LGBT people to live and/or holiday, as well as locations to avoid. Generally, urban areas were seen as better, whilst international locations with repressive LGBT rights were seen as places to stay away from. Whilst holidays usually only mean staying in a location for a short space of time, it was thought to be important to go somewhere where people could feel comfortable and safe to express themselves, particularly if they were with their partner. Travel could also offer some the opportunity to experience forms of LGBT community they would not otherwise have access to. The significance of some people's visits to Brighton or San Francisco was apparent in that they became comparator spaces against which the rest of their lives could be judged. Online spaces were also important for many, as they enabled communication between people who did not share physical or geographical space, thus helping to combat some, particularly young and/or trans, people's isolation. Forms of virtual community were thought to support information sharing, especially for trans people, and offer opportunities for exploring identities. Web-based communications could also boost political activism and enable opportunities to seek intimate relationships and/or sexual encounters. Across a range of 'public' and 'private' spaces, varied forms of community were felt to facilitate friendships and mutual support, which many people identified as important for LGBT people.

## Notes

1  Hebden Bridge is a small town in the North of England known for having a large lesbian population.
2  Responses were not mutually exclusive and therefore add up to more than 100%. In total, 78% of responses to this question ticked two or more options.
3  *Little Britain* was a popular comedy sketch show aired in Britain 2003–2006.

## References

Barker, M., Richards, C., Jones, R., Bowes-Catton, H., Plowman, T., Yockney, J. and Morgan, M. (2012) *The bisexuality report: Bisexual inclusion in LGBT equality and diversity*. Milton Keynes: The Open University.
Bell, D. and Valentine, G. (1995) 'Introduction: Orientations' in Bell, D. and Valentine, G. (eds) *Mapping desire: Geographies of sexualities*. London: Routledge, pp. 1–27.
Brown, G. (2008) 'Urban (homo)sexualities: Ordinary cities and ordinary sexualities', *Geography Compass* 2(4): 1215–1231.
Brown, G. (2009) 'Thinking beyond homonormativity: Performative explorations of diverse gay economies', *Environment and Planning A* 41(6): 1496–1510.
Brown, G. (2012) 'Homonormativity: A metropolitan concept that denigrates "ordinary" gay lives', *Journal of Homosexuality* 59(7): 1065–1072.
Browne, K. (2008) 'Imagining cities, living the other: Between the gay urban idyll and rural lesbian lives', *The Open Geography Journal* 1: 25–32.
Browne, K. and Bakshi, L. (2013) *Ordinary in Brighton: LGBT, activisms and the city*. Aldershot: Ashgate.
Browne, K. and Ferreira, E. (eds) (2015) *Lesbian geographies: Gender, place and power*. Farnham: Ashgate.
Cant, B. (ed) (1997) *Invented identities? Lesbians and gays talk about migration*. London: Cassell.
Cant, B. (2008) 'Gay men's narratives and the pursuit of wellbeing in healthcare settings: A London study', *Critical Public Health* 18(1): 41–50.

Casey, M.E. (2010) 'Even poor gays travel: Excluding low income gay men from under-standings of gay tourism' in Taylor, Y. (ed) *Classed intersections: Spaces, selves, knowl-edges*. Aldershot: Ashgate, pp. 181–198.

Casey, M.E. (2013) 'Belonging: Lesbians and gay men's claims to material spaces' in Tay-lor, Y. and Addison, M. (eds) *Queer presences and absences*. Basingstoke: Palgrave Macmillan, pp. 141–158.

Choi, Y. (2013) 'The meaning of home for transgendered people' in Taylor, Y. and Addison, M. (eds) *Queer presences and absences*. New York: Palgrave Macmillan, pp. 118–140.

Craig, S.L. and McInroy, L. (2014) 'You can form a part of yourself online: The influence of new media on identity development and coming out for LGBTQ youth', *Journal of Gay and Lesbian Mental Health* 18(1): 95–109.

Cresswell, T. (2004) *Place: A short introduction*. Oxford: Blackwell.

Cronin, A. and King, A. (2014) 'Only connect? Older lesbian, gay and bisexual (LGB) adults and social capital', *Ageing and Society* 34(2): 258–279.

Delanty, G. (2010) *Community*. London: Routledge.

Donovan, C. and Hester, M. (2014) *Domestic violence and sexuality: What's love got to do with it?* Bristol: Policy Press.

Ellis, S.J. (2007) 'Homophobia, rights and community: Contemporary issues in the lives of LGB people in the UK' in Clarke, V. and Peel, E. (eds) *Out in psychology: Lesbian, gay, bisexual, trans and queer perspectives*. Chichester: John Wiley and Sons, pp. 291–310.

Formby, E. (2013) 'Understanding and responding to homophobia and bullying: Contrast-ing staff and young people's views within community settings in England', *Sexuality Research and Social Policy* 10(4): 302–316.

Formby, E. (2015a) 'Limitations of focussing on homophobic, biphobic and transphobic "bullying" to understand and address LGBT young people's experiences within and beyond school', *Sex Education* 15(6): 626–640.

Formby, E. (2015b) *From freshers' week to finals: Understanding LGBT+ perspectives on, and experiences of, higher education*. Sheffield: Sheffield Hallam University.

Ghaziani, A. (2014) *There goes the gayborhood?* Princeton: Princeton University Press.

Gieseking, J. (2013) 'Queering the meaning of "neighborhood": Reinterpreting the les-bian-queer experience of Park Slope, Brooklyn, 1983–2008' in Taylor, Y. and Addi-son, M. (eds) *Queer presences and absences*. New York: Palgrave Macmillan, pp. 178–200.

Guibernau, M. (2013) *Belonging: Solidarity and division in modern societies*. Cambridge: Polity Press.

Heaphy, B. (2011) 'Critical relational displays' in Dermott, E. and Seymour, J. (eds) *Dis-playing families: A new concept for the sociology of family life*. Basingstoke: Palgrave Macmillan, pp. 19–37.

Hines, S. (2010) 'Queerly situated: Exploring constraints and negotiations of trans queer subjectivities', *Gender, Place and Culture* 17(5): 597–613.

Holt, M. (2011) 'Gay men and ambivalence about "gay community": From gay community attachment to personal communities', *Culture, Health and Sexuality* 13(8): 857–871.

Homfray, M. (2007) *Provincial queens: The gay and lesbian community in the North-West of England*. Bern: Peter Lang.

Howe, A.C. (2001) 'Queer pilgrimage: The San Francisco homeland and identity tourism', *Cultural Anthropology* 16(1): 35–61.

Howes, R. (2011) *Gay West: Civil society, community and LGBT history in Bristol and Bath, 1970 to 2010*. Bristol: SilverWood Books.

Hughes, H.L. (2006) *Pink tourism: Holidays of gay men and lesbians*. Wallingford: CABI.

Johnston, L. and Valentine, G. (1995) 'Wherever I lay my girlfriend, that's my home: The performance and surveillance of lesbian identities in domestic environments' in Bell, D. and Valentine, G. (eds) *Mapping desire: Geographies of sexualities*. London: Routledge, pp. 99–113.

Knocker, S. (2012) *Perspectives on ageing: Lesbians, gay men and bisexuals*. York: Joseph Rowntree Foundation.

Lefebvre, H. (1991) *The production of space*. Oxford: Blackwell.

Lehavot, K., Balsam, K.F. and Ibrahim-Wells, G.D. (2009) 'Redefining the American quilt: Definitions and experiences of community among ethnically diverse lesbian and bisexual women', *Journal of Community Psychology* 37(4): 439–458.

Mason, G. (2001) 'Body maps: Envisaging homophobia, violence and safety', *Social and Legal Studies* 10(1): 23–44.

Massey, D. (2005) *For space*. London: Sage.

May, V. (2013) *Connecting self to society: Belonging in a changing world*. New York: Palgrave Macmillan.

Moran, L., Skeggs, B., Tyrer, P. and Corteen, K. (2003) 'The formation of fear in gay space: The "straights" story', *Capital and Class* 27(2): 173–198.

Moran, L., Skeggs, B., Tyrer, P. and Corteen, K. (2004) *Sexuality and the politics of violence and safety*. London: Routledge.

Myslik, W.D. (1996) 'Renegotiating the social/sexual identities of places' in Duncan, N. (ed) *BodySpace: Destabilising geographies of gender and sexuality*. London: Routledge, pp. 155–168.

O'Riordan, K. and White, H. (2010) 'Virtual believers: Queer spiritual practice online' in Browne, K., Munt, S.R. and Yip, A.K.T. (eds) *Queer spiritual spaces: Sexuality and sacred places*. Farnham: Ashgate, pp. 199–230.

Oswald, R.F. and Lazarevic, V. (2011) '"You live where?!" Lesbian mothers' attachment to nonmetropolitan communities', *Family Relations* 60(4): 373–386.

Pritchard, A., Morgan, N.J., Sedgley, D., Khan, E. and Jenkins, A. (2000) 'Sexuality and holiday choices: Conversations with gay and lesbian tourists', *Leisure Studies* 19(4): 267–282.

Rosser, B.R.S., West, W. and Weinmeyer, R. (2008) 'Are gay communities dying or just in transition? Results from an international consultation examining possible structural change in gay communities', *AIDS Care* 20(5): 588–595.

Sanders, D. (2002) 'Some say Thailand is a gay paradise' in Clift, S., Luongo, M. and Callister, C. (eds) *Gay tourism*. London: Continuum.

Scourfield, J., Roen, K. and McDermott, E. (2008) 'Lesbian, gay, bisexual and transgender young people's experiences of distress: Resilience, ambivalence and self-destructive behaviour', *Health and Social Care in the Community* 16(3): 329–336.

Simpson, P. (2013) 'Differentiating the self: The kinship practices of middle-aged gay men in Manchester', *Families, Relationships and Societies* 2(1): 97–113.

Simpson, P. (2014) 'Differentiating selves: Middle-aged gay men in Manchester's less visible "homospaces"', *The British Journal of Sociology* 65(1): 150–169.

Simpson, P. (2015) *Middle-aged gay men, ageing and ageism: Over the rainbow?* Basingstoke: Palgrave Macmillan.

Simpson, P. (2016) 'The resources of ageing? Middle-aged gay men's accounts of Manchester's gay voluntary organizations', *The Sociological Review* 64(2): 366–383.

Smith, D.P. and Holt, L. (2005) '"Lesbian migrants in the gentrified valley" and "other" geographies of rural gentrification', *Journal of Rural Studies* 21(3): 313–322.

Soja, E.W. (1996) *Thirdspace: Expanding the geographical imagination*. Oxford: Blackwell.

Taylor, V., Kaminski, E. and Dugan, K. (2002) 'From the Bowery to the Castro: Communities, identities and movements' in Richardson, D. and Seidman, S. (eds) *Handbook of lesbian and gay studies*. London: Sage, pp. 99–114.

Taylor, Y. (2007) *Working-class lesbian life: Classed outsiders*. Basingstoke: Palgrave Macmillan.

Taylor, Y. (2008) ' "That's not really my scene": Working-class lesbians in (and out of) place', *Sexualities* 11(5): 523–546.

Taylor, Y. and Falconer, E. (2015) ' "Seedy bars and grotty pints": Close encounters in queer leisure spaces', *Social and Cultural Geography* 16(1): 43–57.

Taylor, Y., Falconer, E. and Snowdon, R. (2014b) 'Queer youth, Facebook and faith: Facebook methodologies and online identities', *New Media and Society* 16(7): 1138–1153.

Traies, J. (2015) 'Old lesbians in the UK: Community and friendship', *Journal of Lesbian Studies* 19(1): 35–49.

Valentine, G. (1993a) 'Desperately seeking Susan: A geography of lesbian friendships', *Area* 25(2): 109–116.

Valentine, G. (1993b) 'Negotiating and managing multiple sexual identities: Lesbian time-space strategies', *Transactions of the Institute of British Geographers* 18(2): 237–248.

Valentine, G. (1993c) '(Hetero)sexing space: Lesbian perceptions and experiences of everyday space', *Environment and Planning D: Society and Space* 11(4): 395–413.

Valentine, G. (1994) 'Toward a geography of the lesbian community', *Women and Environments* 14(1): 8–10.

Valentine, G. (1995) 'Out and about: Geographies of lesbian landscapes', *International Journal of Urban and Regional Research* 19(1): 96–111.

Valentine, G. and Skelton, T. (2003) 'Finding oneself, losing oneself: The lesbian and gay "scene" as a paradoxical space', *International Journal of Urban and Regional Research* 27(4): 849–866.

Valentine, G., Skelton, T. and Butler, R. (2003) 'Coming out and outcomes: Negotiating lesbian and gay identities with, and in, the family', *Environment and Planning D: Society and Space* 21(4): 479–499.

Valentine, G., Wood, N. and Plummer, P. (2009) *The experiences of lesbian, gay, bisexual and transsexual staff and students in higher education*. London: ECU.

Waitt, G. and Markwell, K. (2006) *Gay tourism: Culture and context*. Binghamton: The Haworth Press.

Wakeford, N. (2002) 'New technologies and "cyber-queer" research' in Richardson, R. and Seidman, S. (eds) *Handbook of lesbian and gay studies*. London: Sage, pp. 115–144.

Walkerdine, V. and Studdert, D. (2011) *Concepts and meanings of community in the social sciences*. Swindon: Arts and Humanities Research Council.

Weeks, J., Heaphy, B. and Donovan, C. (2001) *Same sex intimacies: Families of choice and other life experiments*. London: Routledge.

Weston, K. (1995) 'Get thee to a big city: Sexual imaginary and the great gay migration', *GLQ: A Journal of Lesbian and Gay Studies* 2(3): 253–277.

Whittle, S. (1998) 'The trans-cyberian mail way', *Social and Legal Studies* 7(3): 389–408.

Woolwine, D. (2000) 'Community in gay male experience and moral discourse', *Journal of Homosexuality* 38(4): 5–37.

# 6    The Pleasures and Pains
of Scene Spaces

## Introduction

This chapter examines the scene as a form of space. Twenty-five years ago, Weston (1991: 403) argued that "bars remain a central symbol of identity, and almost everyone has a story about a first visit to a gay club". Given the legislative and social changes that have occurred within this period, one could be forgiven for thinking that this might no longer be the case. Yet the recent shooting in the Pulse nightclub in Florida led to a series of media discussions about the ongoing importance of such spaces. A Guardian newspaper article in the UK had the tagline 'sanctuaries that are like therapeutic spaces that patch up invisible wounds and provide unconditional acceptance' (Mahdawi, 2016). Another had the headline 'Gay bars are not only places to have fun, they are havens of freedom and relief' (Tóibín, 2016). Given the context, it is not surprising that people were moved to write about such spaces in this way, but my point is that they do still attract people—to frequent them, and to write about them in such positive terms. Positive experiences are not universal, however, as I will go on to explore. As a particular spatial understanding of community, scene spaces are important, so it is particularly significant that not everyone feels able to access such spaces. This chapter will show how, for some, the scene is experienced as an enjoyable space that can offer (at least the possibility of) friendship, feelings of comfort and safety and 'diversion' away from heteronormativity. It forms part of the night-time economy, but it is more than this. Even when people do not or cannot access these spaces, they can still have symbolic significance. However, scene spaces can also undermine some people's identities because of the existence of norms and attitudes that can render those who are not seen to 'fit' as out of place, and therefore excluded. Heterosexual customers within scene spaces were regularly deemed 'out of place' within the research, because of their challenge to LGBT majorities that resulted in LGBT people feeling less safe and/or comfortable. Despite these and other weaknesses, there was a sense that scene spaces are still necessary, and I show that some people felt they had no choice but to visit venues with which they were not entirely happy. The chapter will thus demonstrate that whilst the concept of community is frequently understood in positive terms (Day, 2006), those who base their understanding of community on the scene can often experience 'their' community as inadequate. I suggest in part this is due to a lack of ownership, with tensions evident in conceptualisations of community based on a space over which people have limited control.

Following an overview of existing literature to set the context for my research, this chapter will explore experiences of scene spaces within the following four sections: The Scene as 'Community'; Positive Experiences; Scene Exclusions; and 'Invasion', Choice and Ownership. Whilst exclusions and problematic norms have already been explored within Chapter 3, this chapter focuses on how they intersect with scene spaces, and therefore their implications for understandings of community.

## Overview of Existing Literature

The scene has been the subject of much geographical and sociological attention. Here I offer a précis of key themes within this work, before going on to examine my own. A body of previous research has linked the notion of community with what is frequently called 'gay' social space, particularly the commercial scene (e.g. see Holt, 2011; Moran et al., 2003). Bars and clubs therefore often feature prominently in discussions of LGBT communities and/or life in general. Lesbian and gay people choosing to socialise together based on an assumed shared 'difference' from heterosexuals can be understood as a "bond of sorts" (Coleman-Fountain, 2015). Accessing scene spaces can be experienced as a 'homecoming' (Valentine and Skelton, 2003), accompanied by feelings of affirmation and validation. Such 'subcultural-specific spaces' have therefore been interpreted as 'difference-affirming' forms of political organising and/or 'community building' (Ghaziani, 2011). However, scene spaces may offer more than physical space alone. It has been argued that the Village, as some scenes are known, helps create a sense of belonging "simply by being there" (Homfray, 2007: 106), suggesting that symbolic importance can sometimes supplement or outweigh people's physical experiences.

However, the idea of the scene as a basis for LGBT community or a sense of belonging has been questioned. As a form of space it has been subject to repeated criticisms within research, which Browne and Bakshi (2013) dubbed 'scene bashing'. Often concerns have focussed on people's age, ethnicity, gender or social class, though my research also evidenced other negative experiences, as I explore in this chapter. Research with ethnic minority gay men, for example, has suggested that sexualisation of the scene can override possibilities for community development, friendship building and mutual support (Keogh, Henderson and Dodds, 2004). Focussing on gender rather than sexualisation, Browne and Bakshi (2013: 75) have noted that "a focus on the gay scene as a locus of community and belonging" affords it "power that some women questioned", given levels of male domination and control common within scene spaces. The scene can therefore be experienced as sexist (Cronin and King, 2014). Weston (1991) noted that if people experienced 'trouble' getting into bars then they could feel peripheral to community. Browne and Bakshi (2013: 87) also commented that "the illusion of the scene as 'community', combined with the enjoyment of the scene made marginalisation from scene spaces more than just 'missing a good night out'". In other words, where the scene is held up as a site of safety and/or belonging away from 'the rest of' the city and/or society, then feeling or being emotionally, physically or financially denied entry to this space has particular significance because it can leave people feeling as if they do not belong anywhere. As the scene is not experienced as universally welcoming (Cant, 2008), where the scene is understood to be the basis for an LGBT community, then such a community is not always safe or inclusive. The conflation of the scene with LGBT identity and/or community can therefore be experienced as alienating (Browne and Bakshi, 2013).

Practices within scene spaces can make these forms of space physically and/or emotionally inaccessible to some. Staff actions, for example, can deter or restrict some people's admission. Highlighting the power of door staff at commercial venues, Rogers (2012) identified a need for black British gay men to 'camp it up' in order to gain entry. Woolwine (2000) also illustrated how racist door practices (in America) impacted upon his participants through door staff requiring more or excessive ID for black patrons when they were not accompanied by a white person. Once within venues, staff can still be influential. Casey (2007), for example, has identified how venue staff refusing to turn up lighting and/or turn down music can restrict deaf people's ability to communicate. A lack of facilities within venues can also make them less accessible for some people. Cant (2008), for example, found that gay pubs do not always have 'disabled-friendly', accessible toilets for those in a wheelchair. However, it is not only the venue or staff that can have a negative influence, but so too can other customers. It has been suggested, for example, that the scene is experienced as unwelcoming to LGB people with learning difficulties, which can limit their ability to meet and maintain friendships with other LGB people (Abbott and Howarth, 2005). Cant (2004, 2008) has also identified how groups of Asian men entering scene spaces felt 'stared at', whilst white customers were thought to be 'threatened', 'apprehensive', 'confused' or 'shocked' by their presence. Keogh, Henderson and Dodds (2004: 30) identified ways in which black gay men are objectified and sexualised on the scene. Though in their study sexual commodification was accepted as an integral component of the scene, it became particularly "animated, painful or significant" for participants when it mobilised wider social inequalities, such as racism (Keogh, Henderson and Dodds, 2004: 40). In conclusion, they emphasised strong links between objectification, sexual stereotyping, bodily commodification and ethnicity on the scene (Keogh, Henderson and Dodds, 2004). 'Workings' of the scene can therefore act to make some people feel less welcomed, whether by staff or other customers.

In addition to prejudices connected to people's identities, the body is also subject to scrutiny within scene spaces, which can influence people's experiences. Common 'standards' of body image on the scene, particularly for gay men, are experienced as off-putting (Cant, 2008), whilst focussing only on youth, attractiveness and sex can alienate older gay men (Casey, 2007; Cronin and King, 2014; Ellis, 2007; Yip, 1996) and older women (Cronin and King, 2014). However, Simpson (2013b, 2014, 2015) has argued that whilst middle-aged gay men might feel a loss of bodily 'value' on the scene, they can, as middle-aged men, also resist such cultural pressures. Nevertheless, Taylor (2007b) has identified how devaluations can occur when people (in her research, working class lesbians) fail to display the 'correct' gay signifiers or 'bodily capitals' on the scene, meaning that for some, the scene is not experienced as 'their' space, or I might add, community. Working class lesbians, amongst others, can therefore miss out on the affirmation that this space is often thought to offer, whether through avoiding scene venues or through feeling out of place when they are there. However, Browne and Bakshi (2013: 87) have suggested that a focus on 'scene bashing' can result in neglecting "the importance of these spaces for many people". At the same time, they argue that we should not view those who do not feel able to use the scene as 'victims' (Browne and Bakshi, 2013). Scene spaces are thus complex because whilst they can be affirming and enjoyable to some, they can be painful and exclusionary to others.

A further area of scene-based enquiry relates to non-LGBT people's entry into these spaces. Scene spaces are frequently marketed as signifiers of a cosmopolitan city (Johnston, 2005), which suggests the bringing together of diverse groups of people (Moran et al., 2004). However, this process can also be felt as the 'colonisation' (Moran et al., 2003), 'dilution' (Hughes, 2006) or 'erosion' (Pritchard et al., 2000) of LGBT space, where non-LGBT people's presence is understood as reducing LGBT people's feelings of safety (Moran et al., 2004). This 'touristification' of gay space is also read as (re)establishing heterosexual control (Hughes, 2006). Heterosexual consumption on, or of, the scene is thus thought to impact on lesbians' and gay men's enjoyment, affirmation and/or feelings of belonging (Binnie, 1995; Skeggs, 1999; Taylor, 2007b). Heterosexual 'invasion' can lead to lesbian and gay people feeling 'gawked at' (Moran et al., 2004) and that they are losing ownership of 'their' space (Hughes, 2006). A narrative of nostalgia regularly accompanies this narrative of invasion, which frequently harks back to (perceptions of) less commercialised and/or more political spaces or communities of the past (Holt, 2011; Moran et al., 2003; Taylor, 2008; Traies, 2015). As Moran et al. (2003) note, these narratives are often linked because a 'pre-invasion' time can be imagined as 'pure' gay space, without 'straights', and without danger. These narratives support Bauman's (2000) suggestion that community is nearly always viewed nostalgically as a 'paradise lost', or alternatively, as a 'paradise to be found' or (re)made. A sense of lost paradise can be seen in the frequent laments about closures of, and/or campaigns to save, particular venues in the 'gay' press. There are also similar debates about the decline of gayborhoods in the United States (Ghaziani, 2014). I now draw on my research to explore these themes further.

## The Scene as 'Community'

The physical spaces most often associated with the term LGBT community were commercial scenes. The term 'scene' was most often used to describe commercial 'gay' bars and clubs, which were rarely referred to as 'LGBT' bars and clubs.

These spaces were seen as "different to the heteronormative spaces in which many LGBT people worked, went to school and at times lived" (Browne and Bakshi, 2013: 67). As such, they formed part of the night-time economy, but were also visited outside of these hours. There was not always agreement about whether it was customer base or ownership that resulted in a venue being identified as gay. A minority of participants thought that gay book shops and coffee shops (outside of the night-time economy) also form a part of the scene:

> I interpret the scene as . . . the gay book store . . . the shop run by the gay couple, you know, it's all of those things, so it's not just going out and being hedonistic. It's about a broader gay network.
>
> (Gerry)

> I'm referring to clubs, bars . . . there isn't a unified scene, it's just thinking geographically there is often a space. So something like a gay book club or a gay coffee [shop] would both be part of the scene.
>
> (Helen)

Some saw the scene as a form of community in which they participated, albeit sometimes made up of only a small 'core' of people:

> In terms of the scene, I think there will always be like a kind of core member-ship, like a kind of scene queen. I mean that's definitely a community. If you go to [a particular pub] there's always the same core 20 people in there, and if you go to [a particular club] there's always the same core 100 people there, I mean I'm one of them.
>
> (Matt)

Though participants did not necessarily think that the scene was the only form of LGBT community, many did think, because of its visual nature, it was most often associated as such in the non-LGBT public imagination. Within this, many also identified a lack of diversity:

> [The scene] tends to be very Caucasian and younger and more male-dom-inated and I'd describe that as quite a visual, what people think of as the, LGBT community.
>
> (Helen)

Matt also felt that visual forms of community based on the scene only represented certain LGBT people:

> I think it's so easy to assume that an LGBT community revolves around gay bars . . . [for example] people assume that Canal Street [in Manchester] is the nucleus of their community . . . [but] the people who go out on the scene are

almost always white, young, rich gay men, which is only a smidgen of LGB and T.

(Matt)

Not everybody was happy to engage with the scene or 'other collective activities' associated with community:

> I am comfortable being out, but I really, really do not like the gay scene or those other collective activities often referred to as the gay community.
> (Survey respondent 179: Gay man aged 45–54)

Where participants understood community to be based around the commercial scene, they might distance themselves from the notion of community, because they did not wish to socialise on the scene:

> I am an out lesbian both at work and home, and over many years have found the concept of an LGBT 'community' to be a myth. I don't wish to base my social life around the pubs/clubs on the 'scene', but even now that's all there seems to be. As an older woman I have no choice but to go to hetero-sexual venues and join heterosexual groups as they provide more choice and variety.
> (Survey respondent 487: Female lesbian aged 45–54)

For those who were less familiar with scene spaces, these forms of community were thought to be 'superficial' and even 'scary':

> I've only just brushed up against the . . . scene, not necessarily in [my home town], in London briefly, but I never really participated or looked much further into it, it scared me too much so I backed away . . . That to me seems like a very sort of superficial community.
> (Charlie)

Feelings of exclusion from particular spaces or venues are important when considering how people understand community. This is because exclusion from the scene can be experienced as exclusion from community. Perhaps as a result, one participant rejected the word community when applied to the scene, preferring instead the term 'clique' to describe a scene he had experience of:

> There's definitely like an LGB clique, but there isn't necessarily a community . . . If you look at like the main core people specifically that are out on the scene, it's all the same people, they all know each other, they all sleep with each other . . . especially gay men . . . and they all look the same, dress the same, everything!
> (Ed)

Ed suggested that in larger urban areas forms of LGBT community might involve more than the scene, which meant that 'scene' and 'community' would be easier to identify and differentiate. This could be, for example, by distinguishing between commercial venues and a broader range of social groups and events. However, in smaller cities Ed thought LGBT space was focussed solely on the scene, perhaps because there were not enough people to sustain varied social groups. Perceptions of 'cliques', as opposed to communities, were also identified within the survey:

> Often there is very little sense of community, and cliques form as [they] do anywhere else . . . the commercial scenes are so one-dimensional.
>
> (Survey respondent 109: Female lesbian aged 45–54)

Concern was also expressed about the visibility of the scene, which was thought to influence how some people understand LGBT communities or people in general, and which might reinforce particular stereotypes:

> There are a group of people who the general population think is the LGBT community, and it's the people who are on the scene, the pill-poppers, the posers, the ones who are pulling constantly.
>
> (Julie)

> The external view I would guess . . . would be walking down the street half naked, normally drunk, snogging and maybe having sex, you know, all that sort of stereotype view . . . If that is the external view of the LGBT community, then it's the wrong view.
>
> (Timothy)

These views were attributed to the 'general population', and echo concerns about how non-LGBT people might view Pride events, explored in the following chapter. However, the views of some participants, such as Julie and Timothy, also appear to reveal their own assumptions about people on the scene. In doing so, they demonstrate how certain people can be homogenised or 'othered' by people perceived to be from within the same community. There was also no acknowledgment from Timothy and some others that non-LGBT people may also get drunk, snog and so on, creating the impression that this was only a scene issue.

   In the following exchange between participants, othering is clearly used to distance themselves from other people on the scene. This was linked to their own feelings of exclusion on, or from, the scene, which meant they saw that particular community as only being for certain people, at the same time as believing that was the only place they could go for acceptance (see further discussion on choice below):

> It [the local scene] is a community for the . . . fashion lesbians and the scene queens . . . That's just a group of people who are like pulling, posing and pill-popping, simple as that, and . . . we're excluded from that community.
>
> (Julie)

It's quite aggressive, but at the same time it's almost a fearful scenario . . . if you were to take a girl that had not been seen before, it's almost as if like, they become vultures, don't they?

(Jo)

A predatorial lesbian . . .

(Julie)

Very predatorial, but at the same time, about the acceptance, if that's the only place you are going to be able to go to, you've almost got to go . . . unless you go like out of town.

(Jo)

It is clear that LGBT community is often understood spatially, particularly based around the scene, which meant that not everyone could access the concept of community because they did not, or could not, access the scene. To be denied entry to these spaces is therefore to be denied more than simply a night out, or access to a pub or club, as I explore further below.

## Positive Experiences

Despite some doubts about whether the scene should be thought of as a form of LGBT community, many participants had positive feelings about scene spaces, at least for part of their lives. This was frequently related to a sense of 'freedom' already explored within Chapter 4. As such, the scene was regularly thought of as a place where LGBT people would feel more comfortable:

When I was younger the scene was like a Mecca for me, like I grew up in a small town which is just short of an hour on the train from [this city], and making that journey was really important . . . It's just more comfortable sometimes to go there and it's as simple as that.

(Gemma)

Participants also looked towards scene-based venues to provide a safe place for themselves and/or their partner:

Because we've spent years and years of so much oppression, sometimes you kind of get like forced into this group and it becomes a safety barrier for you. And now we have clubs that we can go to and events we can go to because we know it's safe and we'll be accepted. So I see that as a really positive thing.

(Julie)

You need a safe space. If you go down the local pub and sit there holding your girlfriend's hand and kissing her you aren't going to stay there for very long . . . you need to know that you can be safe there.

(Dilys)

Some identified that for themselves and others, needing to feel safe contributed to their routine of socialising on the scene:

> For some people [the scene] is their sense of community, it's being part of that, a routine of going to a particular bar, or bars or clubs, meeting up with familiar faces, having a laugh, having a carry on . . . People feel safe in it, it's the only place you feel safe.
>
> (Ben)

'Safe' scene spaces were often contrasted with how people experienced non-scene or non-LGBT venues elsewhere:

> My partner would feel quite uncomfortable going to a non-LGBT club because of the potential homophobia she might experience, because of the gender policing in toilets and things like that.
>
> (Fiona)

Helen discussed the 'hassle' of sexual and/or homophobic harassment, meaning that for her and others, scene-based venues could offer a respite from the 'male gaze' (Skeggs, 1999) elsewhere:

> You can go for lunch there with your partner or someone and no-one stares at you and no-one comments and you get much less sexual harassment . . . If I go to a straight bar with my partner you get so much hassle . . . I think that's why a lot of straight people actually go there as well sometimes.
>
> (Helen)

Elsewhere, Timothy and Carl focussed on feeling comfortable and able to be themselves amongst their 'own kind':

> What I do in my social life, my personal life, does tend to rotate around being able to go to places where I feel comfortable going, so for example this weekend I'm going to Blackpool and we'll go round the bars . . . It gets me through the week . . . it keeps me going . . . I know there's almost a certainty that I'm with my own kind.
>
> (Timothy)

> Gay bars don't exist because gay people don't like straight people; gay bars exist because we feel we need them so we can be ourselves.
>
> (Carl)

What these comments share is a sense of 'escape' from the 'outside world'. This supports Browne and Bakshi's (2013) argument that the scene creates majorities, and therefore makes (some) LGBT people feel 'ordinary', with this ordinariness predicated, in part, on the continuing presence of heteronormativity and homophobia in LGBT people's lives. The creation of LGBT majorities and ordinariness can clearly be seen in Timothy's feeling of being with his 'own kind', which gets him through the—one can perhaps assume heteronormative and/or homophobic—week. Similarly, within the survey, community was seen as offering the possibility of feeling ordinary:

> Providing a space from which being the Other is turned on its head.
> (Survey respondent 10: Post-heterosexual female aged 35–44)

Drawing on Goffman's (1959) notion of front and back stages, the scene can perhaps be understood as offering a sense of figurative home, akin to a 'back stage' area where Carl and others feel more comfortable being themselves. By contrast, the 'front stage' area is made up of non-scene or 'heterosexual' space. Many people conceptualised such space as the 'rest' of society, i.e. the neighbourhoods, workplaces and educational establishments in which they spent much of the rest of their time. However, this is not to suggest that the back stage metaphorical home should be idealised or romanticised, given the multiple experiences of oppression and exclusion some people faced, or avoided, there.

Overall, the scene was thought to enable people to make friends, often operating as a 'starting place' to establish contacts when people moved to a new area:

> Suppose you moved into [a city] for the first time, as a gay person, the most likeliest places that you would aim for are the gay clubs initially to start making contacts and get to know people.
>
> (Dilys)

As previous research has attested (Aggleton, Davies and Hart, 1995, 1999; Davies et al., 1993; Weeks, Heaphy and Donovan, 2001), the scene is also somewhere people, particularly men, go when seeking sex and/or physical intimacy:

> I don't think we should underestimate sexual desire. I used to go to pubs to pick somebody up, unless things have changed a lot.
>
> (Peter)

> A lot of going out in our culture is to do with . . . having a drink, having a dance, and having a bit of a snog at the end of the night.
>
> (Carl)

Binnie (1995) developed the notion of 'diversionary' consumerism, which can be seen in Timothy's reference to the scene as something that gets him through the week. This was also discussed by Petra, who believed that positive aspects of the scene came out of difficult times:

> You have . . . oppression in the first place, which gives birth to a consciousness, and these people are very political and . . . they make a big effort to

be visible in a time and a place where it's very difficult to be visible, but of course sometimes they still need to go and have a drink, so the social thing develops . . . and then of course commercial interests get involved . . . None of these things are separable . . . [but] if you're talking about going down Old Compton Street for a drink, that's a wonderful thing.

(Petra)

Even for those who did not visit Old Compton Street[1] or other scene locations, these visible spaces operated to a certain extent as symbolic sites of safety and connection where people could validate their LGBT identities. As Browne and Bakshi (2013) noted, even when the scene is not used or felt 'needed', it can have symbolic importance simply by people knowing it is there. In their study, for example, gay men from working class areas discussed feeling 'part of' the scene, even when they could not afford to go there (Browne and Bakshi, 2013).

As much as scene spaces were understood to offer the possibility of friendship, and feelings of comfort, safety and escapism, or at the very least 'diversion', they are more complex than this. As the basis of some people's understanding of community, scene spaces can also offer a feeling of being part of something, even when they are not physically accessed. However, not everyone shared this view, as I will now explore.

## Scene Exclusions

As discussed above, people can feel excluded from, and by, the scene—often, but not always, related to people's physical appearances. This section therefore focuses on a range of emotional and practical exclusions that rendered the scene less accessible or welcoming to some. Given these experiences of exclusion, the scene was not always conceptualised as a form of community. Nor can these spaces always be thought of as 'back stage' areas (Goffman, 1959), because whilst they may allow some people to feel more comfortable or relaxed, they nevertheless contain expectations that can restrict or limit people's 'performances' within them. The section will look at the importance of 'dress codes', embodied practices, gender, age and financial resources as factors able to render people included or excluded. As Gemma observed, 'standing out' on the scene can lead to experiences of disdain:

I have had negative experiences on the gay scene in [this city] because it's very homogenous and it's very mainstream and people don't necessarily like the way I dress or that kind of stuff . . . My ex, who had a lot of piercings and stuff, was often kind of treated with quite a lot of disdain in mainstream gay places.

(Gemma)

Implicit 'dress codes' could therefore deter or prevent people from socialising in particular spaces. They could also be experienced as pressures to conform in order to access particular venues or communities (Simpson, 2013b; Valentine, 1993b; Valentine and Skelton, 2003), where failure to conform could result in access being refused (Taylor, 2007b). In particular, dress codes could operate as physical barriers to people accessing a form of 'LGBT space' due to the actions of door staff at some scene venues. Helen, for instance, thought that she was sometimes denied entry to places because of the way she looked:

> I normally wear dresses and skirts and have long hair and I often don't get into clubs, or I won't get in if I'm not with my partner . . . There's this very strict stereotype . . . around who is and who isn't . . . in a very physical way . . . allowed in . . . That's part of the reason sometimes I can't be bothered to go out because I can't be bothered to argue with somebody on the door.
>
> (Helen)

Carl also identified visual norms on the scene, and representations in 'gay' media, that for him, suggested that gay men should have "ripped" bodies. He thought this influenced gay men's experiences of, and interactions within, scene spaces. Carl believed that the domination of men in gay nightclubs heightened these pressures, precisely because they were not 'mixed' environments:

> There is this theme in the gay community . . . what the image of the ideal man is . . . There's more pressure because . . . the emphasis isn't like a normal club that you'd go to where it's a mixed crowd . . . [and] there's different kind of opinions, different views, different kinds of needs and wants going on in that environment. If you go to a gay club it's all about the men and so it's heightened.
>
> (Carl)

Ben similarly suggested that gay bars could be dominated by "very hyper-masculine young men". For those who did not conform to this presentation of masculinity, the scene was a space in which they could feel uncomfortable:

> [I'm] not totally comfortable on the commercial gay scene . . . from being fat and therefore often feeling out of place.
>
> (Survey respondent 26: Queer male aged 25–34)

Even when people did not feel out of place themselves, some were aware of their privileged position in being:

> Good looking 'enough' not to feel excluded from the pick-up scene, which if I'm honest has made the scene more accessible for me and the place where I have been able to make friends (friends of mine with disabilities experience those places in a totally different way).
>
> (Survey respondent 225: Gay male aged 45–54)

Some young men can derive pleasure from paying attention to their image, and having it emulated (Valentine and Skelton, 2003), which shows that pressures to conform to particular bodily ideals are not always experienced negatively. For those who do not or cannot conform, however, the 'wrong' image can lead to them being excluded on, and from, the scene.

Previous research has suggested that the scene can also be experienced as male-dominated (Binnie, 1995; Browne and Bakshi, 2011; Casey, 2004; Moran and Skeggs, 2001). In my research, Carl believed that the dominance of men on the scene was to do with gendered choices about who people prefer to socialise with:

> A lot of the gay clubs are very male-focussed . . . In an ideal world the gay community would feel linked, whether they're men or women, but the differences between men and women are still there . . . A group of lesbians would still rather go out together and get drunk and talk about other girls, and a group of gay lads would rather go out [together].
>
> (Carl)

Shourjo also believed that 'divisions' on the scene were about people grouping themselves together:

> What I've experienced is that . . . you tend to see, for example, in the scene in Manchester, the trans people tend to be together, the lesbians tend to be together, the gays tend to be together.
>
> (Shourjo)

However, it might be that exclusions and oppressions operate in scene venues that limit or prevent some people from occupying particular spaces. Such 'segregation' may also point to practices amongst bar owners, and the ways in which they market their venue and target particular customers. Casey (2007), for example, has argued that spaces are male-dominated because scene-based establishments do not focus on the 'lesbian pound'.

Aside from gender, a range of others factors, including age, could make people feel out of place on the scene. More specifically, ageist attitudes towards how old people looked were found to be oppressive on the scene:

> When I have been out on the scene . . . I've found it a thoroughly depressing experience . . . I find the normative pressures from the gay scene over appearance, behaviour, taste in music, attitudes towards age, etc. etc. etc., far more oppressive than anything I've experienced within my non-gay social network.
>
> (Survey respondent 179: Gay man aged 45–54)

> There is more discrimination . . . because I'm kind of like an older guy, I'm plus 30 so therefore I'm kind of on the scrap heap, nobody will sort of entertain you, nobody will want to talk to you . . . It's purely about sexual attraction and if there is no sexual attraction, then they've got no interest in you whatsoever.
>
> (Colin)

For Steve, such negative experiences were particularly unhelpful around the time of his 'coming out', which calls into question the popular idea that the scene is especially useful around the time of coming out:

> I've known I've been gay for years, but I only came out as a mature man . . . Coming out was like huge . . . and you go to the so-called gay scene and it's like you're feeling really tender and you go in there and it's slap! You know, 'do I really want this?' . . . It was a really bad experience and I just backed off instantly.
>
> (Steve)

Whilst older people might experience discrimination on the scene, young people could also be excluded on a practical level. Those aged under 18 found notions of, at least visual, LGBT communities as being scene-based particularly problematic as they could not yet legally access this scene/community. This limited their ability to meet other LGBT people to specific organised groups located outside the scene:

> Being a young person, it's hard for me to find people my age . . . I'm just fed up of being single, me, and I want to find a nice boy, but you can't round [here] because it's just not open enough.
>
> (Jason)

As a way to open up scene spaces to younger LGBT people, Jason wanted a 'pop and crisps' (i.e. underage) night in the only gay bar where he lived:

> [It] is a gay bar but it's only older people who can go. They should do like a younger gay night for people who are younger who want to go . . . a gay pop and crisps night . . . I've never been to a pop and crisps night [elsewhere] because I don't feel safe enough.
>
> (Jason)

Inaccessibility of the scene was not always restricted to age, however. Participants also identified lack of money, which could result in them being excluded from venues on the basis of their limited financial resources:

> Two weeks ago I was invited to go down to [a local gay pub]. They had a £10 door charge. I'm on benefits, and I'm not even on full benefits, I only get £57 a week so £10 for me . . . [is too much].
>
> (Fin)

In addition, Gemma felt that limited financial resources could make people feel less welcome on the scene if they did not have the money to look a certain way. This made her doubt whether the scene should be understood as a form of community:

> If you don't have money to go to the club and money to buy the clothes that are in H&M that week, you're not really welcome here . . . That's where the

concept of community tends to not really mean very much . . . That's just a bunch of people in a room.

(Gemma)

In general, it was thought that expectations and stereotypes connected to the scene could put people off, or prohibit them, accessing such spaces:

> [People] feel that they have to fit into a particular stereotype . . . I know younger people who will not go down to [a Village] because they don't want to be defined in a certain way.

(Tony)

A number of participants suggested that expectations connected to the scene could even make some people reluctant to identify as LGBT:

> [For some people] expectations placed on them by the gay scene are a barrier to them identifying as LGBT; that you have to go on the scene, or that you have to be a queenie, or you have to be promiscuous.

(Gemma)

As I have shown, there are a range of factors that can deter or prevent LGBT people from accessing the scene or particular venues. Not only does this limit their opportunities for socialising and consumerism, but as scene spaces are associated with communities, it might also exclude them from benefiting from a feeling of community belonging.

## 'Invasion', Choice and Ownership

This section turns to look at issues of 'choice' and 'ownership' within people's use of scene spaces. Building on Valentine's (1999) suggestion that space can be endowed with meaning in relation to both distance and difference, it could be argued that the scene is often constructed and symbolically situated as 'far away' from the 'rest' of society. As a result, non-LGBT people accessing scene spaces could be understood as an 'invasion' of LGBT space, or community:

> I remember going into [city] once, and like I was getting quite annoyed because I was thinking, 'look, you've got the rest of bloody [city]! You know, you've allowed us this area, sod off! Go away!'

(Jackie)

Whilst some participants were unhappy with such invasions, others felt much more strongly, wanting to go back to what they saw as a 'golden age' of exclusive LGBT spaces:

> LGBT people are made to feel isolated within their own communities by a cheap and nasty invasion of hen parties and homophobic bigots who come

into the village, because it's safe and they are far less likely to get the slap they deserve as a consequence of their anti-social behaviour. I wish we could . . . simply revert back to exclusively LGBT environments.

(Survey respondent 218: Gay female aged 45–54)

Talk of invasion clearly constructs boundaries and 'safe' scene spaces in opposition to 'dangerous', 'straight' spaces that are constructed as 'elsewhere' (Moran et al., 2003), or in Jackie's eyes, 'the rest of' the city. As participants suggested, the presence of heterosexual people could make lesbian and gay people feel less safe and/or that they were being 'gawked at':

I go in this bar and there are all these heterosexuals dancing on the floor and I felt myself going like, 'what the hell are you doing here?', but not only that . . . I didn't [dance], because immediately after all these years of not having gone to places like lesbian bars or anything I felt I don't want these men watching . . . I just feel less comfortable, [less] safe.

(Luce)

I think we all know sort of on [a particular street] there are certain bars you don't go to because it's going to be mainly heterosexual people and you're going to be sort of gawked at.

(Adam)

Participants acknowledged that LGBT people might currently access 'heterosexual' venues, but this was seen to be on unequal terms:

It's about equality rights . . . If you want to come and go in our bars, and I say our bars because that was the original intent, it was somewhere where we would feel safe . . . then you've got to reciprocate. So if we want to go into [a 'straight' chain pub] in [a small city] for our Sunday dinner and sit there and hold hands, then we don't want to get gawked at as we tuck into our Yorkshire pudding, right, and that to me is the equality bit.

(Timothy)

Linked to the notion of invasion, sometimes there was particular nostalgia for how the local scene had once been. In one town, participants suggested that there were only commercial LGBT spaces left in a nearby city, unlike an earlier 'golden age' when there were more varied forms of commercial and non-commercial spaces. They argued that things had "gone backwards" and that 'gay bar owners' did not support 'gay communities'. As Homfray (2007) has argued, spaces believed to be metaphorically owned by their gay and lesbian clientele are invariably owned by commercial breweries and chains, and hence are not often gay-managed or gay-owned. This has implications for who 'controls' the space, who is welcomed to participate, and even how 'gayness' is constructed:

The reason it [this city's scene] is so homogenised is because it's mainly owned by one group . . . It's a constant pain in the somewhere . . . It's very controlled, it's very corporate, it's very money-driven, it tries to stamp out DIY things that start. It sells to young people a concept of this is how you are gay . . . and I say gay for a reason . . . because actually that outfit is not really interested in LGBT . . . They are not community-minded.

(Gemma)

If heterosexual owners guided by capitalist motivations prioritise profit, they are unlikely to turn away heterosexual people and/or support LGBT customers in other ways they may desire. A space that some people understand as the basis for LGBT community can thus become conceptualised as not 'community-minded', when being 'community-minded' may never have been the intention of the venue owners.

Alongside concerns about invasion, participants frequently talked about their local scene as 'limited', whether in size or variety. However, dissatisfaction with the scene was most often voiced in relation to the quality of venues. As Gerry commented:

Having tried out gay pubs and gay clubs . . . most of them are 90%, 95% of the time, disappointing . . . You just think why do we put up with so much shit? . . . In towns and cities across the country, in towns in particular . . . where there might be only one pub . . . why does it have to be that bad?

(Gerry)

Nevertheless, a broader social environment that was assumed to be unwelcoming often led people to believe it was unsafe for them to go elsewhere:

I try to explain to people who are not LGBT . . . you have the supermarket, you have the rugby club, you have the library, you have all these places where we've historically learnt that it's not safe . . . [so] we're almost stuck [now] . . . I don't know of any other group that kind of subjects itself to . . . three really bad bars with broken toilet seats . . . Under any other circumstance anyone who had any sense of self-belief would not go in these places and put up with sticky floors and everything else.

(Jodi)

Believing they needed to seek safety in specific venues led some participants to feel that they had little choice in where they could go:

There's some bars and clubs in [city] centre where I don't go anywhere near because . . . I won't feel safe . . . so I feel more happier going to [club] or [other club] . . . My only issue is that where you can go is very limited.

(Ben)

Broken toilet seats within venues on the scene was a recurring theme in my research, and evidenced in Taylor and Falconer's (2015) study. Huw exhibited a clear sense of resignation about the toilets in venues that he felt he had little choice but to visit:

> Obviously no-one wants to go to toilets like that, but then you're just sort of, 'OK, that's how it is'.
>
> (Huw)

When participants socialised in non-scene venues, they sometimes had poor experiences that proved to them there was still an ongoing need for gay venues in order for gay customers to feel, and be, safe from homophobia:

> There's a big nightclub in [city] called [name] and the most homophobic [thing] that ever happened was somebody poured a drink over me in there while I was kissing another man. And I think there will be a demand for gay bars until those things are long in the past.
>
> (Matt)

Others also identified a need for gay spaces:

> When a group of straight blokes can be in a club and see two blokes getting off with each other and it's not an issue, there won't be the need for gay bars and gay clubs.
>
> (Carl)

A lack of choice was implicit where people wanted to be able to socialise on and off the scene, but felt that poor responses to same-sex couples in non-scene venues restricted where they could go:

> Things will be fine and great when I can walk into *any* place and my partner doesn't get harassed and I don't get some muppet trying to pick a fight with me because he thinks I want his girlfriend.
>
> (Jodi, emphasis added)

It was not only same-sex couples that anticipated poor experiences in non-scene venues. For Rachel, concerns about responses to which toilet she used meant that she felt her choice of pub was limited:

> I would like to go to a *normal* pub, but due to stupid things like using the facilities, in many cases that dictates where you go.
>
> (Rachel, emphasis added)

Some people therefore felt that venues exploited their lack of choice within small towns and cities where there were few LGBT venues. Taylor and Falconer (2015) have argued that 'disgust' within scene venues is saturated with moral values about other customers, for example related to their consumption of alcohol. However, I would suggest that my participants' dissatisfaction was more with bar owners for not fixing the toilet seats, possibly because owners believe that LGBT people have no choice but to put up with them. There is perhaps no need for owners to spend money on venue facilities when people in small towns and cities have so few 'gay' bars to choose from.

Ghaziani (2011) has suggested that some gay people may wish for 'difference-affirming' spaces, but I would suggest that a desire to socialise on the scene is more about wanting to avoid other spaces that are perceived and/or experienced as 'cisgender/heterosexual-affirming', rather than a wish to necessarily create 'LGBT-affirming' spaces. In other words, it is more of a push than pull affect. Matt also reflected on what he saw as a need for gay spaces:

> It's a sad reflection on our society that the only kind of places where these [gay] comings together are, are on the scene . . . Why can't it be in our [university students'] union bar? Why can't it be in the park?
>
> (Matt)

To answer Matt's question, this research suggests that LGBT people may choose to not socialise together in the students' union bar, in the local park or in a 'normal' pub because they are apprehensive about reactions they may receive if they are deemed to be 'different', for example by holding hands with a same-sex partner or going to the 'wrong' toilet. It is not always that LGBT people are fearful, although some people were consciously trying to avoid violence, but that they feel more relaxed in spaces where they are in the majority. Even if these fears are unfounded, it might be that for some they have become habit (see Chapter 4 for further discussion).

As I have shown, scene spaces can be understood and/or experienced as invaded spaces, where invasion by non-LGBT people is thought to reduce LGBT people's safety and challenge LGBT majorities. LGBT people do not want to be 'gawked at' for being 'different' in what was perceived to be 'their' space. There was a common feeling that scene spaces were still necessary, and hence some people felt they had no choice but to go to venues they found unsatisfactory, whilst simultaneously bemoaning the owner's lack of 'community-mindedness'. It may be, however, that it is an expectation that scene spaces will be more than 'just' a bar or club that fuels this dissatisfaction. Whilst people might prefer better toilet facilities, arguably they would also prefer more control over 'their' space. Many people might prefer more control over their local or favourite pub, but I suggest this lack of control becomes more significant when that pub is thought to be the basis of one's community.

## Chapter Summary

The research indicates that scene spaces regularly form the basis of LGBT people's understanding of community. Whilst they were very much appreciated and enjoyed by some, they could also be experienced negatively because of limited norms and other discriminatory or 'othering' practices. These experiences could undermine some people's identities and identity 'performance', and subject them to exclusion. Contrary to Mahdawi's (2016) belief, scene spaces do not offer 'unconditional acceptance'. For some, they are therefore not (always) synonymous with community. However, scene spaces were often thought to enable friendships and facilitate feelings of comfort, safety and 'diversion' away from heteronormativity. This illustrates how the scene can be felt as both inclusionary and exclusionary by different people, or by the same people at different times. The chapter has thus demonstrated how scene spaces can include some people, and in doing so facilitate a sense of belonging for some, but simultaneously exclude or marginalise others within this same, supposedly 'safe', space. The presence of non-LGBT customers could also result in LGBT people feeling less safe. As spaces which are frequently thought to exemplify or signify community they are therefore fundamentally problematic. However, despite varying degrees of dissatisfaction, there was often a sense that scene space is necessary, so people felt they had no choice but to visit scene-based venues or communities with which they were not always satisfied. Conceiving a community based around a space over which people have limited ownership and control is thus intrinsically problematic. Yet even for those who did not or could not access a scene, they could still have symbolic significance, suggesting they are a contested yet influential space, and a complex foundation for community.

## Note

1  Old Compton Street is within the Soho area of London and houses several 'gay' bars, cafes and restaurants.

## References

Abbott, D. and Howarth, J. (2005) *Secret loves, hidden lives? Exploring issues for people with learning difficulties who are gay, lesbian or bisexual.* Bristol: Policy Press.

Aggleton, P., Davies, P. and Hart, G. (eds) (1995) *AIDS: Safety, sexuality and risk.* London: Taylor and Francis.

Aggleton, P., Hart, G. and Davies, P. (eds) (1999) *Families and communities responding to AIDS.* London: UCL Press.

Bauman, Z. (2000) *Community: Seeking safety in an insecure world.* Cambridge: Polity Press.

Binnie, J. (1995) 'Trading places: Consumption, sexuality and the production of queer space' in Bell, D. and Valentine, G. (eds) *Mapping desire: Geographies of sexualities.* London: Routledge, pp. 182–199.

Browne, K. and Bakshi, L. (2011) 'We are here to party? Lesbian, gay, bisexual and trans leisurescapes beyond commercial gay scenes', *Leisure Studies* 30(2): 179–196.

Browne, K. and Bakshi, L. (2013) *Ordinary in Brighton: LGBT, activisms and the city.* Aldershot: Ashgate.

Cant, B. (2004) 'Facilitating social networks among gay men', *Sociological Research Online* 9(4).

Cant, B. (2008) 'Gay men's narratives and the pursuit of wellbeing in healthcare settings: A London study', *Critical Public Health* 18(1): 41–50.

Casey, M.E. (2004) 'De-dyking queer space(s): Heterosexual female visibility in gay and lesbian spaces', *Sexualities* 7(4): 446–461.

Casey, M.E. (2007) 'The queer unwanted and their undesirable "otherness"' in Browne, K., Lim, J. and Brown, G. (eds) *Geographies of sexualities: Theory, practices and politics.* Aldershot: Ashgate, pp. 125–136.

Coleman-Fountain, E. (2015) *What's the difference? Lesbian and gay youth 'after equality'.* [Online] Available at: http://discoversociety.org/2015/03/01/whats-the-difference-lesbian-and-gay-youth-after-equality/ [accessed 31.10.2016].

Cronin, A. and King, A. (2014) 'Only connect? Older lesbian, gay and bisexual (LGB) adults and social capital', *Ageing and Society* 34(2): 258–279.

Davies, P., Hickson, F., Weatherburn, P. and Hunt, A. (1993) *Sex, gay men and AIDS.* London: Falmer.

Day, G. (2006) *Community and everyday life.* New York: Routledge.

Ellis, S.J. (2007) 'Homophobia, rights and community: Contemporary issues in the lives of LGB people in the UK' in Clarke, V. and Peel, E. (eds) *Out in psychology: Lesbian, gay, bisexual, trans and queer perspectives.* Chichester: John Wiley and Sons, pp. 291–310.

Ghaziani, A. (2011) 'Post-gay collective identity construction', *Social Problems* 58(1): 99–125.

Ghaziani, A. (2014) *There goes the gayborhood?* Princeton: Princeton University Press.

Goffman, E. (1959) *The presentation of self in everyday life.* New York: Doubleday Anchor Books.

Holt, M. (2011) 'Gay men and ambivalence about "gay community": From gay community attachment to personal communities', *Culture, Health and Sexuality* 13(8): 857–871.

Homfray, M. (2007) *Provincial queens: The gay and lesbian community in the North-West of England.* Bern: Peter Lang.

Hughes, H.L. (2006) 'Gay and lesbian festivals: Tourism in the change from politics to party' in Picard, D. and Robinson, M. (eds) *Festivals, tourism and social change.* Clevedon: Channel View, pp. 238–245.

Johnston, L. (2005) *Queering tourism: Paradoxical performances at gay pride parades.* Abingdon: Routledge.

Keogh, P., Henderson, L. and Dodds, C. (2004) *Ethnic minority gay men: Redefining community, restoring identity.* London: Sigma Research.

Mahdawi, A. (2016) *Kissing my girlfriend at the Zodiac: Gay bars are everything straight people take for granted.* [Online] Available at: www.theguardian.com/world/2016/jun/14/kissing-my-girlfriend-zodiac-gay-lesbian-bars-safe-spaces [accessed 31.10.2016].

Moran, L. and Skeggs, B. (2001) 'Property and propriety: Fear and safety in gay space', *Social and Cultural Geography* 2(4): 407–420.

Moran, L., Skeggs, B., Tyrer, P. and Corteen, K. (2003) 'The formation of fear in gay space: The "straights" story', *Capital and Class* 27(2): 173–198.

Moran, L., Skeggs, B., Tyrer, P. and Corteen, K. (2004) *Sexuality and the politics of violence and safety.* London: Routledge.

Pritchard, A., Morgan, N.J., Sedgley, D., Khan, E. and Jenkins, A. (2000) 'Sexuality and holiday choices: Conversations with gay and lesbian tourists', *Leisure Studies* 19(4): 267–282.

Rogers, A. (2012) ' "In this our lives": Invisibility and black British gay identity' in Rivers, I. and Ward, R. (eds) *Out of the ordinary: Representations of LGBT lives*. Newcastle: Cambridge Scholars Publishing, pp. 43–60.

Simpson, P. (2013) 'Differentiating the self: The kinship practices of middle-aged gay men in Manchester', *Families, Relationships and Societies* 2(1): 97–113.

Simpson, P. (2014) 'Differentiating selves: Middle-aged gay men in Manchester's less visible "homospaces" ', *The British Journal of Sociology* 65(1): 150–169.

Simpson, P. (2015) *Middle-aged gay men, ageing and ageism: Over the rainbow?* Basingstoke: Palgrave Macmillan.

Skeggs, B. (1999) 'Matter out of place: Visibility and sexualities in leisure spaces', *Leisure Studies* 18(3): 213–232.

Taylor, Y. (2007) 'If your face doesn't fit . . .': The misrecognition of working-class lesbians in scene space', *Leisure Studies* 26(2): 161–178.

Taylor, Y. (2008) ' "That's not really my scene": Working-class lesbians in (and out of) place', *Sexualities* 11(5): 523–546.

Taylor, Y. and Falconer, E. (2015) ' "Seedy bars and grotty pints": Close encounters in queer leisure spaces', *Social and Cultural Geography* 16(1): 43–57.

Tóibín, C. (2016) *Gay bars are not only places to have fun, they are havens of freedom and relief.* [Online] Available at: www.theguardian.com/world/2016/jun/17/gay-bars-are-not-only-places-to-have-fun-they-are-havens-of-freedom-and-relief [accessed 31.10.2016].

Traies, J. (2015) 'Old lesbians in the UK: Community and friendship', *Journal of Lesbian Studies* 19(1): 35–49.

Valentine, G. (1993) 'Negotiating and managing multiple sexual identities: Lesbian time-space strategies', *Transactions of the Institute of British Geographers* 18(2): 237–248.

Valentine, G. (1999) 'Imagined geographies: Geographical knowledges of self and other in everyday life' in Massey, D. and Allen, J. (eds) *Human geography today*. Milton Keynes: Open University Press, pp. 47–61.

Valentine, G. and Skelton, T. (2003) 'Finding oneself, losing oneself: The lesbian and gay "scene" as a paradoxical space', *International Journal of Urban and Regional Research* 27(4): 849–866.

Weeks, J., Heaphy, B. and Donovan, C. (2001) *Same sex intimacies: Families of choice and other life experiments*. London: Routledge.

Weston, K. (1991) *Families we choose: Lesbians, gays, kinship*. New York: Columbia University Press.

Woolwine, D. (2000) 'Community in gay male experience and moral discourse', *Journal of Homosexuality* 38(4): 5–37.

Yip, A.K.T. (1996) 'Gay Christians and their participation in the gay subculture', *Deviant Behaviour* 17(3): 297–318.

# 7 Pride Spaces, Rituals and Symbols

## Introduction

Building on previous discussions about 'space', this chapter focuses specifically on Pride events as creating temporary spaces that were of particular significance for many participants. Drawing on participant data and existing research, the chapter will demonstrate how Pride events have the potential to create or support feelings of community, and offer spaces which can facilitate safeties and freedoms not always experienced elsewhere. I will also explore how Pride events offer possibilities to celebrate identities and party with others, which may or may not be conceived as political and/or involve elements of protest. The research identified a range of perspectives regarding previously documented tensions between 'party' and 'politics' or 'protest', though this assumed dichotomy has been questioned by Browne (2007), who argues that Pride events are 'parties with politics'. A strong presence of capitalism and commercial interests, including those related to the sale of alcohol, at many Pride events could be experienced as off-putting. Linked to commercialism, a lack of resources and the intersections of some people's identities could also contribute to the exclusion of some LGBT people within and from Pride events. In addition, tensions were evident about 'flamboyant' displays of 'queerness' that unsettled some participants who did not want to be (seen to be) 'different' or 'extreme'. Following an overview of existing literature on Pride events and how they relate to notions of ritualism and symbolism, the above sub-themes will be examined within nine headings: Creating Communities?, Safety and Freedom, Celebration, Protest, Partying with Politics, Commercialism, Alcohol at Pride Events, and 'Excess' and 'Extreme' Displays of Pride.

## Overview of Existing Literature

It has been suggested that Pride events offer liminal safe spaces in which 'transformations of self' can occur, 'consolidating' identities and 'building' communities (Howe, 2001). They allow "unapologetic expression[s] of identity, defiance of conservative sexual norms, and claiming of space and power beyond the confines of the gay ghetto" (Kates and Belk, 2001: 420). Other existing scholarship has also drawn attention to the relationship between Pride events and use of 'public' space. Browne (2007: 66), for instance, has argued that Pride events enable the enactment of otherwise hidden identities, creating a "temporary LGBTQ public" and "visible presence of sexual otherness", which points to the everyday hetero-sexualisation of space, and the presence of homophobia and heterosexism more generally. Browne and Bakshi (2013) suggested that Pride events 'allow' LGBT people to represent themselves whilst refusing homonormative agendas. They suggest that Pride events can bolster and celebrate gay identity, facilitate visitors' opportunities to express their sexualities more than 'daily life', and challenge fear and shame experienced elsewhere (Browne and Bakshi, 2013). Thus, "dancing on a float, experiencing the wonder of being part of Brighton Pride, or tentatively watching from the street, can be 'life affirming', even life changing" (Browne and Bakshi, 2013: 166). This is not to negate their flaws and imperfections, but to suggest that Pride events should be interrogated both in relation to their posi-tive possibilities *and* normalising and commercial impetuses (Browne and Bak-shi, 2013). Others have focussed on Pride events changing over time. Hughes (2006), for example, has argued that festivals that originated as protest marches for gay rights now appear less political and more about celebration, commer-cialism and attracting tourists. The attendance and participation of heterosexual people in Pride events has been described as 'de-gaying' Pride (Casey, 2004) and contributing to the 'depoliticisation' of these spaces, linked to their marketing as tourist attractions that draw heterosexual dominance and/or revulsion (Browne and Bakshi, 2013). These tensions concerning commercialism and tourism echo observations and concerns about visitors to scene spaces, discussed in Chapter 6.

Literature drawing on anthropological traditions can be applied to Pride events, highlighting their ritualistic and/or symbolic nature, as well as their potential as shared cultural rites of passage (Kates and Belk, 2001). Cohen (1982), for exam-ple, referring to the annual Notting Hill Carnival in London, suggested that rituals and ceremonies signify 'membership'. He argued that such events are "complex social practices, through which individuals are able to identify themselves with the symbols, show that they understand them, and thereby exclude others who lack the same awareness" (Cohen, 1982: 160). Symbols thus facilitate mutual recognition and understanding, helping to distinguish between group 'insiders' and 'outsiders' (Guibernau, 2013). Kates and Belk (2001), in their discussion of Pride, similarly suggested that an 'out-group' (in this example, 'straights') can strengthen feelings of unity and communitas within the 'in-group'. In suggesting membership and communitas, Pride events also indicate distance from others, which this chapter will go on to explore. Within her wider work on belonging, Guibernau (2013) also highlighted the importance of 'rituals of belonging', sug-gesting that rituals aim to generate a sense of closeness and solidarity among their participants. She sees 'rituals of inclusion' in positive terms, due to their ability to promote a sense of belonging, solidarity and/or feeling of community (Guiber-nau, 2013). Whilst 'ritualised' events in the UK may involve habit or routine, the overriding motivation behind Pride events in non-Western/Global South contexts are likely to be different. Brown (2009: 1506), for example, points to such events as "politically important expressions of public visibility that seek to challenge dominant social and moral conservativism (especially, at present, in much of Central and Eastern Europe, and countries in the Global South)". As this chapter goes on to show, whilst some people also saw UK Pride events as politically important, this was not the case for everybody. We should therefore remember that Prides are complex, and certainly not homogenous events (Browne and Bakshi, 2013).

Weeks (1996: 76) has suggested that a community must be "sustained over time by common practices and symbolic re-enactments" that reaffirm identity and difference. As Jenkins (2014: 179, original emphasis) argued, "we have to be made to *feel* 'we'". Whilst these arguments can be applied to Pride events as common rituals, I would suggest they can also be applied to people's 'affinity' with the rainbow flag as a symbol of LGBT presence and pride. Guibernau (2013: 4) has highlighted the importance of symbols in bringing "to the fore their own power as pillars of individual as well as collective forms of identity", which may or may not be recognisable by individuals outside the group. She argues that belief in a common identity and community comes from the use of symbols and rituals that strengthen (and visually represent) feelings of unity (Guibernau, 2013). Similarly, Cohen (1985: 12) also stressed the role of symbols as "ideal media through which people can speak of a 'common' language . . . [and] participate in the 'same' rituals". It is not difficult to apply these arguments to the visible presence of rainbow flags within Pride events, and more generally. Indeed, the rainbow flag was designed by Gilbert Baker to evoke (symbolic) pride and unity for the San Francisco Gay Freedom Day Parade in 1978 at the request of Harvey Milk (Lipsky, 2006). Whilst the rainbow flag may now be more widely understood or linked with LGBT people, it is (only) among LGBT people that it is more likely to have an emotional connection. Using a nation's flag as an example, Guibernau (2013) suggests that a soldier willing to die for 'his flag' does so because of its signification of 'his' country, rather than an emotional connection to the actual fabric. Though not suggesting that people are necessarily willing to die in defence of the rainbow flag as a symbol of LGBT rights (though that might be a possibility within some international contexts), Guibernau (2013) stresses the power of emotional attachments in generating a sense of shared identity, belonging and solidarity, which can be applied to the rainbow flag, as well as the Pride events within which it features. Symbols and rituals can therefore help mask group differences by highlighting commonality and fostering a sense of belonging (Guibernau, 2013). Pride events can thus feature as symbolic markers on a calendar, for some people the one day a year that the notion of LGBT community is realised.

Existing empirical research has indicated that there are a variety of current concerns connected with Pride events, which this chapter will go on to explore. Hughes (2006), for example, has suggested that as, and in part because, gay festivals have been promoted as tourist attractions, they have become less politicised and more about the 'party'. Johnston (2007: 30) has also observed that as tourist 'spectacles', Pride events can "strengthen western dichotomous categorizations of homosexuality and heterosexuality as distinct, separate and hierarchical subjectivities". In Browne and Bakshi's (2013) research, a desire for more politicisation was often framed by nostalgic narratives of creating community and solidarity through coming together (as 'us') in resistance and mutual support against a unified aggressor ('them'). They found that participants wanted a 'uniting' message against something, such as bullying, so that a common opposition could assist this coming together, especially where participants may not have much else in common (Browne and Bakshi, 2013).

Related to these themes, Brown (2009: 1506) has observed that it has become fashionable for academics and activists to deride Pride events as "the epitome of all that is wrong with contemporary 'homonormative' gay life", including significant levels of corporate sponsorship, but he argues that they are still culturally and politically important events, which many people enjoy. Browne and Bakshi (2013: 178) agree that "commercialisation is often used as a homogenous and supposedly unified trope against most large scale Pride events in the Global North", despite the lack of shared understanding about what makes a Pride event 'commercial', which might include paying to attend, making money for businesses and/or the involvement of business-focussed people. They propose that 'colluding' with state business interests does not necessarily make Pride events apolitical, because (commercial) parties can still be political, arguing that the 'celebratory politics of Pride' creates 'ordinariness' in spatially and temporally specific ways, which challenges the idea that protest is the only form of political action (Browne and Bakshi, 2013). The visibility and 'overt sexuality' of Pride events is in itself political to some (Waitt and Markwell, 2006). Just as the commonly assumed party/politics dichotomy has been questioned, so too has the politics/commercialism binary (Browne, 2007; Kates and Belk, 2001). Kates and Belk (2001), in their Canadian study of Toronto's Lesbian and Gay Pride Day, also complicate commercialism by suggesting that consumption can offer a way to resist dominant culture(s). They note that the event can be commemorated and remembered throughout the year by the wearing of a souvenir purchased on the day, such as a T-shirt, key-ring or badge, highlighting that this is in "contrast to the rather simplistic contention of a hegemonic commercial presence taking over the day" (Kates and Belk, 2001: 423). However, Waitt and Markwell (2006: 246) have suggested that because white middle class professionals "constitute the most lucrative market segment . . . it is their interests that typically dominate". Events premised on the notion of inclusiveness can therefore be experienced as anything but, because a shared sexual identity does not overcome "social divisions based on class, ethnicity, and gender" (Waitt and Markwell, 2006: 246). In the remainder of this chapter I will explore these themes in relation to participant accounts of their experiences of Pride events.

## Creating Communities?

I now examine how Pride events were linked with conceptualisations of community within the research. Hughes (2006: 240) has argued that "[Pride] parades are vehicles for the expression of commonality". Supporting this idea, some participants suggested that Pride events could aid or create community through bringing people together, combating isolation and facilitating a sense of commonality. This, in turn, can support affirmation and wellbeing:

> When one goes to events which are designed for LGBT [people] like Pride or the recent gay fringe festival in East London, the community is visible and this feels reaffirming.
>
> (Website contributor)

Visibility is therefore important, and symbolic flags and ritual events offer ways that LGBT people can set the 'tone' of a neighbourhood (Ghaziani, 2014a). Events and flags can also foster a sense of ownership and belonging, themes which run throughout this book. As a symbol of LGBT pride, participants drew attention to the rainbow flag and how it made them feel, alongside other readings of the flag:

> [Recently] I passed a newly opened children's nursery and on the gates there was a giant rainbow flag. What did it mean? The kids liked the colourful flag, there was a peace group, or just imagine a place where gay parents and workers could be open and the kids would grow up to be honest and accepting about their own and others' sexuality . . . It's funny how just seeing a flag made me part of a community.
>
> (Website contributor)

> You see the rainbow flags hanging over the shops and you feel 'these are my tribe, this is where I belong'.
>
> (Ruth)

Shared symbols as well as ritual practices can therefore support a notion or feeling of community (Weeks, 1996). Even when particular elements, such as the music, did not appeal to everyone, Pride events were often identified as important for bringing about a sense of unity:

> I am a big fan . . . I think they have a big role to play in bringing people together, even if just once a year. When I lived in [city] . . . there was always some trashy trance music playing, but it was still fun to go along and be part of that.
>
> (Andrea)

Fiona felt that large Pride events could facilitate a sense of community and pride that was particularly important for young people to witness or be a part of as they could feel isolated at other times:

> They [young people] go there with their banner and walk and see thousands of people and that's quite a big thing for them . . . having that community and having people to make it so that you aren't the only person, because it can be SO isolating.
>
> (Fiona, original emphasis)

Ben similarly suggested that Pride could validate young people's identities and raise awareness about diversity:

> I think that there's realisation that not only is it just not me and my little group, my group of friends, but there is a lot more of us and we come in all shapes and sizes, all different ages and ethnicities . . . I think that's good for young people, and for adults.
>
> (Ben)

Ben's feelings thus support Brown's (2009: 1506) assertion that Pride events can offer "a free sharing of embodied knowledge of the diversity of ways to do 'gay'". Pride events were therefore understood as supporting individuals, as well as creating or supporting communities. One of the ways in which Pride events often impacted upon individuals was in offering feelings of safety and freedom, which I explore below.

## Safety and Freedom

Building on themes of safety and regulation explored in Chapter 4, here I examine the potential value of Pride events for allowing people to feel safe and less 'censored' than in other 'everyday' spaces. Pride spaces were often conceptualised as 'community' spaces, and came into being in temporally and geographically specific ways. Whether predominantly described in relation to 'party' or 'politics', the importance of Pride spaces in offering safety and freedom from self-censorship was frequently highlighted by participants. Pride events facilitated people 'flouting' the usual 'risk' that such 'open' behaviours engender (Mason, 2001), with holding hands potentially seen as 'political' or a 'protest' in itself (Ghaziani, 2014b; Nygren, Öhman and Olofsson, 2015). Browne and Bakshi (2013: 167) identified "ongoing safety issues [which] means that Pride events, for some, mark a difference 'one day out of the whole year'". This contrast to every other day of the week was often explicit in participant accounts, where perceptions of risk may explain participants' inhibitions:

> Being . . . a community that can take over some street and act like every other straight person could on any other day of the week is important to us because we can't do that on a Monday through Sunday usually.
>
> (Jackie)

In some cases, participants were not aware of their own inhibitions until they attended Pride events:

> I sometimes wonder to myself, do I have such ingrained habits that are actually really sad, because if I go to a Pride I suddenly notice a change. That must mean that I have been inhibited although I didn't really . . . feel suppressed, repressed or whatever, but when there's a moment I can come out completely open, then there's a difference.
>
> (Luce)

Pride events can therefore be experienced as 'fortifying', like a "good shot in the arm to help us throughout the rest of the year" (Kates and Belk, 2001: 416), echoing how participants talked about certain holiday destinations and scene spaces within Chapters 5 and 6. The contrast between Pride and 'every other day' was often illustrated by participants in relation to public displays of affection. In Browne's (2007: 76) research, many women suggested they could show affection, express their sexuality and 'be themselves' at Pride events in ways that were not ordinarily possible. These sentiments were also evident amongst men in my research, who were aware of the potential risk of violence or discomfort at other times of the year:

> It was much easier to hold hands [at Pride] . . . Much easier to be intimate and kiss . . . All the things we've been consciously trying to do here [where we live] but obviously still aware of who's watching, you know, you need to be mindful of being bashed by somebody.
>
> (Shourjo)

> On the Friday night I wouldn't have felt comfortable walking down Regent Street with my partner, kissing and holding hands, whereas on the Saturday it was more than acceptable and we relished every minute of it.
>
> (Timothy)

For some, their everyday practices of self-regulation were contrasted with feelings of 'liberation' within (temporary, geographically bounded) Pride spaces:

> It's liberating sometimes to be able to do that [hold hands at Pride events], but it's quite a sad reflection on our society that we still have to think, you know, there's certain days of the year when we can be ourselves and do our thing.
>
> (Tony)

However, as Johnston (2005) identified, Pride spaces can, paradoxically, be both positive and dangerous, because whilst they can offer empowerment and support, they can also be sites where LGBT people face public abuse and/or social exclusion. Whilst Johnston (2005) alluded to social exclusion from 'mainstream' and/ or 'public' society, in my research there was also discussion of exclusion of LGBT people within Pride events (discussed below). In the following section, I discuss differences of opinion about the role or purpose of Pride events.

## Celebration

Pride events clearly meant, or provided, different things to different participants, supporting Cohen's (1985: 55) suggestion that "people can participate within the 'same' ritual yet find quite different meanings for it". In my research, there was a clear contrast between those who saw Pride, essentially, as a 'party', and those who saw Pride more politically or as a 'protest'. This section focuses on understandings of Pride as being about celebration, and it was this that had most appeal to some participants. Shourjo, for example, compared the celebratory aspect of Pride events to Indian weddings:

> The thing I like the most about Pride, especially London Pride, was that it was a celebration, it was joyous, and it's on a huge scale . . . I remember when my brother got married in India, I remember the whole family came together in celebration and joy, and I remember thinking at that time I would never have this, and Pride is sort of a substitute because you can celebrate who you are, and your relationships.
>
> (Shourjo)

Shourjo's reflections are reminiscent of Bassi's (2006) research, which compared Birmingham's British Asian 'gay' club scene to Indian weddings, because of the music and 'congregation' of people, though we also might assume sense of joy.

Carl alluded to people's different motivations in his references to 'flag waving' and 'a fight for who we want to be', but stressed that for him celebration was the key:

> I've never been a rainbow flag waver, I've only gone to Pride because it's an excuse to drink on the streets for a few days and not get arrested . . . It's more of a party and I think it's more of a celebration of who we are, rather than a fight for who we want to be.
>
> (Carl)

Jodi also stressed that for them Pride was a celebration, though they were aware that this might not be the case elsewhere:

> It's about celebration . . . at least in this country, it's a lot more of a party atmosphere, and I think it's more of a celebration of the contribution of LGBT people.
>
> (Jodi)

Pride events can thus provide 'life affirming moments' for LGBT people (Kates and Belk, 2001), reminding us that LGBT lives are not only, or always, about suffering and exclusion (Airton, 2013; Browne and Bakshi, 2013; Formby, 2015). Celebration can thus be challenging, and one could argue 'political' (Johnston, 2007), though not necessarily radical (Browne and Bakshi, 2013). I now turn to look at participant perspectives on Pride events as being about protest.

## Protest

Here I explore tensions around participants' views of Pride as political or celebratory. For some, there was an evident desire for Pride to be more political:

> I think that it could be, and should be, more politicised. I think that you have the march for 45 minutes to an hour and then after that it's a good piss

up . . . I would like to see more political awareness raising and consciousness building.

(Ben)

Ben clearly felt that Pride should be political, and his use of the word 'march' might also emphasise his beliefs about Pride events as being political, at least ideally. By contrast, other participants referred to Pride 'parades', though this did not necessarily indicate (wanting) a lack of protest within them. Some thought that Pride events were more political in the past, and therefore wanted contemporary Pride events to 'reclaim' this political focus:

> I think those [commercial] kind of Prides maybe do need to be reclaimed back into something a bit more tangible or meaningful . . . There is stuff which needs to be campaigned on, and there's a danger of people becoming too apathetic.

(Matt)

Some linked a lack of politics with a lack of community:

> Unfortunately Pride has been side-lined as kind of a carry on and a chance to get pissed . . . I think the community needs to be put back into Pride . . . I would like to see politics get put back into Pride.

(Gemma)

There was also a tension in how some participants talked about Pride explicitly in opposition to a 'party':

> For me Pride is definitely a protest. I can take or leave the party. It's nice, but I can go out any day and it's cheaper and there's less people, so that's definitely for me what it's about . . . trying to keep the marches political and ensure that those messages around what's happening in the UK, what's happening abroad, what's happening in our asylum process, are present in the parades.

(Helen)

> From sort of a trade union point of view, it absolutely drives me insane when people see Pride events as a big party.

(Colin)

As Nicky suggested, you can go to Pride without participating in 'the piss up':

> I go for the parade and to like show unity and to support people . . . but I'm not going for the piss up.

(Nicky)

Not everyone agreed that Pride events should have (more) political focus, however, with some, such as Matt, being reticent about what were referred to as 'shouty' methods. Matt also critiqued a politics based on assuming everyone is the same and therefore has equal 'need' to protest:

> There's something which happens quite a lot . . . is the phrase 'Pride is a protest', which kind of pisses me off a bit because for some people Pride is a protest, but for lots of people now it's really not . . . maybe like the tipping point came when there was just less to be angry about.
>
> (Matt)

Carl questioned the degree to which politics is a uniting force, suggesting that a shared party can be equally, if not more, unifying:

> I don't necessarily think the political aspect of it would tie too many of the younger generation together like a massive party would . . . which isn't really a bad thing . . . At the end of the day, surely . . . the end result for [activism] is for people to be able to be happy with who they are . . . so if the younger generation are . . . doing that already, then that's great.
>
> (Carl)

Matt's lack of connection with the 'Pride is a protest' slogan may reflect uncertainty about what this protest is and/or what there is for him to be 'angry about'. I observed a similar lack of clarity whilst walking within the trade union block at World Pride in London in 2012, where I was surrounded by chants of 'Pride is a protest' but without any visual or oral indications as to what or who this protest was about. Whatever their reasoning for, and/or preferred methods of, protest, it was clear that some people thought that Pride events should have a political focus or element. The extent to which this necessarily excludes a party is explored below.

## Partying with Politics

In the above sections I have focussed on celebration and protest, but this distinction can be blurred. Here I examine the idea that Pride events are 'parties with politics' (Browne, 2007). However, only a minority of participants in my research felt that Pride events could be both 'party' and 'protest' at the same time:

> The two can co-exist and you don't have to chuck one overboard just because of the other.
>
> (Jodi)

> To me it can be both . . . Why label it at all in those ways? It seems a little bit narrow-minded really as what's wrong with having a party and what's wrong with protesting?
>
> (Huw)

Petra suggested that Pride events need not be political all the time, but that people may need to be 'reminded' what they are celebrating. In doing so, they raised questions about what is 'political', commenting that the motivation and resultant safety levels might be political, but implying that because London Pride was not 'dour' or overtly addressing 'the war', that it was not (explicitly) political:

> It's very easy to go to London Pride and think that the war's been won and it quite clearly hasn't . . . I had a fantastic day, but it wasn't political at all . . . I mean it's political in the sense that the motivation is political, and it's political in the sense that . . . you can walk right across the middle of town and not only were you not beaten up . . . [but] tourists loved it! . . . It's so easy to be dour and political all the time but I think that people need to be reminded of why it's a celebration . . . It's easy to forget what underlies this whole thing.
>
> (Petra)

Helen also thought that some people distinguish between 'party' and 'protest' because they believe protest is 'depressing'. In thinking that protesting can be fun, she felt that Pride spaces could support both 'party' and 'protest' at the same time:

> It happens in the same space which is kind of interesting, but I think a protest doesn't have to be depressing and I think a lot of people associate it with that so they assume you can't have fun.
>
> (Helen)

Though it was suggested by only a small number of participants, the notion of partying with politics does clearly complicate an assumed dichotomy between party and protest. Participating in a (fun) 'ritual of belonging', which can contribute to a sense of LGBT solidarity, can in itself be understood as political. Yet the research raised questions about how politics is often understood, namely as dour and depressing, which meant that some people did not view protesting as fun. However, within discussions about what motivated people to participate in Pride events, participants raised concerns about levels of commercialism involved, which is explored below.

## Commercialism

This section focuses on perspectives on commercialism within Pride events, which has already been linked to differences between party and protest. Closely linked to debates about the place of politics and protest within Pride events, some people were concerned about what they saw as rising levels of commercial interest in Pride events and the negative effect this was having:

> The commercial side of things and the money-making side of things . . . have turned it [Pride] into sort of raping the pink pound rather than . . . a sense of

community and a sense of standing together, fighting against issues . . . That's all . . . fallen by the wayside.

(Colin)

A number of participants went as far as to suggest that some Pride events are *only* about making money, echoing widespread concerns about commercial Pride events documented, and critiqued, elsewhere (e.g. see Brown, 2009; Browne and Bakshi, 2013):

> I think there's nothing more horrendous than locking down [a] street with a metal gate around it and paying 20 quid a day or whatever it is to get in. It's not that it's not political, there's just nothing. That's not even a celebration of diversity or culture, it's an exclusive party to make lots of money.
>
> (Matt)

However, for some of my participants, the rise in commercialism offered the possibility for size that they compared favourably to their own city's Pride, which could serve to "legitimize and strengthen the event" (Kates and Belk, 2001: 401). As Gemma reflected:

> I've been to Manchester Pride, which I know some people think that's become a bit corporate . . . but as an outsider going to that event, it felt, well it was big. To be honest, stuff here often feels a bit cheap.
>
> (Gemma)

Gemma's view that her local Pride was 'cheap' compared to Manchester's might suggest that she equated validation and celebration with the level of commercial input, i.e. she was 'worth' that level of investment, which contributed to her memories of what she saw as impressive size. Pride events are clearly felt to be commercial by many people, but this can still feed into enjoyable feelings of 'ordinariness', and indeed pride. This is not to dismiss participants' concerns, however, as the remainder of this chapter explores.

## Alcohol at Pride Events

Linked to views about commercial input into Pride events, here I explore participants' concerns about alcohol at Pride, and how this made them feel. A perception of increasing levels of alcohol during Pride events was viewed as problematic by some participants. This was often linked to what they saw as decreasing levels of politics:

> I have attended local Pride events for over 10 years and have found that of late they have become less about equality and more about how much alcohol can be consumed.
>
> (Survey respondent 487: Female lesbian aged 45–54)

Fiona and Ben thought that the emphasis on alcohol during Pride events was particularly problematic for young people, which was a cause for concern for them as practitioners. They suggested:

> There is still far too much of Pride, as an event, shaped by alcohol and the pubs and clubs.
>
> (Ben)

> It's a load of men in hot pants getting pissed most of the time.
>
> (Fiona)

For some, the presence of what they saw as 'undesirable' elements, such as 'pulling' and 'pills', contributed to their criticisms. These were similar to some criticisms of the scene, as discussed in Chapter 6. Julie explicitly compared Pride events to the scene:

> It's lost its sense of pride. It's ridiculous, it's called Pride, but it's nothing to do with pride . . . it is about piss up and it's about a chance to pull . . . Pride has changed into the scene, that's all it is, like it's merged into it.
>
> (Julie)

A perception about the prevalence of pills limited or curtailed some people's participation in Pride events:

> I'm going to [city] next week but . . . I'm just going during the day, listening to some of the bands, and then coming home on a night because I'm not really . . . like pills and all that shit, I'm not really into all that.
>
> (Nicky)

For Laura, Pride events were "a bit much". Rather than just 'not being into all that', she found them "quite shocking". Whilst she noted the potential for "a great feeling of community" at some she had visited, she described some of the attendees as "virtually naked", and felt that the general environment was "very alcoholic" and hedonistic, which she did not approve of:

> My bad experience with Pride last summer . . . was very disappointing really, because I'd looked forward to going and I just thought . . . 'this is one of the reasons why I don't go into the Village' . . . You've got to enjoy yourself to meet somebody but you don't want to have things really hedonistic . . . [That has] definitely put me off going to Pride and getting involved with Pride ever again.
>
> (Laura)

The presence of alcohol at Pride events could therefore be off-putting to some participants who did not drink (much) alcohol themselves. This was also a concern for those who worked with young people who thought Pride events were potentially positive experiences, but who felt that levels of alcohol consumption detracted from this potential. The possibility of some people being excluded from and within Pride events was also identified as problematic by some participants, which is explored below.

## Exclusion

This section examines ways in which Pride events might (not) be experienced, with significant risk of exclusion a concern for some participants. Whilst many participants saw Pride events as (only) important and positive, others acknowledged that such events are not universally accessible to everyone. Helen, for example, felt that the cost of some Pride events could exclude some groups, such as the homeless and/or young people:

> Actually look, here's all the people that that community is excluding because they can't afford it, because they can't drink, or they don't want to drink, or you know, we do have homeless people in our community. I don't think they're welcome at Pride.
>
> (Helen)

Some contrasted who they perceived to be financially and emotionally 'comfortable' middle class Pride participants with those who they thought were not so comfortable or able to access such resources:

> The most comfortable people at Pride are white, middle class . . . and walking around comfortably with their wealth and resources, and each other. I spoke to some young people who were on the periphery and we had a debate about why they wouldn't enter . . . they were young unemployed people.
>
> (Eva)

However, it was not only the young and/or unemployed who were (at least partially) excluded, or who did not 'fit'. Some participants observed that, when combined with alcohol, levels of racism could hinder their enjoyment of LGBT space. As Gerry said of Soho immediately following Pride:

> Soho was great . . . the atmosphere there, people were spilled out onto the streets . . . I enjoyed it . . . [but] I think I was just a bit cautious . . . I was aware that people, as they were getting more drunk, were just getting a bit more careless . . . and I would be sensitive to that.
>
> (Gerry)

Though Gerry's concern here specifically related to the likelihood of racism, he is not alone in his concerns about alcohol. Other research has suggested that some gay men view all 'young drunk men' as threatening or 'risky' (Nygren, Öhman and Olofsson, 2015), with 'straights' associated with 'unreasonable' levels of drunkenness (Moran et al., 2003). However, Gerry's caution was notable in that it occurred in what might be described as 'safe' (scene) space, reinforcing that 'LGBT' space is not always or equally experienced as safe (see also Chapter 3). Gerry's 'caution' is an example of how participants sometimes modified their behaviour, discussed further in Chapter 4. However, for Gerry, awareness of the potential for homophobia *and/or* racism led to spatially specific risk-management strategies, explicitly connected to perceived safety levels in differing spaces and concerning differing intersections of his identity at any one time.

Gerry and Shourjo described World Pride as "brilliant" and "great", but both recognised the low(er) representation of South Asian people:

> You saw a lot of East Asian people and Latin American people but very few black or people from the subcontinent . . . It was quite a pleasant surprise to see a bunch of South Indians in a group and we hooked up with them and had a nice chat . . . It would be nice to see more Asian people and black people I think.
>
> (Shourjo)

Because of this underrepresentation, and possibly because of what he perceived to be underlying racism, Gerry felt that it was important to be 'counted' and seen at Pride events:

> We need to be counted, we need to be seen, and unless people like us . . . are seen at such events, maybe we'll never see anyone.
>
> (Gerry)

Though concerns were only raised by a small number of participants, this chapter has shown that Pride events have the potential to exclude, reinforcing themes running throughout this book, that feelings of belonging, sense of community and access to 'safe' space are not universal.

## 'Excess' and 'Extreme' Displays of Pride

In this final section I examine 'excessive' displays of/at Pride, closely linked to some participants' feelings about their own identity and how they wished to be perceived. Whilst Pride events are arguably about 'display', precisely because celebration with excess is an act of resistance to the status quo (Kates and Belk, 2001), they were troubling to some when associated with 'extreme' displays. A disadvantage of Pride events for some people was that LGBT people might become associated with excess in the public eye. Thus, "sites of carnivalesque transgressions, where normatively heterosexual streets are re-performed" (Browne and Bakshi, 2013: 159) were uncomfortable for some who, whilst wanting to 'claim' those spaces (for a day), did not necessarily want this to be in 'extreme' or challenging ways, or ways which drew attention to LGBT people or relationships as 'a freak show'. However, quite what concerned participants varied. Colin, for instance, worried about the 'dangers' of being viewed in the 'wrong', 'freakish' way:

> The danger is that if it does become too much of a spectacle, it becomes a freak show and then it doesn't become a celebration, it becomes a place for people to come and point and laugh, because it does become too extreme and it does become too extravagant, and then people start and look at it from the wrong angle.
>
> (Colin)

Carl, however, identified Pride as more about 'excessive', rather than 'dangerous', celebration:

> Pride is basically the gay cousin of . . . the Notting Hill Carnival . . . You don't eat that much food normally, you don't listen to that much steel music normally. It's about celebrating it to the excess and it [Pride] is about seven foot drag queens and fire eaters . . . It isn't a true reflection of what it is like to be gay, but I think that's what a lot of straight society would think.
>
> (Carl)

The following survey respondent also appeared less vehement than Colin: on the one hand he lacked empathy with certain people's 'queer' practices; on the other hand he found their flamboyance beautiful:

> I was brought up in a conservative/religious/upper-middle class family that rejects the 'Pride behaviour' portrayed by the media (showing the most beautifully flamboyant segments of the LGBT community) . . . I am very supportive of the LGBT community . . . [but] I can still feel not-so-empathetic with the most queer representations at Pride.
>
> (Survey respondent 4: Mostly masculine, performatively gay, aged 18–24)

Colin was thus most clearly 'resisting resistance', in not wanting to participate in "a carnivalesque celebration of excess" (Kates and Belk, 2001: 393). Kates and Belk (2001: 420) found that for some of their participants, "public sexual excesses of the celebration are too much and conflict with personal constructions of sexual identity". Shourjo also felt that visibility at Pride could be a 'two-edged sword':

> That's the danger . . . I think it's a two-edged sword. Whilst visibility in public can normalise things, it can also create an impression in certain aspects of the public that this is what it is, and I suppose I'm as guilty as anybody else because I associated LGBT with men in hot pants, and I didn't want to be associated with that.
>
> (Shourjo)

The 'flamboyant' visibility of Pride events had also not appealed to Gerry, at least in the past:

> A visible LGBT community through things like Pride . . . never spoke to me . . . If anything it was wanting to do the opposite . . . wanting to disassociate from them because . . . what they do show on news reports is something very limited. They normally show the more flamboyant, the more loud . . . men in underpants.
>
> (Gerry)

He linked his past desire to disassociate from Pride with wanting to fit in, "in a heteronormative environment", particularly as a young Asian man attracted to "male heterosexuality as a role model . . . [It] did appeal". Both Shourjo and Gerry had therefore gone on a significant journey from feeling some disgust at photographs of Pride events, to having attended their first (local) Pride in 2011 to "support the broader community", and then World Pride in London in 2012. Shourjo felt that it now "made sense" to him to be part of a community, so that LGBT people could support each other, which was a shift from his previous feelings of distance and disgust:

> I happened to look at [the] Pride march in London and there was a certain curiosity, but also certain disgust and, you know, 'I'm not really them' . . . 'I'm not that gay person'.
>
> (Shourjo)

Whilst many research participants clearly enjoyed the 'excesses' of Pride, others sought to distance themselves from other Pride participants who they saw as 'extreme', or even 'freaky'. Johnston (2005) has proposed that it is the flamboyance of Pride performances that attracts heterosexual tourists, as they can easily distance themselves from the bodies on display. However, this potential distance might have created the 'border anxiety' (Johnston, 2005) felt by some research participants who did not want to be distinguishable from the heterosexual tourists. Whilst Johnston (2005) referred to border anxiety for 'straight' tourists, I suggest that this also occurred for some LGBT people who were discomforted by visible 'queer' displays.

## Chapter Summary

As this chapter has shown, there are complexities regarding Pride events and their place within constructions of community. Whilst Pride events were largely understood as positive temporary LGBT spaces that facilitated people coming together and which could enable a sense of community, a range of concerns were identified that limited the potential for community and/or which help explain uneven access to community. Pride events can offer time-limited and spatially specific feelings of safety and freedom to some people, but not necessarily all. Those who do not drink alcohol, who cannot afford to participate or who do not 'fit' in some other way, can feel, or are literally, excluded. Others are not physically excluded but clearly feel in a minority, and/or the need for caution, due to the possibility of racism. As sites of celebration and/or protest, Pride events are nevertheless still sites of potential oppression, whether from within or without. These different experiences of Pride demonstrate that such events do not universally engender a sense of community or feeling of belonging. 'Flamboyant' displays of 'queerness' could be unsettling for those who did not want to be so easily distinguished from non-queer/heterosexual onlookers. Feelings of safety could therefore be simultaneously allied with feelings of exposure at being 'different'. As Pride events differ and change, and LGBT people differ and change, so too do people's responses to, and experiences of, Pride vary. Nevertheless, this chapter indicates that such events can still play an important part in some people's lives, both experientially and symbolically, contributing to potential feelings of community and/or belonging. Once a year, they represent a visual and/or imagined community that might not exist at other times. It is to these feelings of belonging and/or imagined community that the next chapter turns.

# References

Airton, L. (2013) 'Leave "those kids" alone: On the conflation of school homophobia and suffering queers', *Curriculum Inquiry* 43(5): 532–562.

Bassi, C. (2006) 'Riding the dialectical waves of gay political economy: A story from Birmingham's commercial gay scene', *Antipode* 38(2): 213–235.

Brown, G. (2009) 'Thinking beyond homonormativity: Performative explorations of diverse gay economies', *Environment and Planning A* 41(6): 1496–1510.

Browne, K. (2007) 'A party with politics? (Re)making LGBTQ Pride spaces in Dublin and Brighton', *Social and Cultural Geography* 8(1): 63–87.

Browne, K. and Bakshi, L. (2013) *Ordinary in Brighton: LGBT, activisms and the city*. Aldershot: Ashgate.

Casey, M.E. (2004) 'De-dyking queer space(s): Heterosexual female visibility in gay and lesbian spaces', *Sexualities* 7(4): 446–461.

Cohen, A.P. (1982) 'Belonging: The experience of culture' in Cohen, A.P. (ed) *Belonging: Identity and social organisation in British rural cultures*. Manchester: Manchester University Press, pp. 1–18.

Cohen, A.P. (1985) *The symbolic construction of community*. London: Tavistock.

Formby, E. (2015) 'Limitations of focussing on homophobic, biphobic and transphobic "bullying" to understand and address LGBT young people's experiences within and beyond school', *Sex Education* 15(6): 626–640.

Ghaziani, A. (2014a) *There goes the gayborhood?* [Online] Available at: www.youtube.com/watch?v=sB-yyD5qGuo [accessed 31.10.2016].

Ghaziani, A. (2014b) *There goes the gayborhood?* Princeton: Princeton University Press.

Guibernau, M. (2013) *Belonging: Solidarity and division in modern societies*. Cambridge: Polity Press.

Howe, A.C. (2001) 'Queer pilgrimage: The San Francisco homeland and identity tourism', *Cultural Anthropology* 16(1): 35–61.

Hughes, H.L. (2006) 'Gay and lesbian festivals: Tourism in the change from politics to party' in Picard, D. and Robinson, M. (eds) *Festivals, tourism and social change*. Clevedon: Channel View, pp. 238–245.

Jenkins, R. (2014) *Social identity*. Abingdon: Routledge.

Johnston, L. (2005) *Queering tourism: Paradoxical performances at gay pride parades*. Abingdon: Routledge.

Johnston, L. (2007) 'Mobilizing pride/shame: Lesbians, tourism and parades', *Social and Cultural Geography* 8(1): 29–45.

Kates, S.M. and Belk, R.W. (2001) 'The meanings of lesbian and gay Pride day: Resistance through consumption and resistance to consumption', *Journal of Contemporary Ethnography* 30(4): 392–429.

Lipsky, W. (2006) *Gay and lesbian San Francisco*. San Francisco: Arcadia.

Mason, G. (2001) 'Body maps: Envisaging homophobia, violence and safety', *Social and Legal Studies* 10(1): 23–44.

Moran, L., Skeggs, B., Tyrer, P. and Corteen, K. (2003) 'The formation of fear in gay space: The "straights" story', *Capital and Class* 27(2): 173–198.

Nygren, K.G., Öhman, S. and Olofsson, A. (2015) 'Everyday places, heterosexist spaces and risk in contemporary Sweden', *Culture, Health and Sexuality* 18(1): 45–57.

Waitt, G. and Markwell, K. (2006) *Gay tourism: Culture and context*. Binghamton: The Haworth Press.

Weeks, J. (1996) 'The idea of a sexual community', *Soundings* 2: 71–84.

# 8    Imagined Communities and a Sense of Belonging

"Most of all, community, as difficult as it is to articulate, is a feeling, a sense of belonging"

(Survey respondent 38: Female lesbian aged 35–44)

## Introduction

The possibility of imagined LGBT groupings and communities has already been established in previous chapters. Here, I explore further how these connections and a sense of belonging were felt and articulated by participants, often being described as a sense of 'something'. A sense of belonging was often hard to define or explain, but imagined connections between LGBT people were identified based on what participants saw as similarities, together with a belief that this created mutual understanding. This could gloss over degrees of difference and diversity within imagined communities. However, drawing on ideas of 'sameness' did not always mean that participants did not recognise the potential for differences between LGBT people. Whilst LGBT people might not always be 'similar', some participants identified the potential for shared values, as well as the likelihood of shared experiences. As I show, most often these shared experiences were related to discrimination, and to a lesser extent experiences of 'coming out' or 'living in the closet'. Significantly, I found evidence of participants 'imagining' (Anderson, 2006) or 'inventing' (Said, 2003) LGBT communities. This demonstrates how some LGBT people understand community in a broader, more amorphous way than has been documented in some previous research, such as that largely focussed on friendship-based families of choice (Weeks, Heaphy and Donovan, 2001) or personal communities (Heaphy, Smart and Einarsdottir, 2013).

Following an overview of previous literature on the concepts of belonging and imagined communities, this chapter proceeds within four headings: Belonging and Connection; Commonalities, Similarities and Mutual Understanding; Differences and Values; and Shared Experiences and the 'Bond' of Discrimination.

## Overview of Existing Literature

Yuval-Davis (2011) has suggested that 'belonging' is an emotional attachment and a feeling of being 'at home'; May (2013: 50) has proposed that when we feel at home, we feel "bodily comfort and ease". In acknowledgment of its multi-faceted nature, she drew attention to three different aspects of belonging: "relational (between people); cultural (the institutional order); and material (space and objects)" (May, 2013: 5). Drawing on Bourdieu (2000), she argues that in a setting where we feel at home, we have a 'feel for the game' and know how to behave and what to say, because we feel "a sense of affinity with people who share our habitus" (May, 2013: 50). Habitus therefore contributes to a sense of belonging with people 'like me' (May, 2013). May (2013: 3) suggests that belonging is fundamentally important to the self because, in part, we "come to understand who we are . . . on the basis of where and with whom we belong". As Guibernau (2013) argues, it is 'the group' that offers a home, which is a familiar space, whether physical, imagined or virtual, where people share common interests, values and principles. She proposes that a group can offer 'non-material assets', such as 'emotional closeness', 'moral support' and solidarity, likening this to a sense of belonging to a nation (Guibernau, 2013). Building on notions of belonging in relation to nations, Anderson's (2006) influential idea of an imagined community is based on the premise of comradeship and fraternity, regardless of inequalities or exploitations, to the extent that some people are willing to die for an imagined nationhood. Nationhood therefore becomes related to the feelings of people who think they belong, rather than to the world 'out there' (Yuval-Davis, 2011), and has similarities with imagined (Soja, 1996) or conceived spaces (Lefebvre, 1991).

For Guibernau (2013), nationalism is based on five distinct components: a sense of belonging and felt connection; a sense of shared history, including victory and defeat; a shared culture, including language, symbols, customs and rituals; attachment to clearly demarcated territory or landscape; and people's right to be recognised and able to decide upon their destiny. In this way, the nation forms a community based on five dimensions: psychological, historical, cultural, territorial and political. We can see parallels between this description of nationalism and imagined LGBT communities, for example in people's sense of belonging, shared history, cultural symbols and rituals such as the rainbow flag and Pride events, and attachment to particular spaces, most often the scene. Psychological feelings of belonging to an imagined community or 'quasi-nation' of LGBT people can help explain feelings of empathy and similarity across difference and/or geography, which might be described as " 'neotribes' united around shared sentiments" (Day, 2006: 222). Brown-Saracino (2011) used the term 'ambient community', as distinct from 'real' place-based community, to describe people's sense of belonging or connection based on shared tastes and activities, and an assumption of safety and acceptance. In contrast, Woolwine (2000) found that imagined community was experienced and believed in, but less important overall than experiences of community as friendship or community within and through participation in local organisations.

Notions of similarity and difference have long been the subject of scholarship. Guibernau (2013: 33, original emphasis) has suggested that "belonging automatically brings about the distinction between *members* and *aliens or strangers*", and the assumption that those who belong share similar norms and values. By feeling a sense of belonging with other LGBT people, people are simultaneously invoking both similarity to LGBT people and difference from non-LGBT people. As Cooley (1902) argued in his 'looking glass self' thesis, we think of ourselves both in relation to whom we resemble *and* to whom we are different, so that even those we do *not* identify with are part of how we construct our selves. Constructing a selfhood therefore involves *distance from* as well as *closeness to* others, as there is no sense of 'I' without a correlative sense of 'you' or 'they' (Cooley, 1902). Cohen (1982) saw communal identification as being evoked through, and reliant on, a comparative framework of similarity and difference, such as our similarity to each other, and our difference from others. People construct belonging in response to, or as a defence against, their categorisation by 'outsiders' (Jenkins, 2014). Difference is then asserted against these outsiders, thus symbolically constructing a mask of similarity amongst those 'inside'. This similarity is imagined, and yet "inasmuch as it is a potent symbolic presence in people's lives . . . it is not imaginary" (Jenkins, 2014: 137). These ideas clearly link to notions of 'them' and 'us' that have flowed throughout this book, and which continue to be salient in explorations of belonging and the desire to feel comfortable with people 'like me'.

The idea of belonging relates to boundaries and 'boundary maintenance' (Casey, 2013), and therefore who should and should not be included. As Ghaziani (2011) proposed, a sense of 'we-ness' is established through boundaries, as boundaries mark the difference between members and non-members. Moran et al. (2003) similarly drew attention to boundaries as a necessary strategy for building identities and communities. However, not only do these boundaries exclude non-LGBT people, they can also exclude LGBT people. Empirical research with and about LGBT people has evidenced such complexities with regard to belonging and imagined communities. Weston (1995), for example, noted that when people tried to realise a gay imaginary the results could be disappointing, and not equally accessible to all. She suggested that individuals are 'differently positioned' and have different trajectories, hence "the imagined community incarnated in gay neighbourhoods has been gendered, racialized, and classed" (Weston, 1995: 270). This has 'fixed' gay neighbourhoods as being dominated by wealthy, white gay men. For those who fall outside this group, knowledge of gay neighbourhoods does not mean that they will be affordable or guarantee that they will find people 'like me' (Weston, 1995). This casts doubt on Anderson's (2006: 7) notion of a "deep, horizontal comradeship". As Weston (1995) argued, 'the great gay migration' in 1970s and early '80s America both contributed to and undermined an imagined gay community. It perpetuated the idea that an urban life was required, at the same time as demonstrating to some people that this was a disappointment.

## Belonging and Connection

This section examines participants' perceptions of belonging and/or sharing a connection with other LGBT people. On the whole, participants thought that sharing a sexual or gender identity contributed to a sense of belonging. Many imagined that they shared something with other LGBT people, not necessarily forming an LGBT 'nation' (Guibernau, 2013), but an LGBT community at an abstract rather than physical level. When survey respondents ordered a number of options in terms of how 'true' they thought they were in explaining the development of historic communities, a 'sense of "belonging" or "connectedness" with other LGBT people' was ranked fifth out of 11. In explaining the existence of current communities, a 'sense of "belonging" or "connectedness" with other LGBT people' was ranked second out of nine, indicating that people thought LGBT communities of the past were less amorphous than they are today.

As previous chapters have suggested, having something in common does not equate to sharing the same intersectional identities, preferences for spaces in which to socialise or political views. This meant it was sometimes hard for participants to describe what the shared something was. Where they were unable to describe connections based on 'solid' experiences, participants often equated a feeling of belonging with being among what they referred to as 'kin':

> The concept of belonging to something, however kind of intangible that is as a concept, the feeling that you belong to something is part of your identity . . . I think that that's probably my best understanding of what a community means . . . finding your kin.
>
> (Gemma)

Perhaps even more intangibly, some participants suggested that the idea or concept of a community was more important than their own personal connections:

> I feel that the 'idea' of an LGBT community is actually more important that anything solid that exists in the real world. I've met plenty of LGBT people throughout my life . . . but I don't think I can say that I feel part of a group of people/sector of society just because they are LGBT.
>
> (Survey respondent 215: Gay—a bit queer too! man aged 45–54)

> A lot of LGBTQ* interaction takes place in bars and clubs which does mean I have more of a sense of commitment to 'the community' as a concept and group than I do to individuals that I know.
>
> (Survey respondent 486: Trans*, masculine gay queer attracted to masculinity, aged 25–34)

For Julie, a sense of belonging was linked to feeling in the minority, and/or the subject of ridicule. Reflecting Cohen's (1986) argument that being made to feel different by some people can lead to a feeling of being similar to other people,

Julie's feeling of being ridiculed contributed to her sense of having something in common with other gay people:

> There are more heterosexual people in this town than gay people, therefore gay people are entwined together and create their own community . . . Realistically you are going to have more in common with someone who is going through the same thing as you and that brings people together . . . It's the sense of belonging and being part of something that you have been ridiculed for in the past.
>
> (Julie)

Carl also referred to the idea of sameness, which he suggested was in part because of a shared difference that non-LGBT people might have an 'issue' with. This means that LGBT people could see value in grouping themselves together, whether physically or psychologically:

> When society . . . continues to be more accepting and more accepting . . . I still think there will be a sense of community . . . I can't imagine there ever being a point in time where everyone is perfect and . . . hasn't got an issue with someone being different . . . As long as it's like that, people are always going to feel the need to group themselves with people that are the same as them.
>
> (Carl)

A sense of belonging with other LGBT people, alongside some sense of separation from non-LGBT people, was common in participant discussions. This was often illustrated in participants' references to belonging with their 'kin', 'tribe' or 'own kind'. However, whilst many talked about a sense of belonging, others also talked of being excluded, which means we need to question assumptions of *universal* belonging or inclusion within a community, imagined or otherwise. Some participants did not feel that they belonged with other LGBT people, suggesting that some may need more than just a shared identity to share a feeling of belonging:

> As an LGBT person myself, I wouldn't say I belonged to those [LGBT] communities . . . I think it's important for people to find that sense of belonging but it's not automatic just because they identify with that label.
>
> (Andrea)

In the comment below, the participant distinguishes between his political views and his identity, and suggests that he once thought that he would feel a sense of belonging based on his politics, which had not turned out to be the case. This once again illustrates that feeling part of a community is not automatic:

> I am politically committed to equality, including sexual(ity) and gender(ing) equality, but this does not create my identity or sense of belonging, although I once thought that it would.
>
> (Survey respondent 196: Gay man aged 65+)

Whilst belonging might not be automatic, Ruth argued that if people are told or made to feel that they do not belong, they will make a place where they do:

> People want it . . . We want to be part of a community and if we're not part of one we jolly well make one . . . we just do need to belong somewhere . . . [and] if you're told you don't belong then you make a place where you can.
>
> (Ruth)

For those made to feel that they do not belong in a heteronormative world, the space they imagined was often focussed on a sense of LGBT community. For Weston (1998: 401), 'finding community' means discovering that you are not "the only one in the world". You therefore do not need to meet people to share a community; the connection comes from knowing of each other's existence (Weston, 1998). As one survey respondent suggested, people can feel that they are not on their own just by knowing that there is the possibility of meeting others, even if they do not actually meet those others:

> I don't live near a 'gay scene' but knowing that there are others out there that I can meet if I wish at, for example, Pride or by travelling to the nearest 'scene' means I'm not on my own.
>
> (Survey respondent 61: Gay female aged 35–44)

A sense of belonging is clearly not universal, nor is it straightforward, but the research suggests that a sense of 'something' shared was often experienced by those who identify as LGBT. How this was often explained is explored below.

## Commonalities, Similarities and Mutual Understanding

In this section I explore participants' accounts of feeling similar to, or having something in common with, other LGBT people, which they often viewed as contributing to their feelings of belonging and/or community. The notion of connections based on similarity is not new; the adage 'birds of a feather flock together' attests to this, as do similar academic discussions of the 'homophily principle' (May, 2013). As Browne (2007: 75) suggested, "imagined sameness ('to be with my own') can (re)create the idea(l?) of 'community'". Participants often felt a sense of belonging or shared connection with other LGBT people because they thought they shared something in common, which Wilkens (2015: 95) has referred to as a "community built on sameness". Colin compared the connection he felt with other LGBT people to feeling comfortable with people that supported the same football team as him:

> I'm a [football team] supporter, so if I went to a pub and I saw other [football team] supporters . . . I would talk with those and I would feel more comfortable . . . I think it's that kind of similarity that you can actually feel part of something if there is something that you've got in common . . . It

can manifest itself in various different ways, but it's the connection between people and sharing something in common.

(Colin)

A sense of similarity, based on an assumption that they would share the same issues, meant people often thought they would understand one another, simply because they identified in the 'same' way:

Obviously it's easier to talk to another gay person who understands the same issues you may have . . . there is a want to associate with your own kind.

(Dilys)

Similarly, Huw connected what he assumed to be mutual understanding with feeling comfortable with other gay people:

I've got a lodger and he's gay . . . I made it clear in the advert that I was gay, and I didn't say I wanted someone who was gay living there, but it just so happened that he came round . . . Maybe there are a lot of things that are understood without being spoken about . . . [and] I do feel more comfortable just being with him knowing that he's gay.

(Huw)

This desire for, and/or assumption of, mutual understanding can be linked to a 'vocabulary of values' (Weeks, 1996), which negates the need for explanation or self-censorship, as we saw in Chapter 4. In her research, Ellis (2007) identified lesbians and gay men wanting and believing in a shared perspective or understanding, which one of her participants referred to as a shared 'emotional vocabulary'. Similarly, for Petra what was important, at least at first, was a 'mutually understandable language', and not having to explain themself:

It's very, very nice to have friends that you've found and you can just talk in shorthand and there is a mutually understandable language.

(Petra)

Whilst having a mutually understandable language was felt to be important, this should not be equated with people being, or needing to be, the 'same'. Petra, for example, joined a gay cycling club where they felt comfortable, because even though they were not 'quite the same', they were 'similar enough':

They were supportively quizzical, if you know what I mean. We weren't quite the same but we were similar enough . . . It would be nice to go cycling with other people who I don't have to explain myself to was basically the motivation behind that.

(Petra)

Charlie identified a desire for some degree of connection or similarity with other LGBT people in order to facilitate what they thought of as a 'template' for living:

> There are some people who question the very idea of a network like an LGBT community . . . Straight people say, 'well why do you need that? If you think that you're not any different from us, then why do you need that?', but . . . they don't quite get that straight people . . . are the norm in society. They are given all of these templates to live by and we have none. We have to find our own. We have to find people . . . who are enough like us in that one way that we can connect with them in other ways.
>
> (Charlie)

Charlie's wish for a template to live by is similar to Weeks, Heaphy and Donovan's (2001) notion of 'resources for living' that are, in essence, knowledges and representations about how to 'be' LGBT. Weston (1998: 401) also drew on the idea of 'practical wisdom', which she suggested developed out of bars, friendship networks and gay organisations, and which helped construct sexuality as "a ground of common experience", rather than being purely 'personal'. We can see these ideas in Gemma's account of when she was younger and unsure about what it meant to be LGBT. Not seeing LGBT people in the world around her, Gemma thought that through going out on the scene she would meet other LGBT people and therefore learn what she would be like:

> For me, you know, coming out, I wanted to find out what it meant to be LGBT, I wanted to learn about what people were like, what that would mean that I would be like.
>
> (Gemma)

Overall, it was clear that people often focussed on what they saw as commonalities and similarities, which they assumed led to mutual understanding. For some, this focus could overlook or gloss over internal differences and diversities within (their) imagined communities. As I have shown, a belief in some degree of similarity could enable people to feel comfortable, and/or guide people in ways of living.

## Differences and Values

I now turn to focus on the notions of difference and values within LGBT communities. Although some participants referred directly to the notion of similarity or sameness, others acknowledged that not all LGBT people are the same, and therefore a connection may not be shared evenly amongst LGBT people. Whilst some participants alluded to differences amongst LGBT people, others such as Carl focussed on what he assumed were commonalities. For Carl, other demographics within a community no longer matter:

> If you've got a commonality that brings you together into a community . . . all those other aspects of your demographic go out of the window . . . When you focus on . . . one or two commonalities that you've got with someone that

means you're part of that community, all of those other things that seem to split people off in society generally aren't issues any more . . . Nothing else really matters, I suppose, it's just about that thing that you've got in common.

(Carl)

Within her working life, Gemma valued coming together with other LGBT people despite their differences:

We [colleagues] are from radically different class backgrounds, educational backgrounds, but we come together through our LGBT identities.

(Gemma)

However, participants did not always feel connected or similar to all LGBT people. For Gerry, sharing his experiences with someone of the same or similar ethnicity was particularly significant, reminiscent of Lehavot, Balsam and Ibrahim-Wells' (2009) participants feeling elation and joy when meeting other South Asian lesbians for the first time. Gerry therefore differed from Carl, who suggested that only those aspects of identity that people have in common matter. For Gerry, whilst he might share a sexual identity with others, ethnicity remained important:

Just hearing one of the chaps we met the other day talk about how his mum had caught him and a boyfriend of his when he was 16 kissing on the rooftop . . . Things like that are just wonderful to hear because I've never heard another Indian man say such things.

(Gerry)

Of those who participated in the research, Helen most clearly acknowledged differences between LGBT people. In doing so, she explicitly drew on the concept of intersectionality and suggested that the more identities people have in common, the more likely they are to share similar experiences:

I think the less intersectionalities you share, the less of that experience you share with someone else, and I use that meaning everything from where you went to school to the more traditional things . . . There are definitely some shared things, but the ways they play out in your lives are very personal.

(Helen)

Despite differences in people's identities, some participants suggested that shared values amongst LGBT people could contribute to a sense of community. Gemma, for example, identified that politics was as, if not more, important to her sense of community than a shared LGBT identity:

I don't see myself as belonging to the same community as people who go along to the mainstream gay clubs . . . for me in that sense community really, I hope, is something about politics and it's about shared values.

(Gemma)

Gemma did not think that she necessarily shared similar values with those who used LGBT services:

> As a service provider I'm not actually speaking to people with shared values, I'm speaking to people who need to access services . . . they're two very different things.
>
> (Gemma)

However, she did think that she shared values with others, like herself, who provided LGBT services, including those who did not identify as LGBT themselves. In doing so, she suggested that some people may feel part of an LGBT community even if they do not identify as LGBT:

> I think that even people who work here who don't identify as LGBT, I think they might see themselves as part of the LGBT community . . . What we all share here, I think, is a commitment to overcoming discrimination . . . there is a shared understanding that that is what we're here to do.
>
> (Gemma)

Other participants were keen to note the difference between sharing a sexual identity and sharing values, and they argued that 'like-mindedness' does not necessarily stem from having the same or similar sexuality:

> I think you have to be careful with equating like-mindedness with, like, sexuality, behaviour or identity; it's not the same thing.
>
> (Bryn)

Whilst Bryn critiqued ideas of like-mindedness, a minority of participants believed that LGBT people can share values and beliefs not related to their gender or sexuality, but which might also contribute to a sense of community. For some, this related to political views, whereas for others it was linked to food, and in particular vegetarianism. Gemma, for example, referred to this as 'lesbian food'. Whilst Matt identified vegetarianism amongst gay and lesbian people as stereotypical, he thought it could contribute to a shared outlook on life:

> I think what also brings together some kind of community is . . . those rather ridiculous but non-dangerous stereotypes . . . like the fact that loads of my gay and lesbian friends are vegetarian . . . a kind of shared outlook on life, whether it's serious political things or it's the fact that you love tofu!
>
> (Matt)

Throughout the research, there were varying degrees of acknowledgment of diversities within communities. It was when people understood community to be based on amorphous connections, perceived similarities and/or shared values that differences between people were more likely to be glossed over. Though the idea of shared values could contribute to a sense of community, participants articulated experiences that clearly suggest difference does matter. It is therefore important to take these issues into account when talking of community, rather than risk implying LGBT people are all the same.

## Shared Experiences and the 'Bond' of Discrimination?

This final section looks at the place of shared experiences within constructions of community, particularly with regard to discrimination and 'coming out' or being 'in the closet'. More so than the potential for shared values, what often emerged in discussions about connections and/or community were beliefs that LGBT people will share experiences:

> Whether it be speaking to people online, whether it be meeting them face to face, whether it be in a venue . . . [community] is about . . . sharing experiences.
>
> (Colin)

For some, it was the view that LGBT people share similar experiences that led them to view a community as being able to provide support and acceptance:

> It makes sense to be part of the community so that we can support each other. Because we all have had similar experience, have all been in a minority position and we've had to fight to be accepted.
>
> (Shourjo)

Shourjo's belief that LGBT people will have shared similar negative experiences was also evident within survey findings. When survey respondents ordered a number of options in terms of how 'true' they thought they were in explaining the historical development of communities, 'shared experience of prejudice or discrimination' was ranked third highest out of 11. In relation to current communities, participants ranked 'shared experience of prejudice or discrimination' fourth out of nine. The belief that most LGBT people will have faced negativity or prejudice at some point in their lives was shared by many participants:

> I'm sure most of us have in some way, I expect, experienced some sort of negativity to homosexuality and we have . . . a shared background which we all relate to.
>
> (Adam)

> Most people have experienced prejudice in their day to day lives and that prejudice can vary, but there is a shared sense of prejudice there.
>
> (Helen)

Participants often assumed that a sense of community stemmed from a bond based on previous experiences of discrimination, what Weeks, Heaphy and Donovan

(2001: 28) referred to as a unifying "institutionalised hostility towards homosexuality" (and I would add towards non-normative gender identities). Experiences of prejudice were thus thought to unite LGBT people regardless of other differences, because of the degree of empathy with some shared level of 'struggle':

> What kind of unites us is the fact that we've all struggled through something. Now depending on where you are in the world and what age you are will determine how much you've had to fight [but] . . . I think that's what unites me as a 21 year old white gay man with, I don't know, a 65 year old trans woman . . . I don't want to say her pain is my pain . . . maybe that's patronising to her . . . [but] you can empathise with their situation.
>
> (Matt)

Jason did not necessarily believe he would have much in common with other gay people, but he did identify a sense of *concern* for other LGBT people around the world:

> I'd feel for them [other LGBT people], just in case they'd been through what I've been through.
>
> (Jason)

Many participants suggested that experiences of discrimination and other shared bonds transcended differences within communities. However, Woolwine (2000) found that his participants either denied the existence of community because of diversity, or 'dwelled on the divisions'. This did not necessarily mean his participants rejected the possibility of any form of unifying experience, however. Whilst his participants denied *community* on the basis of division, they did identify *commonality* on the basis of 'alienation' and 'marginalisation' (Woolwine, 2000).

Ruth was clear that a sense of community for her had come from sharing experiences of oppression and 'the effect of the closet' "at a time when we couldn't share it with anyone else". Matt also identified a time when he had not been able to share a particularly difficult experience. Discussing a school trip to Auschwitz[1] before he 'came out', Matt was upset that he had only been able to articulate a sense of connection with what happened to Jews during the holocaust, but not what happened to gay men:

> When I was at school I went on a trip to Auschwitz . . . because everyone knew I was Jewish, but no-one knew I was gay . . . I felt so hurt by the fact that it would have been me who was dragged into that gas chamber . . . because I was Jewish, yes, but [also] because I was gay . . . That really hit me and I couldn't tell anyone about it.
>
> (Matt)

For Ruth, a changing social context since her youth meant that she found more recent communities harder to define than her earlier experiences of community "when it was a kind of ghetto". Whilst her feelings of belonging to a 'ghetto' may have declined, Ruth did still identify some sense of community at particular events:

> We march under banners at Pride with people who we wouldn't speak to the rest of the week [because] there is that sort of sense of community which basically comes from being oppressed . . . You have to have something in common, if you don't feel you've got anything in common, you're not a community.
>
> (Ruth)

Ruth echoed sentiments from Brown-Saracino's (2011) research that found that nostalgia informs a sense of lost 'ghettoised' community, in comparison to more 'ambient' forms of community that might be experienced in the present day.

Jodi also made reference to the importance of shared experiences in the past, suggesting that there might have been stronger bonds or need for community then:

> It was a lot worse 20, 30, 40 years ago and I think that there was a need for that sense of solidarity and to have a beacon that others could aim for . . . That's almost like the grandparents of the community is those little places where we had to go because it was illegal.
>
> (Jodi)

Whilst participants most often identified shared experiences related to prejudice, shared experiences of 'coming out' were also seen as important. Helen, for example, thought that experiences of coming out could facilitate or prompt an, albeit intangible, connection between LGBT people. Talking about experiences of coming out could therefore support or stimulate friendship:

> Everyone's got a coming out story and so there is something to talk about . . . Because my aunt's gay . . . my mum was like, 'you two do share something', and it's not quite tangible . . . I think as long as people are having to come out, as long as there's difficulties they face when they're doing that . . . then there's going to be that sort of shared identity and history and as a result you're naturally going to kind of form friendships.
>
> (Helen)

As we have seen, participants often believed that LGBT people will have shared experiences of prejudice, 'coming out' and/or 'the effect of the closet'. In turn, these experiences were thought to contribute to connections between those who identified as LGBT. Where people did not feel this degree of similarity or sameness, they did still often emphasise a degree of empathy.

## Chapter Summary

This chapter has shown the degree to which belonging and notions of connection are complex and by no means even or universal. Community can be experienced, and valued, as intangible as well as tangible. Whilst sameness was a concept frequently drawn on by participants, this did not always mean that they overlooked difference, as their sense of belonging was not always predicated on similarity. Participants' constructions of LGBT communities were often reliant on what they perceived to be differences from a heterosexual/cisgender 'other' (or 'them') *and* similarities between 'us'. Imagined communities offer a way of believing in collective identities and belonging without necessarily basing this on the idea of similar, or the 'same', identities. However, many participants did commonly focus on what they saw as commonalities or similarities, which they assumed would foster mutual understanding and feelings of comfort, as well as offer guidance for living. Perceived similarities or empathies were often based on experiences of prejudice, 'coming out' or 'the closet'. Some also felt that shared values could contribute to a sense of community, and for some, these values were thought to transcend differences within communities. Use of the term community as a catchall for people often does not acknowledge these complexities, even though they have real implications for LGBT people's lived experiences and wellbeing, which I explore in the next chapter.

## Note

1  Auschwitz was a German Nazi concentration camp in Poland, which is now a memorial and museum.

## References

Anderson, B. (2006) *Imagined communities: Reflections on the origin and spread of nationalism*. London: Verso.

Browne, K. (2007) 'A party with politics? (Re)making LGBTQ Pride spaces in Dublin and Brighton', *Social and Cultural Geography* 8(1): 63–87.

Bourdieu, P. (2000) *Pascalian meditations*. Cambridge: Polity.

Brown-Saracino, J. (2011) 'From the lesbian ghetto to ambient community: The perceived costs and benefits of integration for social ties', *Social Problems* 58(3): 361–388.

Casey, M.E. (2013) 'Belonging: Lesbians and gay men's claims to material spaces' in Taylor, Y. and Addison, M. (eds) *Queer presences and absences*. Basingstoke: Palgrave Macmillan, pp. 141–158.

Cohen, A.P. (1982) 'Belonging: The experience of culture' in Cohen, A.P. (ed) *Belonging: Identity and social organisation in British rural cultures*. Manchester: Manchester University Press, pp. 1–18.

Cohen, A.P. (1986) 'Of symbols and boundaries, or, does Ertie's greatcoat hold the key?' in Cohen, A.P. (ed) *Symbolising boundaries: Identity and diversity in British cultures*. Manchester: Manchester University Press, pp. 1–21.

Cooley, C.H. (1902) *Human nature and the social order*. New York: Charles Scribner's Sons.

Day, G. (2006) *Community and everyday life*. New York: Routledge.

Ellis, S.J. (2007) 'Community in the 21st century: Issues arising from a study of British lesbians and gay men' in Peel, E., Clarke, V. and Drescher, J. (eds) *British lesbian, gay, and bisexual psychologies: Theory, research, and practice.* Binghamton: The Haworth Medical Press.

Ghaziani, A. (2011) 'Post-gay collective identity construction', *Social Problems* 58(1): 99–125.

Guibernau, M. (2013) *Belonging: Solidarity and division in modern societies.* Cambridge: Polity Press.

Heaphy, B., Smart, C. and Einarsdottir, A. (2013) *Same sex marriages: New generations, new relationships.* Basingstoke: Palgrave Macmillan.

Jenkins, R. (2014) *Social identity.* Abingdon: Routledge.

Lefebvre, H. (1991) *The production of space.* Oxford: Blackwell.

Lehavot, K., Balsam, K.F. and Ibrahim-Wells, G.D. (2009) 'Redefining the American quilt: Definitions and experiences of community among ethnically diverse lesbian and bisexual women', *Journal of Community Psychology* 37(4): 439–458.

May, V. (2013) *Connecting self to society: Belonging in a changing world.* New York: Palgrave Macmillan.

Moran, L., Skeggs, B., Tyrer, P. and Corteen, K. (2003) 'The formation of fear in gay space: The "straights" story', *Capital and Class* 27(2): 173–198.

Said, E. (2003) *Orientalism.* London: Penguin.

Soja, E.W. (1996) *Thirdspace: Expanding the geographical imagination.* Oxford: Blackwell.

Weeks, J. (1996) 'The idea of a sexual community', *Soundings* 2: 71–84.

Weeks, J., Heaphy, B. and Donovan, C. (2001) *Same sex intimacies: Families of choice and other life experiments.* London: Routledge.

Weston, K. (1995) 'Get thee to a big city: Sexual imaginary and the great gay migration', *GLQ: A Journal of Lesbian and Gay Studies* 2(3): 253–277.

Weston, K. (1998) 'Families we choose' in Nardi, P.M. and Schneider, B.E. (eds) *Social perspectives in lesbian and gay studies: A reader.* London: Routledge, pp. 390–411.

Wilkens, J. (2015) 'Loneliness and belongingness in older lesbians: The role of social groups as "community"', *Journal of Lesbian Studies* 19(1): 90–101.

Woolwine, D. (2000) 'Community in gay male experience and moral discourse', *Journal of Homosexuality* 38(4): 5–37.

Yuval-Davis, N. (2011) *The politics of belonging.* London: Sage.

# 9   Consequences for Wellbeing

"Belonging is not an option for any of us—a sense of belonging is vital for our wellbeing"

(Kehily, 2007: 173)

## Introduction

This penultimate chapter explores views on LGBT communities in relation to their impact on health, wellbeing and 'quality of life'. It will examine the impact of community 'membership' on some people's physical health and, for larger numbers of people, the beneficial impacts on mental health and emotional wellbeing. In particular, the chapter demonstrates how forms of community can offer support, information and/or friendship, which in turn can aid affirmation and identity validation and foster self-confidence and self-esteem. I will also explore how participants viewed some LGBT people as 'dangerous', particularly in relation to alcohol and/or drug consumption and 'unsafe' sex. The chapter will identify how 'LGBT spaces', such as the commercial scene, can be conceptualised as both (partially) 'safe' from heterosexuals and 'risky' or exclusionary as a result of the practices of other(ed) LGBT people. It will thus demonstrate how the scene can be homogenised and/or demonised by LGBT people, at the same time as scene spaces are often held up as positive evidence of urban cosmopolitanism and/or diversity. As I argue, community can be understood and experienced in positive terms, but also conceptualised and experienced negatively or contradictorily, illustrating the inherent complexities within discussions of community. Following a contextual overview of existing literature, I will explore these tensions and contradictions within six headings: Impacts on Physical and Mental Health; Seeking Support; Friendships, Confidence and Self-Esteem; Finding People 'Like Me'; Alcohol, Drugs and Sex on the Scene; and Paradoxical Spaces.

## Overview of Existing Literature

There is a wealth of evidence on LGBT health inequalities that space does not allow me to include here, but I do summarise existing research themes that relate to community. As Kehily (2007) and others suggest, a sense of belonging is important for wellbeing. May (2013) has noted that belonging requires mutual 'seeing and hearing', i.e. recognition and/or acceptance, which in turn contributes to self-confidence, self-respect and self-esteem. Not having a sense of membership in a community or society can therefore have a negative effect on people's sense of self (May, 2013). Ellis (2007) identified the role of community in (re)affirming a positive sense of self through providing physical or metaphorical space 'to be oneself'. 'Community attachment' and 'social engagement' have been significant themes within sexual health promotion work. This has included, for example, exploration of patterns of social relationships and civic engagement and their potential impact on sexual practices, which in turn have implications for HIV prevention policy and practice (Holt, 2011; Wilkinson et al., 2012). Similar ideas have been examined within psychology. Frost and Meyer (2012), for example, suggested that 'community connectedness' was associated with increased psychological and social wellbeing. Pugh (2002) also argued that being or feeling part of a community can be positive in terms of social support for health, wellbeing and 'quality of life', particularly in older age. However, these potential 'abstract' gains can be un(der)acknowledged in some research. Rothblum (2010: 460), for example, has suggested that women may be "yearning for" support, and yet LBQ 'resources' offer only "a good time" in the form of bars, clubs and social events. This view seems to oversimplify perspectives on the role and value of commercial scenes and minimises their potential impact beyond 'a good time' (Browne and Bakshi, 2013; Weston, 1991).

Woolwine (2000: 24) has examined the impact of friendships, suggesting that for his participants "it was only among individuals 'like oneself' that one could relax, let one's hair down", and find "support and acceptance of oneself as a gay man". Heath and Mulligan (2008) similarly found that lesbians felt able to 'be themselves' in certain environments, with 'feeling normal' said to combat isolation and contribute to feelings of comfort, ease and safety. Community participation was seen as facilitating 'respite' and 'resilience'; conversely, 'not being able to be yourself' was linked to the concept of 'minority stress' (Heath and Mulligan, 2008). However, this concept has been critiqued from within sociology for relying too much on individualistic and/or psychological responses to unequal social and cultural contexts (Donovan and Hester, 2014). Nevertheless, sociologists such as Weeks, Heaphy and Donovan have also suggested that "close non-heterosexual friends and sympathetic others" can heighten LGB self-confidence (Weeks, Heaphy and Donovan, 2001: 189).

Research has also examined the provision of care within and between groups of LGBT people. Weston (1991), for instance, found examples of caring relationships between friends as they got older. More recently, Monro (2015: 90) has suggested that organised bisexual communities "actively support mutual care", including 'volunteer counselling', 'cuddle and massage workshops', "the culture of cake-eating" and "the widespread provision of safer sex supplies and workshops". However, there is also a plentiful supply of safer sex resources on the commercial scene, albeit largely targeted at gay men, and the notion of 'organised' support for cake-eating as a form of care-giving could perhaps be questioned (though personally I like the idea!). Hines (2007, 2010) has documented the role of trans community/support groups in enabling information sharing and mutual support, especially at times of transition, and particularly in a context where appropriate and/or desired care may be lacking in broader medical, social and welfare provision. In doing so, she compared these 'practices of care' to those that emerged among groups, particularly gay men, affected by the HIV/AIDS epidemic (Hines, 2007, 2010). Within other research, a similar 'ethic of care' within lesbian and gay friendship families has been identified and distinguished from an 'ethic of obligation' within biological families/families of origin (Simpson, 2013b; Weeks, Heaphy and Donovan, 2001). However, Holt (2011) found that some of his younger respondents said they avoided what they saw as an 'unhealthy' 'over-reliance' on gay networks or communities, which contrasts with these discussions about the importance of gay friendships.

Research exploring LGBT health and wellbeing has also suggested areas of concern, including reportedly higher levels of illegal or 'street' drug use by LGBT people than by cisgender heterosexual people (Buffin et al., 2012; Guasp, 2012; Hunt and Fish, 2008; Rooney, 2012), though this may result from scene-based recruitment of research participants (McManus, 2003). Lesbian and gay men's drug use has been linked to wanting to 'separate' themselves from the heteronormative environment of their everyday lives (Valentine and Skelton, 2003). Gay and bisexual men's drug use has also been linked to a desire to escape stress, loneliness or unhappiness; lessen social or sexual unease; and to the influence of broader social norms on the scene (Keogh et al., 2009). Research has also identified issues related to body image dissatisfaction and/or 'muscle dysmorphia' among gay men, which some have linked to eating disorders and/or steroid use (Bolding, Sherr and Elford, 2002; Chaney, 2008; Levesque and Vichesky, 2006; Tiggemann, Martins and Kirkbride, 2007; Yelland and Tiggemann, 2003).

Other work has highlighted complexities regarding wellbeing. Cant (2008: 45), for example, described the scene as potentially 'damaging' to gay men's mental health "as it draws gay men towards it but then makes them feel inadequate when they are there". However, he also suggested that feeling part of a group can enhance a sense of wellbeing. As such, accessing sexual health promotion material targeted at gay men can be experienced as valuable not only for the information provided, but also for the sense that men are part of a larger group engaging with similar concerns (Cant, 2008). Previous research has shown that "community can be experienced as both enabling and disabling . . . supportive and excluding" (Fraser, 2008: 255), and that on the scene individuals can "experience moments of belonging, entitlement and exclusion simultaneously" (Moran and Skeggs, 2001: 418). Valentine and Skelton (2003) have also identified the ambiguity of the scene, suggesting it can be both a liberating and supportive space that offers a sense of identity, community and belonging, and a dangerous space in which young lesbians and gay men face a variety of risks and exclusions. More recently, research with middle-aged gay men has found that the scene can be a site of self-expression and 'play', as well as exclusion or oppression (Simpson, 2013a). Such complexities and paradoxical relations have been illustrated throughout this book and will be returned to in further detail below. However, it is important to note that much of this literature specifically concerns the scene, and it would be wrong to assume that these same observations apply to people's conceptualisations of community more broadly, although there is often some 'word slippage'/conflation between the two.

## Impacts on Physical and Mental Health

In this section, I focus on participant perspectives on physical and mental health and how these can be influenced by a sense of community. When asked whether they thought feeling part of one or more LGBT communities had any impact on their physical health, survey results were mixed: 37% did not think there had been an impact, 36% reported a positive impact, 4% thought there had been a negative impact and 23% did not know or did not feel part of one or more communities. A small number of participants provided illustrations of positive impacts on physical health. One participant, for example, suggested that belonging to particular social groups can facilitate or encourage sporting activities, which they linked to physical wellbeing:

> In terms of physical health, I have taken part in social sporting activities with lesbian groups—country walks, walking holidays, 5-a-side football tournaments, sponsored charity fun runs, race for life. Being part of the group has made it a lot easier to participate in these activities.
>
> (Survey respondent 513: Female lesbian aged 35–44)

Nevertheless, for some of those who had limited access to particular events or spaces, such as the scene, this was interpreted as restricting their access to LGBT community, which in turn was felt to have a negative impact on their health. In doing so, participants demonstrated how physical ill-health could limit physical access to communities, which then impacted upon their mental health. This not only shows that physical and mental wellbeing can be intrinsically linked, but also the importance of face-to-face interactions for some people:

> I have chronic fatigue syndrome, which prevents me from participating in many ordinary social activities, especially those which take place in the evening or involve physical activity, including LGBT community events. The 'scene' is a particular problem to me. Attempting to participate can make my physical health worse . . . On the other [hand], not being able to attend is tough on my mental health because it is hard to feel connected when you can't see people face to face.
>
> (Survey respondent 394: Queer [bisexual] woman aged 25–34)

It was mental health and emotional wellbeing that was most often the focus of participant discussions about health. Some participants, for example, linked the idea of community to the possibility of gaining mutual support, and even their 'survival':

> I don't think I could survive if I couldn't interact with other lesbians.
> (Survey respondent 263: Female lesbian aged 45–54)

Survey results on mental health and emotional wellbeing were clearer than they were on physical health: 74% reported that LGBT communities had had a positive impact, 6% did not feel any impact, 4% reported a negative impact and 16% did not know or did not feel part of one or more LGBT communities. Results were similar for an equivalent question on 'quality of life': 72% felt that LGBT communities had had a positive impact, 10% did not feel any impact, 2% reported a negative impact and 16% did not know or did not feel part of one or more LGBT communities. Illustrating the importance some people attached to LGBT community for their wellbeing, some participants, particularly women, saw community as a 'lifeline' and a way to experience life more fully:

> As a disabled lesbian with a chronic illness who came out late in life my local community lesbian group has been a lifeline.
> (Survey respondent 497: Female lesbian aged 55–64)

> I think I'd have survived without an LGBT community, but I don't think I would be truly alive in the same sense.
> (Survey respondent 164: Bi/queer/glittery female aged 18–24)

For some, the importance of a sense of community was specifically related to its role as a counterbalance to the presence of homophobia in society. A feeling of belonging to an LGBT community could therefore be perceived as 'vital':

> My sense of community and belonging is vital in balancing the prejudice and resulting anxiety of homophobia.
> (Survey respondent 447: Gay and/or lesbian [I identify
> with neither word less or more than the other]
> female aged 25–34)

The influence of broader social contexts on LGBT communities were also identified, with some participants identifying that varying levels of discrimination impacted upon how 'normal' they felt, which in turn impacted on their wellbeing:

> I used to live in Northern Ireland where discrimination was definitely current and fuelled by religious intolerance. Any LBGT community was either very clandestine or very radical. Leaving that environment and being part of a low key 'normal' LBGT community has enormously helped my wellbeing.
> (Survey respondent 316: Female lesbian aged 35–44)

Changes over the life course were thus perceived to impact on experiences of both wellbeing and community, which, as discussed in Chapter 4, mean that people's feeling towards community can change. Participants' accounts also illustrated this in relation to wellbeing. For the survey respondent below, for example, changes to her health meant that she began to view and experience LGBT community differently, and less positively. She therefore came to see community more narrowly as revolving around only her friends, who she felt were more inclusive:

> Over the years I have always felt being active within community has been enormously beneficial for my self-worth, emotional health and wellbeing, etc . . . . However, having had a serious accident some years ago I've had to reassess this. I find that I am physically unable to be part of my community and that even LGBT services are behind the times in terms of accessibility. There is a real emphasis on the young, the beautiful, the active . . . Instead of feeling part of a wide and inclusive 'community', I feel part of a much smaller but inclusive community of friends.
>
> (Survey respondent 363: Lesbian woman aged 45–54)

Previous scholarship has documented exclusionary practices on the scene that can have a detrimental impact on emotional wellbeing (Browne and Bakshi, 2013; Cant, 2008), and this was also evident in my research. Participants felt that experiences of exclusions and norms associated with the scene or LGBT communities had a negative impact on their health and wellbeing. As Guibernau (2013: 34) suggested, "belonging can . . . become a source of anxiety and stress whenever the individual feels inadequate, undervalued, misunderstood or ignored within the group". Experiences of prejudice or discrimination within LGBT communities, for example, were seen to have a detrimental or harmful effect on some people's wellbeing:

> I have encountered so much discrimination and prejudice in general LGBT communities for being bisexual it has had a very negative impact on my mental health and quality of life.
>
> (Survey respondent 107: Bisexual cisgender female aged 25–34)

Valentine and Skelton (2003: 859) have suggested that the scene can attract vulnerable young people and then reinforce or exacerbate their low self-esteem through "substance or alcohol abuse, and general patterns of self-destructive behaviour". Similarly, participants thought that 'cliques' and pressures to conform on the scene (discussed in more detail within Chapter 3) could direct some people, including themselves, towards 'unhealthy' practices. How unwelcoming or 'unhealthy' the scene can be experienced as was particularly significant when the scene was understood as the most accessible and/or identifiable form of LGBT community. Some participants, for example, felt that scene-based LGBT communities "reinforce stereotypes" and "keep the LGBT ghetto going", with negative implications for emotional and physical health. Echoing existing research about 'ideal' body image for gay men impacting upon 'unhealthy' eating and/or drug-taking practices (Bolding, Sherr and Elford, 2002; Chaney, 2008; Levesque and Vichesky, 2006; Tiggemann, Martins and Kirkbride, 2007; Yelland and Tiggemann, 2003), pressures for gay men to look a certain way were viewed as particularly harmful:

> I find that I suffer from internalised homophobia and body dismorphia which is exacerbated by the scene, a bullying and elitist attitude by gay men, [and] the media (such as Gaydar never portraying happy larger men any more—just muscle guys) . . . I am different, I should be allowed to enjoy that, and it should be celebrated by all and not something that I am made to feel ashamed of.
>
> (Survey respondent 298: Gay man aged 35–44)

> Pressure to look a certain way, especially for gay men, leads to quite bad health habits.
>
> (Survey respondent 159: Gay man aged 18–24)

The research suggests that belonging to a community through interacting with specific groups of people can impact upon physical health. However, physical health can also influence the degree to which people could participate in such communities. Those with little or no access to forms of LGBT community were at risk of isolation and mental ill-health, highlighting that physical health and emotional wellbeing can be intrinsically linked. On the whole, communities were thought to be beneficial to mental health and emotional wellbeing. Some even associated participation in communities with 'survival'. Experiences and understandings of community are not static, but evolve as people choose to disengage due to a range of factors (see Chapter 4), or feel forced to disengage as a result of discrimination or poor access facilities. As a consequence, any impacts on health and wellbeing can also change. For some participants, communities, and the scene in particular, were experienced as discriminatory and/or pressurising, particularly where body image was concerned, which can also have ramifications for health and wellbeing.

## Seeking Support

A consistent theme throughout this book has been the idea that membership of a community can foster support. This featured strongly in the survey: 'social/other support among LGBT people' was the highest ranked answer when respondents were asked to order which options they thought were the most 'true' in explaining the historic development and current existence of communities. This indicates how important social/support needs and LGBT interactions are perceived to be. Although the assumption that LGBT people automatically need support has been questioned elsewhere (Formby, 2015), the assumed link between community and support was evident in some survey responses, even where people did not rely on an LGBT community for support themselves. Some were able to access support elsewhere, but still identified an LGBT community as somewhere where others might access support:

> Being middle class and in an academic profession makes being 'out' much easier, and means that I can rely on economic privilege and liberal structures at work for support, rather than on the LGBT community.
>
> (Survey respondent 46: Lesbian/bisexual female aged 35–44)

Not requiring support was used to explain a lack of identification with community, as if that was the only reason to engage with LGBT groups:

> I personally do not fully identify myself as part of the LBGT community. This is partly as a result of not previously having a 'need' or 'desire' to engage with LGBT groups for support.
>
> (Survey respondent 57: Gay man aged 35–44)

LGBT communities were identified as important in facilitating access to mutual support from people who had gone through similar experiences or feelings. Within this, there was often an implication that such communities would improve and sustain wellbeing. Supportive networks and communities were thus identified as facilitating a feeling of belonging and wellbeing:

> It has been particularly important as a lesbian to have a community of women and the sense of connection and support that brings contributes greatly to the quality of my life: body, mind and spirit.
>
> (Survey respondent 51: Female lesbian aged 55–64)

Sometimes, a sense of belonging and expectation of mutual support was explicitly premised on an assumption of shared experiences:

> I think when I first came out . . . finding a place where you kind of belong . . . is really important . . . like actually having a support network, having people who've gone through the same thing, the stuff from the time when you're coming out to family that can be really difficult, so there's a sort of shared support there.
>
> (Helen)

It was often hard for participants to disentangle the notion of community from wider social influences on wellbeing. Petra, for example, believed that meeting people with "common identities and experiences" is positive and can help people access support, establish networks and make friends. This can perhaps be linked to a feeling of community, which they thought was supported by greater trans visibility and a more welcoming atmosphere within 'gay' clubs. However, they also felt that more supportive environments generally had a positive impact on wellbeing. They linked legislative developments with changing social attitudes, which they felt contributed to being less 'stared at' now than in the past. Participants thought these changing attitudes and increasing awareness supported LGBT wellbeing:

> Because the culture is much more receptive and much more knowledgeable about LGBT people . . . the wellbeing of LGBT people is therefore better supported.
>
> (Petra)

Participants identified both formal LGBT groups and informal networks as being supportive. For some, this was particularly linked to their working lives, and influenced how they managed, or discarded, self-imposed 'barriers' whilst at work:

> For me, a significant thing for community has been the group here at work, so that has made a difference to me because I was not out . . . I just feel easier in myself now . . . A few years ago . . . the stress levels that are associated with doing your job and also trying to put this strange front in there was becoming . . . a bit much . . . [This group] helped me get through that period.
>
> (Jackie)

> LGBT+ communities have been the keystone of my life. They have supported me through . . . exams, placements and unemployment . . . I was a student nurse (now qualified) and it helped so much to discuss placements with other student nurses in the LGBT+ community. I knew they understood the barriers we needed to have up all day. It wasn't that the people in the hospitals weren't accepting, they often were, but they tended to ask so many questions, which . . . was hugely tiring.
>
> (Website contributor)

Whether through formal volunteering or more informally between LGBT friends and acquaintances, the exchange of information can be seen as a specific form of support (Barker et al., 2012; Ryrie et al., 2010; Weeks, Heaphy and Donovan, 2001). Participants suggested that this supported their own health, as well as enabled them to help others. In her research, Hines (2007) identified education as an 'ethic of care', noting that many of her participants began 'giving something back' to the groups and communities from where they themselves had received support. In my research, Rachel also discussed how she gave something back:

> I have found many interesting facts [online] which have helped my transition, facts that I pass on to others to help them.
>
> (Rachel)

Rachel, however, raised the issue of access to formal trans support groups, and was concerned that the implementation of narrow definitions regarding trans identities could restrict some people's access to support:

> Many, especially young, trans men and women . . . end up in crime due to lack of support, which in many cases is not offered by support groups because they don't fit that group's definition of what being trans is.
>
> (Rachel)

Supporting Hines' (2007, 2010) suggestion that trans groups can fill gaps or address inadequacies in statutory services, the quote below suggests that this form of mutual support and information exchange might happen more broadly amongst LGBT people. This might be due to concerns about lack of confidentiality and/or the risk of prejudice within mainstream health service provision (Fish, 2006; Formby, 2011):

> I am a gay single parent living in a heterosexual environment. I have health issues which are not met by usual pathways and I would not discuss with my GP! I turn to the LGBT community for support, advice and help.
>
> (Survey respondent 188: Gay man aged 45–54)

Some participants felt they had a duty to help or 'defend' people from within 'their' community, for example through voluntary work:

> If I can help people because I'm in a different situation to them but I get what it's like to be gay and I get how hard that is then surely I should be able to support people . . . You have to . . . defend the group that you belong to . . . [because] if you don't then no-one else is going to do it.
>
> (Carl)

Carl worked with young people within his job, and had a pessimistic view of the lives of LGBT young people, echoing 'victim' discourses common elsewhere (see Formby, 2015 for further discussion). He therefore felt a particular responsibility to support LGBT young people:

> I work with like 14, 15, 16 year olds and every single day . . . [I] get what it's like to be a 14 and 15 year old . . . I know how difficult it is . . . I've got their back if that makes sense . . . I'm with them all the way, especially, you know, the lesbian and gay ones because . . . I feel like I kind of need to fight for them even more.
>
> (Carl)

However, Petra, who was also involved in working with young people, contrasted their own experiences when younger with the positive role of support groups, which they thought made:

> the various narratives available to young trans people, helping them make sense of their lives.
>
> (Petra)

This supports Hines' (2010) suggestion that contemporary trans activism and discourse has opened up spaces and possibilities for trans identity construction and performance.

Providing support to others can take its toll, however. One survey respondent who worked with LGBT people in a professional capacity felt that his own community engagement and quality of life had been impacted upon in negative ways because of his job:

> I work in a role offering support [to] LGBT people which leaves me exhausted and 'gayed' out at the end of the week, so my own quality of life has suffered in terms of my motivation to be part of an LGBT community in my own time.
>
> (Survey respondent 418: Gay man aged 45–54)

Although providing support to others can have a negative effect on those providing such support, participants often saw community or communities as a source of support and information that they believed would aid their own or others' mental health and wellbeing.

## Friendships, Confidence and Self-Esteem

I will now explore how participants thought that developing friendships and increasing self-confidence or self-esteem contributed to a sense of belonging and facilitated mutual support. In particular, participants often believed that being part of a community helped to combat isolation, which they said helped to maintain their wellbeing. Formal groups and informal friendships were both thought to be beneficial:

> In terms of wellbeing, I have been involved with some sort of group most of my adult life and it would have been a lot poorer without it, so overall it [community] is a huge benefit for wellbeing I think . . . people have got someone to talk to, friends.
>
> (Peter)

> The healthy bit is the coming together and having fun because nothing, for all the therapy and anti-depressants in the world, nothing will cheer you up more as a young miserable gay man than having more gay friends to laugh about stupid gay things and to talk about boys [with].
>
> (Matt)

For those with no long-term partner, the importance of belonging to one or more communities was identified as particularly significant in combating loneliness or isolation:

> I think feeling part of a community, or more than one, is more important, perhaps even vital, at a time when . . . [you] have no long-term partner. Being

'gay' is sometimes anything but (in the old meaning of the word) [and] rather a lonely place to be for some, so that's when belonging matters.

(Survey respondent 547: Female lesbian aged 65+)

People . . . can feel really isolated if all your friends are straight and you're single and you're like 'I'm never going to meet anyone'.

(Helen)

Wilkens (2015) has suggested that older lesbians can be more vulnerable to loneliness than their heterosexual counterparts. However, Ruth's ability to 'tap into' a network was the envy of her single, heterosexual female friends, who felt they had no such network:

I'm quite an old woman, I'm single . . . straight friends have said to me, 'you're awfully lucky, aren't you, because wherever you go you can kind of tap into the lesbian and gay network', and yes . . . it was not difficult to meet people [when I moved].

(Ruth)

For those who could not easily meet people in person, online spaces provided a way to connect with people, and therefore helped combat isolation. A number of participants felt such virtual communities contributed to their confidence and wellbeing:

Not being actively part of the LGBT community in a physical sense has nonetheless NOT stopped me feeling and being part of the LGBT community in a virtual sense, and given this I feel my overall wellbeing is high. I am fairly young so am enormously appreciative of this, as given this virtual world is pretty recent, my sympathy goes out to older LGBT people who did not have this opportunity . . . and were isolated.

(Survey respondent 505: Female lesbian aged 45–54)

My confidence has been helped greatly by meeting online people like myself.

(Rachel)

Interactions with other LGBT people, which aided the sharing of experiences, were thought to enhance confidence and self-esteem, and consequently enable people to have their identities validated. This was particularly important for those whose identity was not always recognised or accepted:

Identifying as gay has not been accepted well by my family . . . Finding others to identify with has been important for me to feel confident and that I am 'OK'/normal.

(Survey respondent 447: Gay and/or lesbian [I identify with neither word less or more than the other] female aged 25–34)

Jason attributed his growing self-confidence, for example feeling able to attend Pride events, with his belonging to and attendance at a local LGB youth group. As he commented:

> I don't get it [self-esteem] anywhere else.
>
> (Jason)

For some, such as Shourjo, the link between self-confidence and wellbeing was clear:

> I think being part of a group is definitely better than being isolated and if you're accepted in that group, even better, and if you're celebrated in that group, fantastic . . . if you could relate to the group and vice versa and you could contribute to the group it definitely boosts your self-confidence, which in turn leads to wellbeing . . . you want to share your experience with somebody who really completely understands.
>
> (Shourjo)

As I have shown, communities, whether physical or virtual, were often understood as a source of friendship, confidence and self-esteem. These benefits were, in turn, seen to contribute to participants' sense of wellbeing.

## Finding People 'Like Me'

In addition to self-confidence and self-esteem, affirmation and mutual understanding were also specific themes examined by participants in relation to wellbeing, which will be addressed in this section. Knowing that there were others 'like them' was important for participants and contributed to them feeling their identities were validated and understood. Helen, for instance, teased out the difference between wanting and needing to seek people who she thought were similar to her at different times in her life, in order to support her self-understanding and mental health. She currently wanted to meet people to enhance her life, but said that in the past this had been more of a need when she was 'coming out'. In the future, she also thought it could become a need rather than a want, if she was beginning to feel isolated:

> At this point [in my life] . . . I want to be around people that are similar to me . . . When you're first coming out I definitely think there was more of a need . . . A need to understand me, and I felt that meeting other people like me would help me do that, and I think it did . . . I'd say if . . . at the end of this summer [I] still hadn't met anyone in [new city] there would become . . . a need because . . . I [would] feel really isolated . . . The want is it would enhance my life, the need is actually my mental health is going to suffer or my ability to understand my world or myself.
>
> (Helen)

Helen was not the only one to identify interacting with other LGBT people as important in helping people to understand themselves. Whilst Helen discussed this in relation to meeting people, Gemma identified the potential for identity validation in more abstract terms. She thought that being able to 'see' yourself in others was particularly important for marginalised people to feel that they were understood and not alone:

> To be able to see yourself in the world around you is really important for anybody at all, but especially I think for people who identify with some kind of marginal identity. I think that sometimes you don't know who you are or what you want to do until you see it somewhere else . . . To have validation that the way you see the world is shared by other people, that there are people out there who get you . . . of course we all need this.
>
> (Gemma)

Participants thought that observing other people that were confident and happy in their identities was particularly valuable during their own 'coming out'. This meant that LGBT communities could be understood as playing a role in validating identities, particularly when those identities might not be validated elsewhere:

> I find the existence of LGBT communities very valuable, especially when I was in the early stages of coming out—knowing that there were other people who were 'like me' and happy and confident about this was immeasurably helpful.
>
> (Survey respondent 380: Gay cis[gender] male aged 25–34)

Many participants identified the importance of identity validation for wellbeing for LGBT young people and during their own and others' 'coming out'.[1] Looking back at her youth, Ruth vividly recalled the importance of having her identity affirmed at a time when lesbian identities were far less visible, contrasting this with her experiences in the present day:

> From my generation, most of us were very hidden and didn't feel that we could be our entire selves . . . except within that . . . group, and so being in that group was actually quite an important part of affirming your own identity and your selfhood . . . I have to say, it's a terrific buzz now being able to be completely out to everybody.
>
> (Ruth)

Gerry and Shourjo linked wellbeing to having their identities affirmed within particular spaces. In particular, they thought that Pride events contributed to people feeling they belonged:

> I would say they [Pride events] definitely are useful in assisting one's wellbeing, or being part of something bigger. You're not the only one, you know.
>
> (Gerry)

Shourjo believed that to be accepted and celebrated at such events was not only "fantastic", but could also boost self-confidence and wellbeing, which he linked to Maslow's (1943) 'hierarchy of needs':

> I think Pride is important but hopefully it becomes less important in the future. We don't necessarily have to shout about, you know, 'we're here, we're queer' . . . Life moves on . . . like we move up Maslow's hierarchy basically.
>
> (Shourjo)

Most participants thought it was important to find people like themselves, but it is important to recognise that not everyone can access spaces where they can meet people like themselves. Some, for example, might have their access to (safe and supportive) LGBT networks, spaces and events constrained or prohibited by an abusive partner. Not only might this limit their opportunities to interact with other LGBT people and thereby validate or affirm their identities, but it might also leave them isolated, undermined and lacking confidence, particularly if they are recently 'out' (Donovan and Hester, 2008). For many people, however, community was viewed as a source of affirmation and identity validation because it was frequently understood to involve finding people who were (assumed to be) 'like them'.

## Alcohol, Drugs and Sex on the Scene

So far, much of this chapter has discussed positive links between participants' experiences of communities and their wellbeing. However, people also identified what they thought were a range of possible 'dangers' to health, which they thought prevalent within LGBT communities. One of these 'dangers' concerned pressures to conform to particular body images or patterns of behaviour, as discussed in Chapter 3. Participants also identified high levels of alcohol or drug consumption and lack of safer sex linked to the scene, which will be examined in this section. For some, the scene represented a defining element of 'gay culture', in part because it was viewed as the primary 'place to go'. For this reason, it was thought to draw, particularly young, people into potentially 'unhealthy' and/or unsafe environments, which could impact upon their health:

> Young people don't have anywhere to go and then they get sucked into a gay scene which often isn't very safe . . . it's not inherently predatory, it just unfortunately has that element to it. And being around alcohol and being around drugs and all that kind of stuff, it's not good.
>
> (Gemma)

> We know that within the adult population there are high amounts of drug and alcohol misuse and part of the gay male culture can be around promiscuity, and for females as well, so in terms of young people accessing LGBT support

networks that are adult focussed there can be a danger of it not being the healthiest . . . There can be quite a predatory element to it.

(Liz)

Some associated alcohol and/or drugs on the scene with what they saw as 'predatory' adults, who might not have young people's best interests at heart. Whilst not dismissing the risk of LGBT young people being sexually exploited (Donovan, 2014; Fox, 2016), it was clear that some of the criticism and rendering of the scene (and those who occupy it) as 'dangerous' came from those who did not, or who no longer, frequent it. Drawing on Casey's (2007) idea that age can mark some people out as 'undesirable' on the scene, it seems that certain assumed behaviours can also be used to render some people, or spaces, 'undesirable'. As Jo commented:

Those are the people [on the scene] that get the attention . . . I've spoke[n] to so many people and they're like almost scared of gay people because of this kind of aggression, the cheating, the kind of prolific pill-popping posing.

(Jo)

Whilst not everyone identified 'undesirable' or 'dangerous' people on the scene, some did identify high levels of drug and alcohol consumption. Julie, for example, recalled her own experiences on a scene which she saw as dominated by a drug culture:

When I was a teenager I was entwined with the scene, being out and doing whatever. It wasn't exactly the best environment. It didn't have a massive positive effect on me . . . The drug culture is massive.

(Julie)

Many participants, however, referred to the dominance of alcohol rather than drugs within patterns of LGBT socialising, which they often saw as problematic:

I'd say the downside in a way is that it [community] is so linked with drinking and if you don't drink you're excluded . . . And also alcohol and stuff are depressants; they're not the best thing to be having lots of.

(Helen)

Some went so far as to suggest that levels of alcohol consumption contributed to them avoiding the scene:

It needs to be clear that the gay 'scene' has . . . had a negative impact. When I first came out I went there a lot and drank far too much . . . I am now part of a queer community which does not focus solely on drinking and tends to avoid the 'gay scene' for the same reasons as me.

(Survey respondent 388: Queer woman cis[gender] pansexual, lesbian aged 18–24)

There was a clear expectation of drinking alcohol on the scene. Browne and Bakshi (2013) noted that 'not drinking' was an unexpected form of exclusion within their research. As a 'non-drinker' myself, this form of 'othering' was not surprising (I have even had people at an LGBT event tell me that 'non-drinkers can't be trusted'!). The common privileging of alcohol in this phrasing is clear, whereby 'not drinking' is used as shorthand for not drinking alcohol, rather than not drinking liquid in any form. The presence of alcohol and/or drugs in scene spaces is therefore complex and contradictory: on the one hand, such consumption is regularly portrayed as physically and mentally unhealthy; on the other hand, to not participate in such consumption can render people 'out of place' (Browne and Bakshi, 2013) and isolated. This has clear implications for people's emotional wellbeing and a sense of not 'belonging'.

Issues related to sexual health and/or unsafe sex on the scene were also identified as problematic by participants, illustrating some people's assumptions that aspects of community or the scene are associated with 'risk' and/or 'disease', particularly for gay men:

> The drawback of meeting men on the gay scene is [the] risk of STDs.
> (Survey respondent 84: Gay man aged 35–44)

> In terms of sexual health, not to be stereotypical, but I know a lot of gay guys have picked up sexually transmitted diseases through their promiscuity in the LGBT community.
>
> (Julie)

Petra discussed the number of clubs in London open 24 hours a day over the weekend, which they felt created an environment that could lead to unsafe sex. In their view, historic marginalisation had led to a 'hedonistic' or 'hardcore' element of LGBT communities, which meant gay men in particular learnt to 'party hard':

> People go out on the Friday night and arrive home on Monday morning . . . and it leads to unsafe sexual practices, and it's not very good . . . for people's lives, their health and stuff . . . It really can be very hedonistic . . . [In] the mid to late 70s, 80s, I think the scene was an outlet, a reaction against that marginalisation . . . [so] they partied hard and I think that established how things were going to be . . . It became part of the culture.
>
> (Petra)

By contrast, Alison associated marginalisation in the past with a sense of family and belonging, but she thought that a changing social context had resulted in a different scene for young LGBT people today:

> What's different for these kids these days is that . . . when I came out and I belonged to the scene, there was a sense of belonging . . . there was a sense of family . . . and I don't think that's there [now] . . . I think going out socially

now is about going out, getting wrecked, getting laid, how many drugs can you take.

(Alison)

Carl believed that it was lack of opportunity in the past that might lead some to seek out a variety of sexual opportunities in the present, likening sexual opportunities on the scene to 'kids in a sweet shop':

> I'm [in my thirties] but really I'm kind of like [in my twenties] . . . in terms of my history of relationships and the window of opportunity that I've had, and I think that's . . . why gay men have a reputation for being, you know, slags I suppose. It's because . . . if you've repressed something for so long and then something's available and you're introduced to gay bars and gay clubs then . . . of course you are . . . You don't not give a kid sweets for a week and then take them to a sweet shop . . . they're going to want some sweets!

(Carl)

Whilst opportunities for sexual encounters could be viewed positively (see Chapter 4), within discussions of wellbeing, sex was often described in quite negative terms. This can be seen in the use of language such as 'unsafe', 'promiscuous', 'gratuitous' or 'competitive', which suggests that for some people opportunities that the scene affords were unwelcome or perceived as dangerous.

Perhaps as a result of people's negative experiences of the scene, participants often desired alternative, non-scene LGBT spaces or services and lamented the lack of such spaces. This was often on a premise that 'community spaces' would be 'healthier' for people. However, not only are there issues about how to fund and support such non-commercial spaces, questions were also raised about the potential for inclusion within and without scene spaces that call into doubt the assumption that 'off scene' necessarily means inclusive and welcoming for all. Nevertheless, it was often the scene (and less so community more generally) that was associated with 'risk', both to physical and emotional health. Largely, this was thought to be due to physical symptoms from alcohol/drug consumption or 'unsafe' sexual practices or due to social pressures and exclusions. Thus, whilst community can be conceptualised and experienced in positive ways, it can also be experienced negatively and/or contradictorily, illustrating inherent complexities within the concept, and use, of community.

## Paradoxical Spaces

In this final section, I examine the notion of paradoxical spaces. As Valentine and Skelton (2003) have argued, as young people seek to express, validate and/or support their identities, accessing the scene can operate as an important marker of transition to adulthood. However, they argue that the scene operates as a paradoxical space because it can provide both support and validation to young people (and others, I would argue), at the same time as posing 'risks' in terms of possible drug use, unsafe sex, exclusion and even violence. Similarly, in my research, the scene, and community more broadly, were seen to offer both affirmation and safety, at the same time as posing 'risks' to wellbeing. This paradox was illustrated by a number of participants, such as in the following example related to the possibility of bullying and exclusion:

> Some of the worst bullying I have experienced/seen was within the community. Part of the reason I am involved is because of wanting to feel connected and some people made this difficult.
>
> (Survey respondent 159: Gay man aged 18–24)

Despite these negative experiences, this respondent believed that he might be 'worse off' without the community.

> I probably would be worse off emotionally if I hadn't joined [the community] and felt isolated. I spent my school years feeling isolated and that was much worse.
>
> (Survey respondent 159: Gay man aged 18–24)

He had spent his school years feeling isolated and this might have led him to seek connections within a community he subsequently experienced as bullying. However, he felt he needed to maintain these connections in order to avoid being isolated, whilst recognising that he was still at risk of being bullied within this community.

Others also identified both positive and negative impacts, suggesting that communities as well as spaces can be understood and/or experienced paradoxically:

> On emotional wellbeing—the impact is both positive (sense of affirmation, connectedness, social support) and negative (body image, sexual competitiveness).
>
> (Survey respondent 573: Gay man aged 35–44)

Whilst supportive networks and connections were often viewed favourably, expectations around body image and sex were more often seen as worrying or even destructive:

> I think LGBT communities have had positive AND negative impacts on my life. Certain aspects are quite destructive—pressure to conform to certain body types and the obsession with gratuitous sex. Other aspects (community groups when people come together with a shared interest or hobby) are really important to build connections and a support network.
>
> (Survey respondent 585: Gay man aged 25–34, original emphasis)

Matt identified tensions between creating a space in which people can enjoy themselves and creating a space which contributes to negative feelings. This might include, for example, a night out which is seen to be lacking for those who do not meet the person 'of their dreams'. Though these messages might be in broader circulation too, they indicate that the scene may (re)produce pressures to be 'coupled' and/or sexually active:

> There's a balance between creating a space where people can enjoy themselves and have a good time, and creating a space where people either have a shit night out because they haven't found the man of their dreams or woman of their dreams.
>
> (Matt)

Some participants disentangled the scene from wider understandings of community, which enabled them to focus on what they saw as positive aspects of community and avoid negative aspects of the scene:

> Some aspects of the commercial scene can be detrimental to my emotional wellbeing (the commercialisation of sex and the overemphasis on anonymous sex); however, overall, the experience of being part of an LGBT community has been positive on my emotional wellbeing.
>
> (Survey respondent 226: Gay man aged 35–44)

One participant observed that whilst LGBT community was thought to have had a positive influence on their emotional wellbeing, the pressures related to appearance were experienced as so detrimental that they had ultimately chosen to 'disconnect' from the scene:

> Although it [community] has helped improve my general emotional and mental wellbeing the focus on how an LGBT+ person 'should look' has impacted me in a negative way . . . it has made it less pleasant to be part of my wider LGBT+ community and I have almost completely disconnected myself from 'the scene'.
>
> (Survey respondent 145: Genderqueer femme female poly bisexual aged 18–24)

A number of participants distinguished between trans and LGB communities. One survey respondent, for example, felt that trans communities had had a positive, informative influence on their life, whilst LGB communities had been experienced as prejudiced and therefore had a negative impact:

> The only reason I have any idea how to transition on the NHS is because of trans* communities. Generally, however, LGB communities have had a negative effect on my life, due to transphobia.
>
> (Survey respondent 382: Panromantic demisexual male, of trans experience, aged 18–24)

Whilst much of the above discussion relates to emotional wellbeing, some participants also believed that LGBT communities could have both positive and negative impacts on physical health. In the example below, the encouragement of physical activity at the gym was viewed as potentially positive. However, this was coupled with the promotion of unrealistic or overly demanding body image and/or pressures to consume alcohol, which were both thought to have a negative impact on physical health:

> The negative impact on my physical health is due to the alcohol consumption and diet which is not compulsory but I undertake in . . . Saying that there is also a strong emphasis on the gym in some LGBT communities.
>
> (Survey respondent 552: Polysexual [or bisexual depending on the person asking] female aged 25–34)

It is clear that LGBT spaces and communities can be experienced or understood as positive environments, providing opportunities for developing friendships, exchanging information and offering support. However, it is also clear that they can be seen as dangerous or 'risky'. People can thus feel 'pulled' towards them to find connections and avoid isolation, but then feel disappointed at best, and at worst oppressed, within such spaces. Some people were able to lessen their negative experiences, however, by avoiding particular scene spaces, illustrating how people exercise agency when relating to, or within, communities.

## Chapter Summary

The complexities surrounding wellbeing discussed within this chapter demonstrate why community should not be conceptualised or portrayed as a homogenous entity, not least because there are differing opinions and understandings about what forms community. The research thus supports and extends similar arguments put forward about the scene (Browne and Bakshi, 2013), which was often viewed as a specific feature of 'gay culture'. However, whilst views on community were complex, there was clear evidence that participants tended to think of the scene as a monolithic entity, though this was not always seen as synonymous with community. Many of the concerns participants identified related to alcohol, drugs and 'unsafe' sex might also be associated with pubs, bars and clubs more generally. Therefore, it was the link between commercial spaces and notions of community that was most problematic. Rather than seeing those spaces as 'just' places to socialise, because they were often imbued with deeper significance then their perceived weaknesses could become more significant for people's wellbeing. Whilst community 'membership' was thought to offer opportunities for friendship, mutual support, affirmation and self-confidence, the scene (and sometimes community) was also implicated in some people's low self-esteem, 'unhealthy' practices and/or social exclusion. Thus, whilst community can be conceptualised and experienced in positive ways, particularly with regard to mental health and emotional wellbeing, it can also be understood and experienced negatively and/or contradictorily, illustrating inherent complexities within the concept, and use, of community. Some people were able to lessen their negative experiences by avoiding particular scene spaces, showing how people can exercise agency in their relationships with(in) communities. However, if people were not able to access alternative sources of friendship, support, affirmation and/or confidence, then their relationship with community, as well as their wellbeing, was likely to suffer.

## Note

1 People also stressed the positive impact of 'coming out' generally, for instance suggesting that being 'out' strengthened people's ability to build and maintain friendships and other relationships. By contrast, 'the closet' was associated with deceit, distress, poor relationships and a lack of productivity and success at work. However, as this book focuses on understandings and experiences of LGBT communities, these wider observations about LGBT life are not included unless they relate to conceptualisations of community.

## References

Barker, M., Richards, C., Jones, R., Bowes-Catton, H., Plowman, T., Yockney, J. and Morgan, M. (2012) *The bisexuality report: Bisexual inclusion in LGBT equality and diversity*. Milton Keynes: The Open University.

Bolding, G., Sherr, L. and Elford, J. (2002) 'Use of anabolic steroids and associated health risks among gay men attending London gyms', *Addiction* 97(2): 195–203.

Browne, K. and Bakshi, L. (2013) *Ordinary in Brighton: LGBT, activisms and the city*. Aldershot: Ashgate.

Buffin, J., Roy, A., Williams, H. and Winter, A. (2012) *Part of the picture: Lesbian, gay and bisexual people's alcohol and drug use in England (2009–2011)*. Manchester: The Lesbian and Gay Foundation.

Cant, B. (2008) 'Gay men's narratives and the pursuit of wellbeing in healthcare settings: A London study', *Critical Public Health* 18(1): 41–50.

Casey, M.E. (2007) 'The queer unwanted and their undesirable "otherness"' in Browne, K., Lim, J. and Brown, G. (eds) *Geographies of sexualities: Theory, practices and politics*. Aldershot: Ashgate, pp. 125–136.

Chaney, M.P. (2008) 'Muscle dysmorphia, self-esteem, and loneliness among gay and bisexual men', *International Journal of Men's Health* 7(2): 157–170.

Donovan, C. (2014) *The ACE project: Developing an agenda for change in the North East and beyond on young LGBTQ people and child sexual exploitation*. Sunderland: University of Sunderland.

Donovan, C. and Hester, M. (2008) ' "Because she was my first girlfriend, I didn't know any different": Making the case for mainstreaming same-sex/relationship education', *Sex Education* 8(3): 277–288.

Donovan, C. and Hester, M. (2014) *Domestic violence and sexuality: What's love got to do with it?* Bristol: Policy Press.

Ellis, S.J. (2007) 'Homophobia, rights and community: Contemporary issues in the lives of LGB people in the UK' in Clarke, V. and Peel, E. (eds) *Out in psychology: Lesbian, gay, bisexual, trans and queer perspectives*. Chichester: John Wiley and Sons, pp. 291–310.

Fish, J. (2006) *Heterosexism in health and social care*. Basingstoke: Palgrave Macmillan.

Formby, E. (2011) 'Lesbian and bisexual women's human rights, sexual rights and sexual citizenship: Negotiating sexual health in England', *Culture, Health and Sexuality* 13(10): 1165–1179.

Formby, E. (2015) 'Limitations of focussing on homophobic, biphobic and transphobic "bullying" to understand and address LGBT young people's experiences within and beyond school', *Sex Education* 15(6): 626–640.

Fox, C. (2016) *'It's not on the radar': The hidden diversity of children and young people at risk of sexual exploitation in England*. Ilford: Barnardo's.

Fraser, S. (2008) 'Getting out in the "real world": Young men, queer and theories of gay community', *Journal of Homosexuality* 55(2): 245–264.

Frost, D.M. and Meyer, I.H. (2012) 'Measuring community connectedness among diverse sexual minority populations', *Journal of Sex Research* 48(1): 36–49.

Guasp, A. (2012) *Gay and bisexual men's health survey*. London: Stonewall.

Guibernau, M. (2013) *Belonging: Solidarity and division in modern societies*. Cambridge: Polity Press.

Heath, M. and Mulligan, E. (2008) 'Shiny happy same-sex attracted woman seeking same: How communities contribute to bisexual and lesbian women's wellbeing', *Health Sociology Review* 17(3): 290–302.

Hines, S. (2007) 'Transgendering care: Practices of care within transgender communities', *Critical Social Policy* 27(4): 462–486.

Hines, S. (2010) 'Queerly situated: Exploring constraints and negotiations of trans queer subjectivities', *Gender, Place and Culture* 17(5): 597–613.

Holt, M. (2011) 'Gay men and ambivalence about "gay community": From gay community attachment to personal communities', *Culture, Health and Sexuality* 13(8): 857–871.

Hunt, R. and Fish, J. (2008) *Prescription for change: Lesbian and bisexual women's health check 2008*. London: Stonewall.

Kehily, M.J. (2007) *Understanding youth: Perspectives, identities and practices*. London: Sage.

Keogh, P., Reid, D., Bourne, A., Weatherburn, P. and Hickson, F. (2009) *Wasted opportunities: Problematic alcohol and drug use among gay men and bisexual men*. London: Sigma Research.

Levesque, M.J. and Vichesky, D.R. (2006) 'Raising the bar on the body beautiful: An analysis of the body image concerns of homosexual men', *Body Image* 3(1): 45–55.

Maslow, A.H. (1943) 'A theory of human motivation', *Psychological Review* 50(4): 370–396.

May, V. (2013) *Connecting self to society: Belonging in a changing world*. New York: Palgrave Macmillan.

McManus, S. (2003) *Sexual orientation research phase 1: A review of methodological approaches*. Edinburgh: Scottish Executive.

Monro, S. (2015) *Bisexuality: Identities, politics, and theories*. Basingstoke: Palgrave Macmillan.

Moran, L. and Skeggs, B. (2001) 'Property and propriety: Fear and safety in gay space', *Social and Cultural Geography* 2(4): 407–420.

Pugh, S. (2002) 'The forgotten: A community without a generation—Older lesbians and gay men' in Richardson, D. and Seidman, S. (eds) *Handbook of lesbian and gay studies*. London: Sage, pp. 161–181.

Rooney, E. (2012) *All partied out? Substance use in Northern Ireland's lesbian, gay, bisexual and transgender community*. Belfast: The Rainbow Project.

Rothblum, E. (2010) 'Where is the "women's community?" Voices of lesbian, bisexual, and queer women and heterosexual sisters', *Feminism and Psychology* 20(4): 454–472.

Ryrie, I., McDonnell, S., Allman, K. and Pralat, R. (2010) *Experiences of and barriers to participation in public and political life for lesbian, gay, bisexual and transgender people*. London: Office for Public Management.

Simpson, P. (2013a) 'Alienation, ambivalence, agency: Middle-aged gay men and ageism in Manchester's gay village', *Sexualities* 16(3–4): 283–299.

Simpson, P. (2013b) 'Differentiating the self: The kinship practices of middle-aged gay men in Manchester', *Families, Relationships and Societies* 2(1): 97–113.

Tiggemann, M., Martins, Y. and Kirkbride, A. (2007) 'Oh to be lean and muscular: Body image ideals in gay and heterosexual men', *Psychology of Men and Masculinity* 8(1): 15–24.

Valentine, G. and Skelton, T. (2003) 'Finding oneself, losing oneself: The lesbian and gay "scene" as a paradoxical space', *International Journal of Urban and Regional Research* 27(4): 849–866.

Weeks, J., Heaphy, B. and Donovan, C. (2001) *Same sex intimacies: Families of choice and other life experiments*. London: Routledge.

Weston, K. (1991) *Families we choose: Lesbians, gays, kinship*. New York: Columbia University Press.

Wilkens, J. (2015) 'Loneliness and belongingness in older lesbians: The role of social groups as "community"', *Journal of Lesbian Studies* 19(1): 90–101.

Wilkinson, J., Bittman, M., Holt, M., Rawstorne, P., Kippax, S. and Worth, H. (2012) 'Solidarity beyond sexuality: The personal communities of gay men', *Sociology* 46(6): 1161–1177.

Woolwine, D. (2000) 'Community in gay male experience and moral discourse', *Journal of Homosexuality* 38(4): 5–37.

Yelland, C. and Tiggemann, M. (2003) 'Muscularity and the gay ideal: Body dissatisfaction and disordered eating in homosexual men', *Eating Behavior* 4(2): 107–116.

# 10 Conclusions and Implications

"Researching how communities come to be imagined as well as how they come to be inhabited in the everyday world may reveal the complexities of the lived experience of 'community', while providing further insights into its enduring appeal"

(Fortier, 2002: 193)

I hope this book has illustrated in detail the complexity and problematic nature of the term 'LGBT community'. In writing it, I support Fortier's (2002) contention that various imaginings and habitations of community reveal its complexity, and I have gone some way to demonstrate its enduring appeal. Overall, the research shows that the diversity of experience may be overlooked in assumptions and/or language relating to LGBT community, particularly when used in the singular. I have demonstrated that the concept of community is clearly socially constructed, but also that it is a construction that matters to many people. The term community was frequently used to refer to groups of LGBT people, whether known to one another or not. Though community means different things to different people, for many, communities were conceptualised in broader terms than 'just' friendship groups, most clearly in a sense of wanting to share space with, and feel connected to, other LGBT people with whom there may be no personal ties. Whilst this might be described as a sense of solidarity, it does not necessarily mean similarity.

How LGBT communities are understood and how LGBT people are talked about was the focus of Chapter 2. I demonstrated that many questioned whether LGBT people necessarily form or belong to distinct LGBT communities. That some people feel less 'welcomed' within the LGBT acronym, and the related concept of community, was clear, and this has implications for service delivery premised on the notion of a monolithic 'LGBT community'. As I have shown, the concept of LGBT community was seen as problematic, at least in part, because the LGBT acronym itself was seen as problematic. However, 'labels' and suggestions of a collective can become useful when they 'work': to facilitate recognition of people's identities, help people to gain access to services or other forms of support, for political gain, or simply to express 'difference' and possible exclusion. On the whole, though, diversities amongst LGBT people, and how these contribute to different life experiences, were often thought not to be captured within the common four letter acronym LGBT, nor in use of the word community that is commonly understood to suggest some form of commonality or shared perspective.

For many, it was the concept of a singular LGBT community that was questioned. The idea of a plurality of communities, recognising diversity within and between LGBT people, was therefore valued more positively, as it suggests that not *all* LGBT people belong to one large homogenous (and harmonious) group. Who was attributing community status to whom was also significant, and levels of discomfort with the phrase LGBT community tended to be less when it was used by LGBT people themselves. However, there may be advantages to the strategic suggestion of community and/or commonality, with some (limited) basis for this in shared experiences of stigmatisation or prejudice. Singular use of LGBT community was therefore tactically deployed in activism and advocacy regarding LGBT rights. Overall, it was clear that the concept of community can be drawn on in critical, agentic and strategic ways, yet these nuances are often missed in much use of the term LGBT community within broader media, policy and practice arenas.

Chapter 3 examined the notion of difference within LGBT communities and demonstrated how recognition of diversity meant that applying the singular term community to groups of LGBT people was neither helpful nor realistic. However, I also showed that the ideas of difference and sameness can be drawn on simultaneously to explain an acknowledgment of diversity at the same time as maintaining a sense of belonging, which might be described as solidarity without similarity. Therefore, despite some recognition of difference, there were often still assumptions of a collective identity, which was frequently contrasted with a cisgender heterosexual 'them'. This assumed monolithic heterosexual, cisgender 'them' was juxtaposed with an LGBT 'us', despite some acknowledgment of diversities and pluralities within this 'us'. Whilst Browne and Bakshi (2013: 70) have noted that scene spaces are experienced unequally because they are "affected by intersectionalities including race, age, class, bodily ideals, gender identities and sexual identities", I would suggest that this can also be applied to the notion of communities.

Conceptualisations of an LGBT 'us' may be as problematic as a monolithic 'them', given some experiences of discrimination, such as ageism, biphobia, (dis) ableism, racism and transphobia from and among LGBT people. Community belonging is therefore not a given, even if people share a gender or sexual identity. The concept of a singular community can minimise or ignore experiences of diversity and/or discrimination. Whilst May (2013: 123) suggested "'community' is produced through a rhetoric of similarity that, to an extent, denies or masks difference", Gilroy (1987: 235) argued that it "is as much about difference as it is about similarity". As I have shown, LGBT people distinguish themselves as different from heterosexual cisgender 'others' as much as, if not more than, similar to each other. Community does therefore not always require similarity in order to be believed in, as "it is diversity, not unity, that constitutes the space of modern communities" (Day, 2006: 211). Overall, I suggest that use of the term LGBT community often overlooks diversities, inequalities and prejudices amongst LGBT people. An awareness and/or experience of these could make people sceptical about the value of such a term, and indeed the desirability or possibility of such a 'reality'. The notion of LGBT community is therefore problematic when it is thought to require a similarity that many felt did not exist.

Chapter 4 focussed on lived experiences of LGBT communities, including changes across the life course. In doing so, I explored friendships, activism, seeking safety and avoiding 'risk', and demonstrated that as much as it may be used as a convenient label by 'outsiders', LGBT community is also actively constructed by LGBT people. In discussing practices of identity management and self-censorship in intimate relationships, I set out how this related to why some people choose to engage with the idea(l) of LGBT communities. As I have shown, understandings of LGBT communities can be, in part, predicated on the assumption that people 'filter' or self-censor their behaviour outside of these communities. This could include not feeling able to hold hands outside of particular friendship groups or spaces, such as commercial scenes and Pride events. Communities were often understood in terms of the degree to which they enabled people to escape 'filtering' or self-censoring practices, thus demonstrating the prevalence of self-censorship amongst some LGBT people and its links to the very concept of (desiring) community. As this shows, beliefs surrounding communities were often predicated on dichotomous notions of safety and comfort amongst LGBT people, and a lack thereof elsewhere.

A desire for safety and wanting to feel comfortable and at ease was often used to explain why LGBT people 'magnetise' towards each other. This was understood as a 'natural' response to external oppression. Notions of 'safety in numbers', 'birds of a feather' and homophily were often drawn on and linked to the concept of community. For others, the idea of a community of friends, or a personal community, was drawn on where forms of community (most often scene-based) were not accessible or lacked appeal. Overall, a social context that was assumed to be negative towards LGBT people was often the reason why people chose to engage with particular communities. Whilst not suggesting that there have been no improvements in relation to legislation and wider social attitudes, there is, for some, persistent apprehension and self-surveillance which, whether necessary or not, are significant. Perceptions of adversity are therefore integral to notions of LGBT community as it is this social context that many feel they need or want to retreat from in order to relax or feel comfortable, even if only on occasion. The 'doing' of community was thus linked to being with LGBT people, or in particular spaces, often as a way to feel safe and supported, and these themes have flowed throughout the book.

In Chapter 5 I examined the idea of space and demonstrated a tendency for 'LGBT space' to be identified, homogenised and constructed in contrast or opposition to (often monolithic) 'non-LGBT space'. Spatial understandings of LGBT community included geographical areas such as Brighton or San Francisco, commercial scenes, and specific groups and services. These understandings illustrate how social (or community) relations are also spatial relations, as "space is both a medium of social relations and . . . can affect social relations" (Gottdiener, 1993: 132). On the whole, those living in rural locations tended to think that urban experiences would be 'better' for LGBT people, with associated beliefs about greater visibility, though this is not to suggest that experiences of rural living were only negative. Holidays and travel can also be important as they provide an opportunity to experience different forms of LGBT community that otherwise might not be possible.

Drawing on Lefebvre's (1991) 'lived' spaces of representation, and Soja's (1996: 6, original emphasis) notion of the "multiplicity of *real-and-imagined* places", I suggest that how places and spaces are imagined becomes important to how they are experienced, in part because of how those places and spaces are subsequently 'lived'. As Browne and Bakshi (2013: 48) argue of Brighton, because it was "perceived as being 'mixed and accepting', people used spaces in ways that reflected these imaginings and such uses reiterated this sense". Different spaces therefore offer different possibilities or conditions for 'ordinariness', suggesting that ordinariness is "spatially contingent" (Browne and Bakshi, 2013: 191) and informed by our imaginings. We can also see this with online spaces, which can be understood as virtual communities that can support communication and information sharing, opportunities for exploring identities and political activism. As such, they can combat isolation, particularly for certain groups, such as young and/or trans people. Across a range of 'public' and 'private' spaces, varied forms of community could facilitate friendships and mutual support, which were important for LGBT people.

The focus of Chapter 6 was on how scene spaces are experienced and viewed. As I have shown, cisgender heterosexual people's use of these spaces can result in LGBT people feeling less safe or comfortable. Jenkins (2014: 137, original emphasis), drawing on Cohen, has suggested that "a 'sense of us' and community stems from the awareness that things are done differently *there*, and the sense of threat" that engenders. This helps explain LGBT people's discomfort with people from 'there' (outside of LGBT communities) coming into scene spaces. Understanding community in terms of 'owning' space can therefore become problematic, with those from 'outside' seen as 'invaders'. Scene-based understandings of community were also problematic for those who did not or could not access these forms of space. Whilst scene spaces could be experienced as enjoyable and offering (at least the possibility of) friendship, feelings of comfort and safety and 'diversion' away from heteronormativity, they could also be experienced as exclusionary. Particular norms and attitudes could leave people feeling out of place, excluded or 'other'. This might relate to people's dress and appearance, or social practices such as (not) drinking alcohol, indicating that marginalisation is not always, or only, related to intersectional identities (Browne and Bakshi, 2013). The scene can therefore be felt as both inclusionary and exclusionary by different people, or by the same people at different times, and so should not be read as synonymous with community. Where the scene is held up as a site of safety or belonging away from 'the rest of' the city and/or society, then feeling or being emotionally, physically or financially denied entry to this space has particular significance because it can leave people feeling as if they do not belong anywhere. This is because space, as well as people (May, 2013), can imbue a sense of belonging. As Browne and Bakshi (2013: 70) have argued, "the desire to be included and to be 'part of it' was a testament to the importance of the gay scene". As such, they suggest that it should be explored for its possibilities as well as its normalisations (Browne and Bakshi, 2013).

Conceiving a community based around a space over which people have limited ownership and control is inherently problematic, not least because exclusions can limit the possibilities of LGBT community based on events and spaces that not everyone can 'occupy'. However, despite their weaknesses, there was a sense that scene spaces are (still) necessary, and therefore some people felt they had no choice but to visit venues with which they were not entirely happy. Whilst the concept of community is frequently understood in positive terms (Day, 2006), for those who base their understanding of community on the scene, 'their' community can be experienced as inadequate. For others, the importance of scene spaces is symbolic as they can engender a feeling of being part of something, even when those spaces are not physically accessed. It may be that it is an expectation that scene venues will be more than 'just' a bar or club that fuels people's dissatisfaction, as they do not always 'measure up'. Feeling excluded or distant from the scene can be experienced or understood as exclusion from LGBT community. Equally, LGBT community is not always safe or inclusive because the scene is not always experienced as such.

The idea of Pride events as temporary spaces, or a temporary claiming of space, was explored within Chapter 7. These events were seen to create or support feelings of community and facilitate time-limited and spatially specific safeties and freedoms not always experienced elsewhere. Within discussions about Pride events, ideas about celebration, protest and commercialism dominated, though interestingly feeling proud was less often mentioned. Supporting Brown's (2009) work, one of the ways in which Pride events were thought to support communities was in offering and presenting diverse ways to 'do' LGBT. However, these spaces could also exclude some LGBT people, reinforcing themes running throughout the book that a sense of belonging and/or community, as well as access to 'safe' space, is not universal. The notion of partying with politics (Browne, 2007), as suggested by some, clearly complicates an assumed dichotomy between party and protest. Participating in a (fun) 'ritual of belonging' (Guibernau, 2013) can contribute to a sense of LGBT solidarity, which can itself be understood as political. Yet the research raised questions about how politics is often understood, namely as dour and depressing, which meant that some people did not think protesting could, or even should, be fun. Pride events often held a complex relationship with notions of community. They were largely understood as positive temporary LGBT spaces that facilitated people coming together and which could foster a sense of community, but this is not experienced evenly. However, Pride events can at least represent a visual and/or imagined community that might not exist at other times.

The focus of Chapter 8 was on belonging and imagined communities. May (2013: 153) has suggested that belonging "is complex and ephemeral, and easily eludes the researcher", and I would suggest it can also elude those who experience it. A sense of belonging was often hard to define or explain, but as I have shown, imagined connections between LGBT people (often viewed as a sense of 'something') could be identified based on perceived commonalities and similarities, which were thought to create mutual understanding. However, drawing on ideas of 'sameness' did not always mean that differences between LGBT people went unrecognised. Constructions of LGBT community often relied on perceived similarities between LGBT people ('us') and differences from a heterosexual, cisgender 'other' (or 'them'). Drawing on May's (2013: 4) argument that people's experiences of belonging offer a window in to their experiences of social change and human interaction, I have shown that a sense of belonging to LGBT communities can illuminate people's feelings of not belonging with others/elsewhere. In other words, LGBT belonging is important because we are still lacking sufficient social change. As a result, some LGBT people feel cautious and believe that they need to self-censor their behaviour in everyday interactions, which is not easily addressed in equalities legislation. Ghaziani (2011: 99) suggested that LGBT activists "construct collective identity using an oppositional 'us versus them'", but I suggest that constructions of 'us versus them' feature more widely in LGBT people's everyday lived experiences and the ways that they make sense of themselves and their position in the world. Whilst LGBT people might not always be 'similar', there is some potential for shared values, as well as the likelihood of shared experiences, which could contribute to a sense of connection. Most often these were related to discrimination, and to a lesser extent experiences of 'coming out' or living in 'the closet'. However, the concept of intersectionality reminds us that 'shared' experiences are still informed by (intersectional) identities, and therefore likely to be experienced differently. There was a tendency amongst some to essentialise LGBT existence, at the same time as criticising others for misunderstanding or stereotyping LGBT people. However, there might be some benefits to this essentialism, as it can contribute to affirmation and a feeling of 'groupness', as well as aiding activist campaigning via 'strategic essentialism' (Spivak, 2006).

The existence of imagined LGBT communities (Anderson, 2006) demonstrates how LGBT people often understand community in a broader, more amorphous way than has been documented in some previous research, such as that largely focussed on friendship-based families of choice (Weeks, Heaphy and Donovan, 2001) or personal communities (Heaphy, Smart and Einarsdottir, 2013). Imagining and marking boundaries between 'us' and 'them' created a sense of 'we-ness' (Ghaziani, 2011), which I argue is integral to the construction of LGBT communities, and the idea of LGBT 'kin', but these boundaries could also exclude LGBT people. We therefore need to question assumptions of universal belonging or inclusion within an LGBT community, imagined or otherwise, because not everyone feels 'at home', or that they belong, within LGBT community. However, the possibility of meeting other LGBT people was enough for some to feel that they were not alone, even if they never actually met them (see also Weston, 1991). Belonging to, or sharing, a community is therefore not always premised on meeting other (LGBT) people, but can be based on something less tangible. As Delanty (2010: xii) suggested, "community has a transcendent nature and cannot simply be equated with particular groups or a place . . . it is both an experience and an interpretation". Just because community is imagined does not mean that it is not real (Delanty, 2010). It could therefore be argued that the distinction between 'real' and 'imagined' is artificial. Imagined LGBT communities offer a way of believing in collective identities and belonging without necessarily basing this on the idea of similar, or the 'same', identities. As Weeks, Heaphy and Donovan (2001) suggested, people want the ideal of community even when it is rejected as a 'reality'. As I have shown, the 'enduring appeal' of community (Fortier, 2002) includes the suggestion of, or opportunities for, friendship, support, affirmation, a sense of 'groupness' and political gain.

Chapter 9 explored the relationship between LGBT community and wellbeing, and in particular the impact of community 'membership' on physical and mental health. Forms of community could be understood to offer support, information and friendship, which in turn can contribute to affirmation and identity validation, and foster self-confidence and self-esteem. Supporting existing research (Barker et al., 2012; Ryrie et al., 2010; Weeks, Heaphy and Donovan, 2001), the exchange of information between LGBT people can be seen as a specific form of support, or an 'ethic of care' (Hines, 2007). However, some LGBT people are viewed as 'dangerous' and potentially harmful to others, particularly in relation to alcohol or drug consumption, and practices of 'unsafe' sex, although it was often scene spaces in particular, rather than LGBT communities more generally, that were associated with risks to physical and emotional health. I suggest that physical and mental health are closely linked, both to each other and to the idea(l) of community. Those who had limited access to particular events or spaces, such as the scene, could feel that their access to LGBT community was restricted, which in turn was thought to have a negative impact on their health. For some, physical ill-health can limit physical access to spaces and communities, and this can in turn impact upon mental health and wellbeing.

LGBT communities and spaces, such as the commercial scene, were conceptualised as both (partially) 'safe' from cisgender heterosexuals and 'risky' or exclusionary as a result of the practices of other(ed) LGBT people. This shows how the scene can be homogenised and/or demonised by LGBT people, at the same time as scene spaces are often held up as positive evidence of urban cosmopolitanism and/or diversity. Some people felt 'pulled' towards LGBT scenes or spaces to find connections and avoid isolation, and then felt disappointed or even oppressed within such spaces. Whilst those with little or no access to forms of LGBT community were at risk of isolation and mental ill-health, LGBT communities were largely thought to be beneficial to mental health and emotional wellbeing. That people were also able to lessen their negative experiences by avoiding particular scene spaces illustrates how people can exercise agency in their relationships with(in) communities. However, where people were not able to access alternative sources of friendship, support, affirmation or confidence, their relationship to community, as well as their wellbeing, was likely to suffer. I suggest it is the link between commercial spaces and notions of community that is most problematic. Rather than seeing these spaces as 'just' places to socialise, because they are often imbued with deeper significance, their perceived weaknesses can become more significant for people's wellbeing.

Overall, the complexities identified and illustrated within this book demonstrate that LGBT community should not be conceptualised or portrayed as a homogenous entity. As I have shown, community is important to many LGBT people, but there are a plurality of opinions and understandings as to what a community is. Supporting Brown's (2008) argument, I have demonstrated that research with LGBT people can explore experiences of community embedded within 'ordinary' towns and other locations, not just 'known' cities with large LGBT populations. I have shown that LGBT community can be understood and experienced in positive ways, particularly with regard to mental health and emotional wellbeing, but also conceptualised and experienced negatively or contradictorily, illustrating the inherent complexities within the concept, and use, of 'LGBT community'. Community was discussed in terms of physicality, cyber space and imagination, with a feeling of belonging or connection experienced within all three. Soja (1996) argued that space embodies the 'real' and imagined, and I would suggest the same can also be said of LGBT community. This does not, however, negate the need to acknowledge inequalities and exclusions within community.

Whilst there have been debates about the 'decline' of gayborhoods, particularly in America (Ghaziani, 2014; Reiter, 2008), the idea of community remains, at least for the time being. However, it is clearly a fluid concept that people identify with differently at different times and within different places, and understand and experience in a multitude of complex ways. It was often understood within a series of binaries, such as people and spaces 'inside'/'outside', urban/rural locations, 'us'/'them' and inclusion/exclusion. However, as Moran et al. (2004: 171) suggest, "Boundaries both divide and join", and we can see that constructions of 'us and them' can be positive, such as when people join together in celebration at Pride events or for political purposes, but they can also lead to resentments when a division is crossed and 'they' begin to occupy 'our' (scene) space. However, experiences were often temporally or relationally specific and spatially located, and thus less 'clear-cut' than these rigid boundaries or binaries suggest. LGBT communities can, for example, be experienced as physical *and* imagined at different times. For some, membership of a community was fleeting or transitional, whilst for others it was experienced as fundamentally discriminatory, illustrating the "messy betweenness of those included and at times simultaneously excluded" (Browne and Bakshi, 2013: 189).

Language is important to people's relationships with, and perceptions of, LGBT community. The term LGBT community has some value, but using it as a synonym for 'people' does not acknowledge the inherent complexities within the concept, even though these complexities have clear implications for LGBT people's lived experience and wellbeing. Though the idea of shared values can contribute to a sense of community, LGBT people's experiences suggest that difference does matter. We should therefore remember that the idea(l) or 'reality' of LGBT communities is not equally accessible or safe for all. This needs to be taken into account when talking of community, rather than risk implying that LGBT people are all the same. It may be useful to draw on the idea of community in relation to shared interests or rights, but it is not useful when it is understood to be homogenising and/or 'lumping together' LGBT people who may not see themselves as, or wish to be, a group. At these times, the term can be read as offensive and denying or rendering invisible people's negative experiences. Use of the term 'LGBT community' can also foster the idea that people should feel part of something, which if they do not, can heighten feelings of exclusion or isolation, which the term 'LGBT people' would avoid. This is not to negate people's feelings or experiences of 'community', but to show how language use can contribute to some people's alienation. It could be argued that, with many caveats and nuances, the phrases LGBT community and LGBT communities have some validity because some LGBT people choose to use them, and in doing so give the terms some meaning, albeit meanings that are not always shared. Particular caution is needed, however, when the terms are used by those who believe that there is one singular community and/or that LGBT people are more alike than not.

The concept of LGBT community, and many of the issues discussed within this book, have implications for the lived experiences of those who identify as LGBT. Use of the term LGBT community can risk minimising or misunderstanding diverse needs of LGBT people, both in terms of their everyday lives and in relation to service planning and provision. Policy and practice that draws on the concept of LGBT community should acknowledge the diversity, inequality and power dynamics embedded within LGBT communities, and within broader society. Use of LGBT communities in the plural is just the start to this. How we understand and use the term LGBT community has implications for the delivery of social policy and service provision, and ultimately LGBT people's lives. The concept is important but when it is used in the singular, which it so often is outside (and sometimes even within) academia, this is not helpful to many LGBT people, not least because not all feel, or wish to be, included within a singular monolithic community. Whilst community can offer 'benefits' to some, in terms of affirmation and the suggestion of safety, it also poses 'dangers' through perpetuating misconceptions and stereotypes about LGBT people. In wishing to open up new conversations, I am mindful that many feel that the language of community should be questioned and critiqued, and at the very least used by us, not about us. I hope that this book will contribute to these new conversations, and support further thinking in this area, within which everyone will bring their own (multiple) perspectives, whether as academics, practitioners and/or LGBT people themselves.

## References

Anderson, B. (2006) *Imagined communities: Reflections on the origin and spread of nationalism.* London: Verso.

Barker, M., Richards, C., Jones, R., Bowes-Catton, H., Plowman, T., Yockney, J. and Morgan, M. (2012) *The bisexuality report: Bisexual inclusion in LGBT equality and diversity.* Milton Keynes: The Open University.

Brown, G. (2008) 'Urban (homo)sexualities: Ordinary cities and ordinary sexualities', *Geography Compass* 2(4): 1215–1231.

Brown, G. (2009) 'Thinking beyond homonormativity: Performative explorations of diverse gay economies', *Environment and Planning A* 41(6): 1496–1510.

Browne, K. (2007) 'A party with politics? (Re)making LGBTQ Pride spaces in Dublin and Brighton', *Social and Cultural Geography* 8(1): 63–87.

Browne, K. and Bakshi, L. (2013) *Ordinary in Brighton: LGBT, activisms and the city*. Aldershot: Ashgate.

Day, G. (2006) *Community and everyday life*. New York: Routledge.

Delanty, G. (2010) *Community*. London: Routledge.

Fortier, A. (2002) 'Queer diaspora' in Richardson, R. and Seidman, S. (eds) *Handbook of lesbian and gay studies*. London: Sage, pp. 183–197.

Ghaziani, A. (2011) 'Post-gay collective identity construction', *Social Problems* 58(1): 99–125.

Ghaziani, A. (2014) *There goes the gayborhood?* Princeton: Princeton University Press.

Gilroy, P. (1987) *'There ain't no black in the Union Jack': The cultural politics of race and nation*. Chicago: University of Chicago Press.

Gottdiener, M. (1993) 'A Marx for our time: Henri Lefebvre and the production of space', *Sociological Theory* 11(1): 129–134.

Guibernau, M. (2013) *Belonging: Solidarity and division in modern societies*. Cambridge: Polity Press.

Heaphy, B., Smart, C. and Einarsdottir, A. (2013) *Same sex marriages: New generations, new relationships*. Basingstoke: Palgrave Macmillan.

Hines, S. (2007) 'Transgendering care: Practices of care within transgender communities', *Critical Social Policy* 27(4): 462–486.

Jenkins, R. (2014) *Social identity*. Abingdon: Routledge.

Lefebvre, H. (1991) *The production of space*. Oxford: Blackwell.

May, V. (2013) *Connecting self to society: Belonging in a changing world*. New York: Palgrave Macmillan.

Moran, L., Skeggs, B., Tyrer, P. and Corteen, K. (2004) *Sexuality and the politics of violence and safety*. London: Routledge.

Reiter, D.F. (2008) *Greetings from the gayborhood*. New York: Harry N. Abrams.

Ryrie, I., McDonnell, S., Allman, K. and Pralat, R. (2010) *Experiences of and barriers to participation in public and political life for lesbian, gay, bisexual and transgender people*. London: Office for Public Management.

Soja, E.W. (1996) *Thirdspace: Expanding the geographical imagination*. Oxford: Blackwell.

Spivak, G.C. (2006) *In other worlds: Essays in cultural politics*. Abingdon: Routledge.

Weeks, J., Heaphy, B. and Donovan, C. (2001) *Same sex intimacies: Families of choice and other life experiments*. London: Routledge.

Weston, K. (1991) *Families we choose: Lesbians, gays, kinship*. New York: Columbia University Press.

# Appendix: Research Methods and Participants

This book draws on an Arts and Humanities Research Council funded research project on understandings and experiences of LGBT communities, which took place throughout the UK in 2012, within the cross-research council 'Connected Communities' programme of work. In this appendix I provide more detail on the research methods and process followed, as well as the research participants. The project involved three methods of data collection, which I outline further below: a short online survey to which there were 627 responses; an interactive project website to which people could post contributions and comments and upload photographs or other files; and in-depth data collection via 12 interviews and five group discussions, involving a total of 44 people. Similar themes were explored in both the survey and in-depth methods. Question areas broadly centred on people's understandings of LGBT communities, currently and historically; their experiences of LGBT communities and their perceived impacts; and views on LGBT communities of the future.

The research was not designed to be 'representative', and I make no claims that it is, not least because of the difficulties of sampling that have been documented elsewhere (Browne, 2005; Heaphy, Smart and Einarsdottir, 2013; Myslik, 1996; Weeks, Heaphy and Donovan, 2001). The research included representation from all four countries within the UK: England, Northern Ireland (survey only), Scotland and Wales. Whilst it might not be 'representative', the research did include people from 'ordinary' towns and suburbs (Brown, 2008), as well as those from outside more 'obvious' scene and Pride spaces (see Stella, 2012; Simpson, 2015 for further discussion). I provide more detail on participants below. Ethical approval was gained from Sheffield Hallam University's research ethics committee and standard ethical procedures were followed regarding informed consent, participants' right to withdraw, confidentiality, anonymity and secure storage of both physical and electronic data.

## Research Process and Recruitment

A project website was established to provide information (and periodic 'news' items) about the research for potential participants and other interested parties. This was designed to be 'interactive' to allow people to post contributions (subject to moderator 'approval'). It also contained further details about privacy and research ethics. Once this was developed, information about the project was disseminated, largely electronically. This consisted of an open 'call' for assistance through providing references or existing literature, completion of the online survey and/or participation in regional discussion groups. This information was sent to approximately 200 individuals/personal contacts, social groups and organisations, and LGBT staff networks, publications and websites. Whilst participants were 'self-selecting' in the sense that they chose to complete the survey and/or be involved in more in-depth research methods, efforts were made to seek varied participants. This was through direct contact with a diverse range of individuals, groups and organisations, but also via a request for information to be cascaded. Emails requested that people forward on the information to their own contacts, in a deliberate attempt to go beyond specific organisations or groups and into more informal networks. However, it is possible that this self-selecting sample may have been more interested in, or opinionated about, community than the wider LGBT population. Equally, my use of 'LGBT' may have dissuaded some people from being involved, though people who do not identify with this grouping did choose to participate. Whilst I have documented a range of opinions and complex engagements with the concept of LGBT community, it should be noted that along with much other research in this field, the potential for certain voices to become more visible within the research is evident (Heaphy, 2012; McDermott, 2010; McManus, 2003).

## Online Survey

The online survey was designed to be short and quick to complete (there were 12 questions). The results therefore only provide a 'snapshot' of opinion, and in all honesty I did not expect as many respondents as I received. The survey was open for a period of six months. The majority of questions were 'closed' (tick-box), though a small number of open questions allowed respondents to write in their own words. One question invited people to provide more detail on their responses to the closed questions and a second asked for more detail on respondents' identities. The varied responses to the latter question go some way to highlighting the complexity and diversity of experience when examining issues about identity. Closed survey questions were used to produce descriptive statistics. Open text survey data was analysed thematically, alongside the in-depth data collection (see below). Detailed demographic information (other than people's age and self-identified gender and sexuality) was not requested within the survey as more complex statistical analysis which might have used this was not anticipated.

## Interviews and Group Discussions

In total, there were two paired interviews (involving four people), ten individual interviews, and five group discussions that involved a total of 32 people. Two participants were involved in both an individual interview and a group discussion, and they have not been counted twice in the overall total of 44 participants. Group discussions involved visits to existing LGBT groups and locations where 'one-off' participants were directly recruited to attend the discussion. These groups lasted between 60 and 90 minutes, whilst individual and paired interviews lasted 30–120 minutes, with the majority taking around 75 minutes. The purpose of the group discussions, and individual and paired interviews, was to provide more in-depth data (from a smaller number of people) that could be analysed alongside the survey results. This 'rich' data adds to the existing literature and the survey data. All qualitative data was digitally recorded, transcribed and analysed thematically.

## Participants

Overall, the project involved a range of participant ages, genders and sexualities, though there were limited numbers of BME people involved. Though Gabb and Fink (2015) 'resist' identifying their participants' quotations with this information, so as not to 'define' people by these categories or 'labels', I maintain these are important to this research, and arguably to the participants who offered this information (as not all did) in discussion of their identities and their place within (or without) understandings and experiences of 'community'. However, this is not to argue that I want to 'define' people by this information or that I do not understand that "identities are fluid, diverse, complex and spatially and temporally created" (Browne and Bakshi, 2013: 211). I also recognise the importance of many other aspects of people's identity, which may or may not have been shared with me. Often participants drew on their identities (e.g. their gender or sexual identity) in relation to their experiences of community, so I do not apologise for including this information with participant quotes. I am thus influenced by Browne and Bakshi (2013: 212) who argue that "There is power in naming and this can be used to address oppression, marginalisations and exclusions . . . Thus, categorisation per se is not necessarily disempowering". Like them, I also use "lesbian, gay, bi and trans . . . recognising that these terms are complex, multiply appropriate, refuted and questioned" (Browne and Bakshi, 2013: 212). I therefore do not suggest that those who identify with particular identities are 'the same', but that their identities are significant—to them, and to this research.

Within the qualitative data collection, there were participants from urban (large cities and small towns) and (to a lesser extent) more rural areas. However, many participants were university educated and/or involved in LGBT service delivery in some way, which may mean that my sample was more 'knowledgeable' or opinionated than the wider LGBT population. Below, I provide further information about my research participants.

Interview participants were aged from 15 to over 65. Of the 627 survey respondents, 14% were aged 16–24, 24% were aged 25–34, 26% were aged 35–44, 26% were aged 45–54 and 10% were aged 55 or over. Unlike these pre-determined categories, questions about gender and sexuality were open so as not to 'force' respondents into particular groups. The question on gender identity produced 31 different responses (and 241 individuals who chose not to disclose this information), which refer to current identities rather than genders assigned at birth. Often, "lesbian and gay *[sic]* surveys" (Browne and Bakshi, 2013: 217) are dominated by gay men, but I had more self-identified women participants. This data is provided by way of summarising those who were involved, rather than as a form of analysis. Individuals' gender was reported in the following ways, which I have cautiously grouped together (where there were over five responses), as a general rule taking the first word supplied as a significant feature:

## *Female/woman* (x 189)

* Female/woman x 173
* Female mostly/mostly female x 8
* Cisgender female/woman x 6
* Female—post op x 1
* Femme x 1

## *Male/man* (x 167)

* Male/man x 163
* Masculine/mostly masculine x 2
* Cisgender male x 1
* Male, of trans experience x 1

## *Trans* (x 12)

* Trans female/woman x 4
* Trans/transgender x 3
* Trans male/man x 2
* M2F x 1
* Transgender FTM x 1
* Trans*, masculine x 1

## *Genderqueer, bigender, genderless or gender neutral* (x 11)

* Genderqueer x 8
* Gender neutral x 1
* I was born in a female body but I feel genderless or somewhere in between male and female mostly x 1
* Male and female x 1

A sexual identity question was also open, and resulted in 44 different responses (and 245 people who said that they did not know or who did not answer this question). These were also, with caution, amalgamated into larger groups where there were over five responses. Again, I have used the first word as a significant feature:

## *Gay/homosexual* **(x 177)**

- Gay x 173
- Homosexual x 3
- Performatively gay x 1

## *Lesbian* **(x 114)**

- Lesbian x 110
- Dyke x 2
- Butch x 1
- Trans lesbian x 1

## *Bisexual, pansexual and polysexual* **(x 48)**

- Bisexual x 38
- Pansexual x 5
- Polysexual x 2
- Polysexual/bisexual x 2
- Bisexual/lesbian x 1
- Pansexual/gay x 1

## *Queer* **(x 24)**

### *Heterosexual/straight* (x 6)

- Heterosexual/straight x 5
- FTM who loves women x 1

The 'pen portraits' of in-depth participants below are necessarily limited to ensure anonymity and confidentiality, but are provided by way of context for the data drawn on throughout the book. Details are taken from oral information supplied and written 'demographic information sheets' that were given to participants. All names are pseudonyms. Overall, within this stage, 21 people self-identified as female, 19 as male and 4 did not identify as 'female' or 'male'. Of these 44 people, 21 identified as gay, 12 as lesbian, 3 as bisexual, 2 as pansexual, 1 as straight and 5 did not disclose their sexual identity.

Bryn, at the time of interview, had been involved in a national gay men's group for many years. They identified as 'pan' with regard to both their gender and sexuality. They were aged 55–64, and educated to university degree level. They lived in a relatively large socio-economically mixed English city. Bryn took part in an individual interview and Group 2.

Carl took part in an individual interview. He was in his early 30s and lived in a small English town. He worked in the public sector and was involved in an online LGB support project in his spare time. He identified as a gay man, and was educated to university degree level. Carl described himself as 'half Indian'.

Gemma was a lesbian in her early 30s. She lived in Scotland and worked for a relatively large LGBT organisation. When asked to describe her gender, Gemma commented "it depends what day it is. I'm happy to go down as female, but I think I would also put in there a caveat that non-gender binary also sometimes applies". She was university educated, and took part in an individual interview.

Helen was a postgraduate student when she took part in an individual interview. She had been involved in a number of LGBT-related campaigns and/or groups during her time as a student. Helen said that she had also been involved in disability politics because she is 'really dyslexic'. She identified as a woman and a queer lesbian/pansexual. She was in her early 20s, and lived in a large city in the North of England.

Julie identified as female and lesbian, and worked for a small LGBT charity. Aged in her mid-late 20s, she lived in a 'deprived' English town (according to the index of multiple deprivation 2015). She was university educated and participated in an individual interview, as well as Group 4.

Laura participated in an individual interview. She was a mature undergraduate student aged 45–54, and lived in a small relatively affluent town in England. She identified as female and lesbian. Her Christian faith was important to her.

Liz identified as female and a lesbian. She was aged between 35 and 44, and described herself as a single parent. In her job, she provided support to young people identifying as LGBT within a broader mental health service. She lived in a semi-rural English county, and participated in an individual interview.

Matt was Jewish, in his early 20s, and recently graduated from university where he was actively involved in a number of LGBT groups. He identified as male, cisgender and gay. Matt lived in a socio-economically mixed English city, and participated in an individual interview.

Petra was in their late 40s and lived in a large city in the South of England. They were a postgraduate student at the time of interview, whilst also involved in trans-related voluntary work. They described themself as trans and pansexual, and participated in an individual interview.

Ruth was involved in an individual interview. She was in her mid-late 60s, educated to postgraduate degree level, and identified as female and lesbian. She lived in an English city 'known' for its sizable LGBT population.

Fiona and Ben took part in a paired interview. They were colleagues employed by a relatively large LGBT organisation based in a Scottish city. Ben was aged 25–34 and identified as a gay man. Fiona was also aged 25–34 and identified as a woman and bisexual.

Gerry and Shourjo are partners and took part in a paired interview. They lived in a socio-economically mixed city in England. Gerry is employed within the arts and identified as British Asian. Shourjo migrated to England from India in adulthood and worked in the public sector. They were both in their 30s and identi-fied as gay men.

Group 1 took place at an existing LGB youth group. All group members knew each other. The group was based within a relatively deprived English town (according to the index of multiple deprivation 2015). Though most group members were drawn from the town, some travelled from slightly further afield to be part of the group. Individuals involved were:

- Alison was involved in supporting the young LGB group in a voluntary capacity.
- Ed supported the LGB youth group in a sessional capacity.
- Fin was also involved in supporting the young LGB group in a voluntary capacity.
- Graham supported young LGBT people (including the group) within his job. He was in his late 20s and identified as gay.
- Jason was a young gay man, and member of the young LGB group. He recently left school.
- Kerry was also a young person and member of the LGB youth group.
- Mark was an ex-student and member of the young LGB group. He identified as gay.

Group 2 took place in a city within a mostly rural county of England. Not all the group members lived within the city itself but were also drawn from more rural neighbouring locations. It was not a pre-existing group so not all members knew each other. It consisted of the following individuals:

- Andrea was a practitioner working in LGBT service provision and identified as female and gay. She was in her early 20s.
- Bryn (see above).
- Eva's professional role included liaison with LGBT populations. She was female, aged 35–44, and did not disclose her sexuality.
- Peter was semi-retired and had been involved in a variety of gay and/or LGBT groups throughout his life. He was male, gay and aged over 65.
- Rachel was aged 35–44 and involved in a variety of trans support networks. She identified as female and gay.

Group 3 took place not far from a large city known for its 'gay scene'. The group was drawn from the LGBT staff network of a large private sector organisation. Most, though not all, of the members had met previously. Group members were:

- Adam was male, gay and aged 25–34.
- Jackie was in her early 50s and identified as a female lesbian.
- Luce was female, lesbian and 35–44 years old.
- Megan described herself as a female lesbian aged 25–34.
- Paul, aged 35–44, identified as a gay man.

- Philippa described herself as a female lesbian aged 25–34.
- Timothy identified as male, gay and aged 35–44.
- Tony described himself as male, gay and 45–54 years old.

Group 4 was conducted within a pre-existing support group for LGBT women, to which a number of additional individuals had been invited. Most participants knew each other. It was based within a deprived English town (according to the index of multiple deprivation 2015). Group members included:

- Colin was a gay man aged 35–44. He was involved in a trade union LGBT group.
- Charlie was aged 25–34 and identified as male (trans) and bisexual.
- Julie (see above).
- Louisa was aged between 45 and 54, and identified as female and bi?
- Jo, aged 25–34, was female and described herself as gay.
- Nicky was a female lesbian aged 25–34.
- Tom identified as male, straight and aged 25–34.

Group 5 took place in a city in Wales. It was not a pre-existing group, though some members knew each other. Individuals involved were:

- Dilys was 45–54 years old and described herself as gay and female. She worked for an LGBT-related organisation.
- Huw was male, gay and described himself as 35–44 years old.
- Jodi identified their gender as 'other', and referred to themself as gay. They were aged 45–54.
- Paula, aged 35–44, described herself as lesbian and MtF trans, though she said she had only been 'full-time' for a number of weeks when the research took place.
- Steve was a gay man aged 55–64. He was involved in an LGBT staff network at his place of work.

# References

Brown, G. (2008) 'Urban (homo)sexualities: Ordinary cities and ordinary sexualities', *Geography Compass* 2(4): 1215–1231.

Browne, K. (2005) 'Snowball sampling: Using social networks to research non-heterosexual women', *International Journal of Social Research Methodology* 8(1): 47–60.

Browne, K. and Bakshi, L. (2013) *Ordinary in Brighton: LGBT, activisms and the city*. Aldershot: Ashgate.

Gabb, J. and Fink, J. (2015) *Couple relationships in the 21st century*. Basingstoke: Palgrave Macmillan.

Heaphy, B. (2012) 'Reflexive sexualities and reflexive sociology' in Hines, S. and Taylor, Y. (eds) *Sexualities: Past reflections, future directions*. Basingstoke: Palgrave Macmillan, pp. 15–31.

Heaphy, B., Smart, C. and Einarsdottir, A. (2013) *Same sex marriages: New generations, new relationships*. Basingstoke: Palgrave Macmillan.

McDermott, E. (2010) *Researching and monitoring young people's sexual orientation: Asking the right questions, at the right time.* Manchester: Equality and Human Rights Commission.

McManus, S. (2003) *Sexual orientation research phase 1: A review of methodological approaches.* Edinburgh: Scottish Executive.

Myslik, W.D. (1996) 'Renegotiating the social/sexual identities of places' in Duncan, N. (ed) *BodySpace: Destabilising geographies of gender and sexuality.* London: Routledge, pp. 155–168.

Simpson, P. (2015) *Middle-aged gay men, ageing and ageism: Over the rainbow?* Basingstoke: Palgrave Macmillan.

Stella, F. (2012) 'The politics of in/visibility: Carving out queer space in Ul'yanovsk', *Europe-Asia Studies* 64(10): 1822–1846.

Weeks, J., Heaphy, B. and Donovan, C. (2001) *Same sex intimacies: Families of choice and other life experiments.* London: Routledge.

# Index